Surviving
the Coming
Mutual Fund
Crisis

Also by Donald Christensen
with Aaron Feigen

INVESTING WITH THE INSIDERS, LEGALLY

Surviving the Coming Mutual Fund Crisis

■ ■ ■

DONALD CHRISTENSEN

LITTLE, BROWN AND COMPANY

BOSTON   NEW YORK   TORONTO   LONDON

First Paperback Edition

LIBRARY OF CONGRESS CATALOGING-IN-PUBLICATION DATA

Christensen, Don (Donald James)
    Surviving the coming mutual fund crisis / by Donald Christensen.
    — 1st ed.
        p.   cm.
    Includes index.
    ISBN 0-316-14145-3 (hc)
    ISBN 0-316-13782-0 (pb)
    1. Mutual funds — United States.   I. Title.
HG4930.C48   1994
332.63'27 — dc20   94-1677

10 9 8 7 6 5 4 3 2 1

MV-NY

Designed by Jeanne Abboud

Published simultaneously in Canada by Little, Brown & Company (Canada) Limited

PRINTED IN THE UNITED STATES OF AMERICA

Contents

■ ■ ■

Prologue

■ ■ ■

S ince 1990 a quiet revolution has changed the mutual fund industry. Unlike political revolutions, which often can be traced to a
single precipitating moment on a specific date, the mutual fund
revolution was achieved through a series of small, seemingly insignificant
events spread out over many dates. February 19, 1992, was one of those
dates. And for thousands of shareholders of mutual funds run by Fidelity
Investments it was a critically important date.

In the fifth-floor conference room at the Boston headquarters of the
mutual fund behemoth, shareholders of Fidelity's Overseas Fund, Global
Bond, and seven other Fidelity international stock and bond funds gathered to consider sweeping changes in the funds' bylaws. These changes,
described in the small print of a 112-page proxy statement, included the
elimination of "fundamental investment limitations" to allow Fidelity
fund managers unprecedented investment "freedoms."

Some proposed changes "standardized" investment techniques that had
once been avoided by most mutual fund companies (including Fidelity)
as too high risk and too speculative — techniques such as buying securities on margin and selling short. They also included the removal of
limitations against buying the shares of high-risk "unseasoned" companies that have been in business for less than three years. Other proposed
changes asked shareholders to approve the removal of limitations against
investment activity that at the time of the meeting was prohibited by state
or federal laws — activities such as buying the shares of mutual funds
run by other companies. Yet other changes gave managers the freedom to
play with a new type of security that few people in early 1992 had ever
heard of — namely, derivatives. Between 1990 and this meeting in 1992,

similar bylaw changes already had been quietly approved and established by nearly every other Fidelity fund — and by many other mutual fund companies as well.

But the February 19 meeting did not produce the unquestioned rubber stamp Fidelity management had previously enjoyed. Several shareholders angrily protested the proposed radical changes. Some voiced concern about removing decades-old limitations that originally had been adopted to protect mutual fund shareholders from the scandals and abuses that had once rocked the mutual fund industry. Others questioned why vast, high-risk investment "freedoms" were needed in 1992, but hadn't been in 1991 and throughout the years since 1946, when Fidelity was founded.

The dozen or so shareholders at the meeting who wanted to ask questions of the funds' trustees easily outnumbered the trustees. In 1991 Fidelity stopped requiring trustees to attend such meetings to hear shareholders' comments or answer their questions. And at the February 19 meeting only one bothered to show up — Fidelity president J. Gary Burkhead.

One question posed for Burkhead focused on the wording in the proxy that modified investment policy limitations from "fundamental" to "*non-fundamental.*" Fundamental limitations carry a legal restriction prohibiting changes without shareholder approval. But redefined as nonfundamental limitations, the investment policies could be changed at any time by the Fidelity board without shareholder approval or shareholder notification prior to the enactment of the changes.

SHAREHOLDER: *In each of these new nonfundamental limitations the proxy says that "the Fund does not currently intend to purchase securities on margin . . ." and ". . . does not currently intend to sell securities short" and ". . . does not currently intend to . . ." for this and that and on and on through all these limitations. But you wouldn't ask for these limitation changes unless you really did have an intention to change the policy. Right?*

BURKHEAD: *Yes.*

SHAREHOLDER: *So, you really have every intention of changing the intentions, don't you?*

BURKHEAD: *Yes.*

Another shareholder commented that the changes were a "sign of the diffusion of mission of the funds."

SHAREHOLDER: *Why do you need these new high-risk investment freedoms?*
BURKHEAD: *We are trying to anticipate changes in the regulatory environment and to standardize investment policy.*
SHAREHOLDER: *Standardize among Fidelity funds or with the entire mutual fund industry?*
BURKHEAD: *With the industry.*

Despite the shareholder protests at the February 1992 meeting, the bylaw changes were overwhelmingly passed based on proxy votes of shareholders who did not attend. Some shareholders may have mistakenly interpreted the "no intentions" declaration printed in the proxy mailed to them in a literal sense instead of recognizing the *real* intentions acknowledged by Fidelity president Burkhead. Others may not have questioned the implications of the sweeping changes and their future effect in heightening the level of risk exposure of their money. Or they may not have questioned — as one protesting shareholder did — how, without the wall of restraining restrictions, shareholders would be protected from the type of excess and greed that had demolished so many financial giants in the recent past following removal of similar restrictions. And — more important — now that Fidelity management could make investment policy changes in secret and enact those changes *while keeping them secret from shareholders,* how any investor could know if the fund invested into yesterday was the same one today.

The shareholders who did not attend the meeting didn't hear Fidelity president Burkhead's simple (and chilling) answer: "Faith."

In less than three years after Burkhead's call for "faith," results of the new high-risk freedoms began to be seen — at Fidelity funds and at many other funds. Specifically, misplaced bets on derivatives contributed to a 1994 plunge of over 16 percent of the value of Fidelity Global Bond Fund shares to make it one of the worst performing funds of the year.

Scores of other funds turned in similar disasters as a result of high-risk forays from new investment "freedoms" that backfired. Some fund companies infused money into their funds to "bail out" the fund shareholders. Other fund companies, including Fidelity, did not.

By late 1994 Americans were beginning to get a glimmer of what the "new" mutual fund was all about.

Surviving
the Coming
Mutual Fund
Crisis

CHAPTER 1

■ ■ ■

It All Started
with a Good Idea

Every financial fiasco in history started out as a good idea. Ironically, as history proves to us over and over again, whenever a good financial idea becomes viewed by everybody as the *only* idea (or an idea too good to miss) it invariably turns into a bad idea.

You may remember, for example, that junk bonds started out as a "good idea" before deteriorating into catastrophe and then, after a period of reform, rebounding into what looked, for a time at least, like renewed life as a good idea.

In 1970 when young Mike Milken issued his now-famous research report "Speculative Bonds: Attractive Yields to Maturity," his good idea provided an alternative to traditional bank loans for corporate financing. Instead of having to satisfy stringent bank requirements to get loans, companies in shaky financial condition could raise needed cash by issuing bonds directly to investors — both large and small. In return for taking on risk that the banks didn't want to assume, the holders of these bonds would be paid interest rates that were higher than they could get just about anywhere else.

Throughout the 1970s Milken displayed analytical genius in assessing the soundness of individual junk bond situations to identify those most likely actually to pay on the bonds. Evidence of his success bred an enormous appetite for this financing concept among corporations and investors alike. It also bred an enormous appetite in Milken himself and others who wanted to follow in his fee-rich footsteps. But then "appetite" began to outstrip the availability of sound situations. Riskier and riskier dishes were added to the groaning board until the good idea became a mania. And as always happens, the out-of-control good idea collapsed in disaster and scandal as we watched the architect of the good idea trotted off to jail. The junk bond idea remains a good idea, however, when prudently approached. In fact, the junk bond market enjoyed a dramatic rebound after collapsing in 1990. But the rebound was largely the renewal of a gluttonous appetite, setting up investors for another round of more of the same. In 1994 the junk bond idea was once again hit with a steep decline.

Whatever direction the junk bond idea takes from its position in the mid 1990s, Mike Milken's original good idea as it was embraced in the 1980s and once again in the early 1990s was not, of course, a *new* idea. It actually was first used in 1921 as a way of saving the then-cash-strapped Goodyear from bankruptcy. Goodyear's success prompted other companies to adopt this good idea. And as the 1920s unfolded, this financing instrument gained in popularity (in much the same way as it did during the 1980s) and was used to great effect in financing take-overs and mergers (again, in much the same way as it was used during the 1980s). But by the end of the 1920s the idea collapsed in disaster and scandal in a near-perfect foreshadowing of the late 1980s–early 1990s experience. After the 1920s, the high-yielding bond was generally shunned for a generation. Most of the people with personal memories and direct (and disastrous) experience with the concept in its original permutation unfortunately had died by the time Mike Milken came along.

But the junk bond is not alone among good ideas gone wrong. Consider the "South Sea Bubble" of early-eighteenth-century England. The original good idea here was the British government's approval for the creation of a company, financed through the sale of shares to the public, that would have a monopoly over any British trade with South American countries. In reality there was very little opportunity for such trade because Spain controlled all the commerce going in and out of those countries. But people clamored for shares of the South Sea Company in expectation of future riches. And the prices of those shares kept going up as more people became willing to pay any price to get in on the action. Seeing how easy it was to raise money by selling securities, scores of other companies, called Bubble companies and promising future riches via such business schemes as trading in hair and insuring horses, were created to satisfy the speculative appetite sparked by the apparent success of the South Sea Company. Eventually the British government outlawed these companies, allowing only the South Sea Company to survive. But then one day everyone suddenly realized that the reality of the underlying "business" of the South Sea Company had no relation to the price of the company's shares and the whole thing collapsed in disaster and scandal. The collapse was so disastrous that the basic good idea of raising money for a business through the sale of securities to the public was not permitted in England for over a century.

Even the Tulipomania that gripped early-seventeenth-century Holland and featured frenzied speculative bidding on tulip bulbs until a single bulb fetched an equivalent of thousands of dollars (before the speculative frenzy collapsed) started out with a good idea: the importation of flowers from Turkey to Northern Europe to beautify the spring landscape.

More recently, a good idea you may remember was the savings and loan association concept. The basis of this good idea was very simple: a financial institution chartered to pool the savings of people in a community and lend that money out as home mortgages to other people in the community. For decades this concept, which was highly regulated by the government, served Americans well.

But in the 1970s the S&Ls started having trouble attracting savings deposits. People could get higher interest rates elsewhere with such new financial instruments as money market funds. Depositors took money out of S&Ls. The S&Ls, limited by laws about the amount of interest they could pay depositors, tried for a time to give away toasters and other trinkets to attract depositors' money. Then S&L industry leaders convinced lawmakers to throw away most of the regulations limiting S&L activities. The well-intentioned goal of the deregulation was to provide S&Ls greater investment "flexibility" so that they, in turn, could provide greater interest payment "flexibility" to depositors.

Unfortunately, although we didn't know it for a few years, abuses and excesses among S&L executives, along with their rank incompetence while pursuing riskier investments, began instantly once the regulations were removed. And the good idea collapsed in disaster and scandal.

Before that happened, however, investors saw a chance to chase after those S&Ls paying the highest interest rates on government-insured deposits. Investment pools were created for the sole purpose of moving large blocks of money from S&L to S&L, following the highest yields — which also happened to be offered by the weakest S&Ls. As each of these weak S&Ls collapsed and government deposit insurance paid off the depositors, the money was moved on to the next one until it created a rippling domino effect.

All in all, a *great* idea.

Of course, the S&L concept as we knew it in the 1980s wasn't an

entirely new concept. An earlier generation experienced the same phenomenon in the 1920s when S&L executives — and to a much greater
degree commercial bank executives — put their depositors' money in
increasingly risky investments as the decade wore on. After the abuses
and excesses of commercial bank and S&L executives of the 1920s (along
with their own style of raw incompetence) led to disaster and scandal,
regulations were adopted in the 1930s to help guard against the opportunities for further abuses and excesses. In the late 1970s and early 1980s,
however, promoters of S&L deregulation told us that things were different; people had changed; and enough regulations remained so that the
mistakes of the 1920s could not be repeated. It turned out otherwise, of
course. As we witnessed, the forces of human nature that spawned the
excesses of the 1920s returned in the 1980s with a grand-scale
vengeance.

The difference between these parallel experiences is that the collapse
of the good idea earlier in this century was borne by the individual commercial bank and S&L depositors. They lost everything. The second time
around, the individual depositors were saved from personal financial disaster by federal government insurance programs that guaranteed the
safety of their money. Instead of each individual depositor paying for the
mistakes and excesses of S&L executives, society as a whole was called
on to pay for them. And as a result, every American old enough to hold
this book will be paying for this experience for the rest of his or her life.

But the very S&L depositors who were saved from personal financial
disaster then took their money and put it into *uninsured* and speculative
instruments — such as those offered by mutual fund promoters — as
they continued to pursue high-rate return on their money that they had
gotten used to during the 1980s. But the return enjoyed in the 1980s
actually was largely illusionary because S&L executives had put money
into fantasy projects with little likelihood of paying on the investments.
As a result, empty office towers, luxury resorts, and corporate parks stand
as monuments to the unreality of the "investment" that was supposed to
support the high-yield S&L depositor accounts. The fantasy basis of the
high-rate return that S&L depositors got in the 1980s ended up costing
American taxpayers, most of whom did not personally benefit from either
the free-wheeling "investments" of the S&L executives or from the artificially high interest rates paid depositors, an estimated $650 billion of very
real money. In fact, the so-called S&L bailout that paid back insured
depositors (and sold off real estate at fire-sale prices) helped finance the

stock market's rebound in the early 1990s from the 1987 crash, as well as the rebound of the high-risk junk bond market from its 1990 plunge. Millions of Americans withdrew billions of their insured dollars from S&Ls and banks and poured them into speculative stock and bond mutual funds. The mutual funds, in turn, flooded those dollars into the stock and bond markets.

Actually, as the good idea of the savings and loan concept and other financial ideas of the 1980s crumbled, Americans became enthralled with the good idea — or, rather, the *many* good ideas — offered by mutual funds. The mutual fund concept offered so many appealing good ideas, in fact, that by early 1995 over 45 million Americans — representing about 35 percent of the country's households — had committed money to some type of mutual fund. This was nearly a fourfold increase since 1980, when there were 12 million mutual fund shareholders representing about 6 percent of American households. The industry needed to serve this popular appetite also grew dramatically. In 1982 there were 882 mutual funds. By early 1995 there were 7,607 mutual funds. During 1994 new funds were created at a rate of three or four a day. In addition, other financial institutions were jumping on the mutual fund bandwagon. Insurance companies, banks, and even those S&Ls that survived the 1980s all pushed to redesign their financial products into forms of mutual funds. The money committed to mutual funds topped $2.5 trillion by 1995, up from $250 billion in 1982 — and more than doubling since 1990. By 1995 the good ideas offered by the mutual fund concept in America had made it the single most popular financial idea in world history — attracting the greatest number of people, the widest range of categories of people, and the greatest amount of money.

But the good ideas that proved so successful in the 1980s and convinced so many people to turn to the mutual fund concept are now becoming distorted under the weight of their own popularity. Massive new — and untested — trends are emerging from the assumptions of those good ideas. And at the same time, Americans quickly elevated the mutual fund concept to mania status in exactly the same way that proved so calamitous for so many good financial ideas of the past.

GOOD IDEA #1: A mutual fund investment provides instant portfolio diversification

The ability of an investor to achieve portfolio diversification in virtually any investment category via a mutual fund is the strongest promise of the concept. Actually, if you peel away all the *implied* "promises" of a mutual fund's promotion materials, you will find that diversification is the *only* concrete promise made by mutual fund promoters.

Diversification, of course, is critically important for any investor. What could be more simple and easily understood than the idea of not putting all your eggs in one basket? For example, how vulnerable you would be to total disaster if you held only one stock in your portfolio. It's simple. That one stock collapses and you're dead. But if you have three or four stocks in a portfolio and one stock collapses, you're not so dead. Simple.

But as simple as the idea of diversification is, it is also limited. Just because you may hold a diversified portfolio of a certain market — stock or bond or real estate or some other — doesn't mean that you'll achieve financial success. Your success depends more on the direction of the market itself than on the diversified nature of your portfolio — no matter how diversified it is.

One dramatic illustration of the limitation of diversification is the diversified portfolios of the now-defunct S&Ls. In fact, it was the call by S&L industry leaders back in the 1970s for flexibility to allow greater diversification of investment — instead of being chained solely to home mortgages — that got the laws changed. Then, through their own peculiar exercise of the idea of diversification, S&L executives flailed in so many directions that it took a special act of Congress and a new government bureaucracy — a bureaucracy that turned out to be bigger than the one that "deregulation" was supposed to eliminate — to sift through the resulting rubble of all that diversification.

Yet, despite this rather gruesome example, diversification via mutual funds provides an undeniable value for people who want convenient access to different types of investment markets but do not have the time, energy, interest, or money to go into the markets directly. In the early 1980s, when current popular interest in mutual funds was beginning to gather steam, the important value of diversification (and its accompanying limitations) was the focus whenever the idea of mutual funds was discussed. General magazine and newspaper articles at the time were typically headlined: "Are Mutual Funds Right for You?" These articles, which were geared primarily to already-active individual investors, presented the mutual fund concept as a convenient alternative to building a personal portfolio.

In the late 1970s and early 1980s, however, only the most adventuresome people were interested in braving the risky waters of bond and stock markets. In those days, no-risk bank CDs were paying, at times, over 15 percent interest. But the bond market, reacting to ever-rising interest rates during the period, had been in the doldrums for over a decade. And things weren't much better in the stock market. The Dow Jones Industrial Average of August 1982, for example, stood at a point *lower* than it had been in 1964. Easy access to those markets — diversified or not — was secondary to the question of whether to have your money in those markets at all. Based on performance charts of the previous fifteen years it appeared that no reasonable or prudent person would put money into those markets. Only bold — if not crazy — risk takers would do it. (There's a very important lesson here that should be remembered: don't ever believe that performance charts tracing markets of the previous fifteen years reveal *anything* about what the next fifteen years will look like. Certainly, the grim stock and bond performance charts of the fifteen years leading up to 1980 did not match what would happen in the following fifteen years. And, similarly, the performance charts of 1995 showing what has happened in the last fifteen years will not likely match the next fifteen years — no matter how many times you see mutual fund promoters printing copies of those charts in full-page newspaper and magazine ads.)

But by the late 1980s, after interest rates began their decline and bond and stock markets began their spectacular rises, the perspective about mutual funds and the portfolio diversification they offered started shifting dramatically. By that time, a typical headline of a general magazine or newspaper would read: "Which Mutual Fund Is Right for You?" or "The Mutual Funds to Buy Now." These articles, instead of weighing the potential pros or cons of mutual fund investment involvement as a way of accessing different markets and the simple (but limited) value of diversification, began with the assumption that mutual funds were perfect. This was a far cry from what the same newspapers and magazines had been saying just ten years before. And then, after the assumption that mutual funds were perfect, the new perspective went on to focus on assessing the nuances of the relative strengths and weaknesses of different funds — across different investment categories and within individual categories.

Not only did the focus of magazine and newspaper articles shift, but the number of articles on the subject exploded. According to data from ABI/INFORM, a computer database that contains the bibliographic information on articles published in about eight hundred American magazines dating back to 1971, there were 8,731 articles published in those magazines dealing with some aspect of mutual funds from 1971 through December 1993. But 2,708 of those articles — or 31 percent of the total articles appearing over the twenty-two-year period — were published in just one year, January 1, 1993 through December 31, 1993. This stunning figure reveals how obsessed Americans had become with the mutual fund idea by the early 1990s.

The shift of perspective and the explosive growth in mutual fund analysis weren't too surprising in light of the growth of mutual fund alternatives. Consider, for example, the growth of the number of mutual funds within just one category: stock mutual funds. In 1982, there were fewer than 400 funds that fit this category. At the beginning of 1995 there were nearly 1,900 of such funds. Or, to put it another way, by 1995 there were nearly as many stock funds as there were stocks that could be reasonably defined as "actively traded" — and almost as many stocks as listed on the New York Stock Exchange.

The number of alternatives became overwhelming and complicated to sort through. As a result, the last ten years have seen an entire industry built up to track and assess the relative performance of mutual funds. Today, you can subscribe to services that provide information such as charts of fund performance, their "relative price strength," and ranking systems that promise to provide comparison measurements of similar funds. They also provide information on historical performance of funds compared to the S&P 500 or other benchmark measurements. In addition, there are now "switching" services that purport to tell you, based on various "timing" techniques, when to leave one fund and go to another. And every three months the horse-race results of relative fund performance are announced by Lipper Analytical Services and printed in articles that typically ask: "How Did Your Fund Do?" All these services focused on mutual funds have largely replaced similar services that in the past provided this type of information on investment choices that are now invested into by proxy via mutual funds.

This shift in focus is a critically important phenomenon. It's not the convenience of diversification of funds as a way to gain immediate access to different types of investment markets that is the appeal anymore. Instead, it's the funds themselves. Now, if you will just pick the *right* fund, you will "win." Or, in other words, speculative attention and expectation have moved from the underlying investment markets *of* funds *to* the funds themselves.

In the past, when large groups of people became removed from involvement with — or, in fact, had any interest in — the reality of investment options and shifted speculative expectation to a *representative* of those options, it served as a classic sign of burgeoning mania. A mania becomes full blown when confidence in the object of the speculative focus is so strong that successful involvement in it is thought of as "easy" and the end result certain. This is what happened, for example, 275 years ago when people focused on the promise of the "South Sea" Bubble companies with full confidence and little information. The people who threw money at the various companies didn't care what those companies were doing with the money that was to deliver the riches. Instead, the people choosing among the ever-growing number of Bubble companies just wanted to make sure that they chose the one that would make them the richest. And, indeed, the focus of a financial mania, like the Bubble companies, *always* delivers self-fulfilling success — for a while — as more and more money is committed to it, because when you strip away all the fancy charts and the convoluted calculations of computer spreadsheets, it all boils down to the simple concept you learned about in fifth grade: supply and demand.

GOOD IDEA #2: *Mutual funds make investment opportunities available to the "little guy" that would normally be limited only to the rich*

There is no question that the mutual fund concept makes nearly any type of investment market and technique available to nearly any type of person. With a mutual fund, anyone with a few thousand dollars or even a few hundred dollars can jump into the speculative fray as easily as a billionaire.

The actual availability of such a wide range of investment options to "everyman" is not in itself a problem. It does become a problem, however, when enough "everymen" join in on the investment options, straining them beyond realistic proportions, until, as one definition of financial mania puts it: "A larger and larger group of people seeks to become rich without a real understanding of the process involved."[1] And, again, when that happens, it can distort the reality — through high "popular" demand — of the valuation of the investment targets. The impact of such a distorted valuation eventually affects everyone — including those people who *do* have an understanding of the process involved.

Moreover, despite the near-mythic ability of mutual funds to deliver "everyman" access to investments, the unprecedented involvement of so many people in mutual funds has in no way democratized the investment world. Instead, it has made it more elitist than ever before. With ownership of stocks of public companies via an equity mutual fund, for example, it is only a fantasy that mutual funds have allowed millions of people to "own" shares of a large public company instead of the 30,000 or 50,000 rich individuals who "owned" them in the past. The reality is that shares of public companies are today concentrated under the control of a *very* few number of people.

By 1993 institutional investors — public and private pension funds, insurance companies, bank trusts, foundations, and endowments, as well as mutual funds — controlled almost 60 percent of all the shares of all public companies. At many of our largest corporations the percentage ownership by institutions is even higher — in some cases, including companies such as Eli Lilly, Bristol-Myers-Squibb, American Express, Texaco, Warner-Lambert, and Philip Morris, reaching up to 70 and 80 percent.

In 1980, institutions controlled only about 30 percent of the shares of public companies. In 1950, institutions controlled less than 10 percent.

Today, only about 3,000 people can be said to effectively control most of the shares of all American public companies. Much of that control is concentrated in even fewer hands. In 1992 the ten largest mutual fund companies represented ownership of more than 20 percent of public companies. In contrast, in 1980 the ten largest mutual fund organizations owned less than 5 percent of American companies. In fact, today at many companies, including some of our largest companies, majority ownership of shares could be represented by a handful of institutional managers sitting around a small table.

One danger of this elitist control of shares of public companies was expressed in 1973 by then-head of the Securities and Exchange Commission (and later head of the Central Intelligence Agency) William J. Casey: "The values established by institutions throwing blocks [of shares] back and forth begin to lose their credibility."[2] Casey's fear here, a fear that he viewed as the "worst possible future," was that too few people participating in the actual trading of shares would bid up the prices of those shares beyond any relationship to reality during "good" periods when money was flowing into the hands of institutions. And, presumably, these same few people could force prices down unrealistically during "bad" periods when the flow of new money into mutual funds and other institutions slowed down, or worse, when the money was taken out and put somewhere else.

One could argue that by 1993 Casey's fear had been realized. And if it had not been realized with nearly 60 percent ownership of all shares of public companies in the hands of about 3,000 people, then it will certainly be realized when 3,200 control 70 percent; or when 3,400 people control 80 percent; or when 3,600 people control everything.

By the early 1990s a few fund managers were already candidly acknowledging that the amount of money committed to mutual funds was causing problems in satisfying the self-interests of shareholders. For example, when superstar money manager Paul Tudor Jones was asked by *Business Week* in January 1992 why his performance for 1991 was subpar, a statement from his office frankly admitted that the size of the assets "makes it difficult to realize the rates of return we want." Despite this candid assessment, Jones, like nearly every other money manager, didn't halt acceptance of new money to his management. But then Jones, like other money managers, has his own self-interest to consider. A blunt description of that self-interest can be found in a June 1991 article in the *ABA Banking Journal* that extolled the benefits of bank sponsorship of mutual funds: "Mutual fund profitability follows its own 'golden rule': the more you rule, the more gold you get." (Jones has been a particularly successful practitioner of this "golden rule." His personal 1991 income, as estimated by *Financial World,* topped $60 million — despite his below-average performance for others.)

Actually, as the 1990s continued there were a few fund promoters who closed some funds to new shareholders, claiming that the funds were becoming too large to be handled effectively. There was loud grandstanding about these closings. Ads blared the news weeks before the closing event. New shareholders rushed to meet the deadline.

But was all this an example of responsible leadership of mutual fund promoters looking for ways to provide better, more efficient service to their shareholders? Or was it just a great marketing ploy? The funds that "closed" certainly didn't stop taking in additional money from existing shareholders. And, indeed, those existing shareholders, now believing they were part of an exclusive group privileged to be allowed to send their money into the now-closed fund, were primed to commit more money in greater concentration to that one fund instead of considering other options. Curiously, the same fund promoters — the same management that had found the size of the closed fund too unwieldy — then went on to open more new funds. It is, therefore, apparently easier for the same people to run many different types of funds — each designed to appeal to the special interests of different types of people — than to run one big fund. Or at least that's what they tell us.

Others, however, took another tack. Instead of closing funds as "too big," some promoters chose to create one huge fund and then sell shares in the same central fund to different people under different fund names. This idea — a new one in the 1990s — became known as "hub and spokes." The big central fund was the "hub." The different names it went under and the slightly different ways the same fund was priced and packaged to different groups of people were called the "spokes." (Critics of the idea characterized it with the less benign image of "octopus.") The reasoning behind the idea was that it would be more efficient to have just one fund that could appeal — with just a twist of a name or promotional brochure copy — to many people instead of incurring the costs of starting up different smaller funds to try to satisfy different investment perspectives of different people.

And which of these ideas is right: multiple "small" funds or one big fund? For the promoters of the funds it was irrelevant (a few fund promoters actually tried both approaches at the same time) because, quite simply, the investment activity of funds is secondary to the simple marketing goal of bringing in more money (as in: "The more you rule, the more gold you get").

A more typical approach of the period — less elaborate than closing funds or creating big ones with multiple guises — was the direct and aggressive push to attract the money of as broad a group of people as possible by making it more and more readily accessible and "easy" to join in. For example, in 1993 the august investment firm of Morgan Stanley lowered the initial minimum investment requirement for entree into the company's mutual funds from $500,000 to $1,000 (and only $250 for individual retirement accounts). Finally, the investment talent of Morgan Stanley was made available to all! It seemed as if Morgan Stanley had embarked on some altruistic campaign to help out the little guy by stretching out a kind, firm hand from a previously impenetrable tower of Wall Street. More realistically, however, it probably had something to do with the marketing team at Morgan Stanley discovering that they were running out of candidates for such an exclusive investment pool as one requiring a $500,000 initial investment. The appetite for wealth that so many small investors displayed in the early 1990s was topped only by the mega-appetite of mutual fund promoters themselves for more and more and more and more of other people's money. And as the 1990s evolved it became increasingly clear that they didn't care what they had to do, what they had to say, or who they had to rub shoulders with to get it.

GOOD IDEA #3: *Professional management of investments*

Of all the good ideas offered by the mutual fund concept, the idea of professional management is perhaps the most alluring. It is also the most elusive of the ideas to define. What exactly does professional management mean? What do you get for the fee paid to the professional managers?

In part, you certainly get — or should expect to get with no argument or complications — accurate bookkeeping and other administrative services involved with the smooth maintenance of your account. Also, you could get such services as telephone redemption, automatic reinvestment or withdrawal plan services, and possibly switching services from one fund to another within a family of funds. You should expect that all the details of managing the portfolio, like stock transactions and payment dividends, are handled correctly. You might also expect to get accurate, straightforward, and clearly explained information not only about how to send your money to the mutual fund but also what you are sending your money *into* — full, clear descriptions of fees and investment policies followed by the fund's managers. (This last hallmark of professionalism, however, cannot and should not be routinely assumed at *any* point during a journey through the world of mutual funds.)

Beyond these basics, the promise of professional management gets foggy. Strictly speaking, the word "professional" means only that the person doing the job is paid for the work being done. Mutual fund promoters try to imply additionally, of course, that the "professionals" are experts. But most mutual fund promoters are very careful not to claim expertise specifically. Professional, yes. But expert? Not necessarily. Mutual fund promotion materials may say something like: "Managers draw on the services of our professional staff of researchers and analysts who have access to the best investment information available." If you look carefully at that message, you'll see that there's no promise the information will be used correctly or prudently or wisely or will, indeed, lead to *any* type of positive experience with the money they have of yours in their hands.

Compare that "professional" profile with the "professional management" profile of a traditional banker. The banker, who promises depositors a set amount return on their money, must make his money primarily through the difference he can get between the investments he makes and the money he promises to pay out to depositors. For years millions of Americans found this relationship with the traditional banker — who must make a living from actual investment expertise — a satisfactory situation. But in the early 1990s, bankers in their professional management role could not find acceptable investment opportunities that would enable them to promise the type of return that depositors apparently wanted, or felt they deserved, or had gotten used to during the age of inflation and high interest rates of the 1970s and 1980s. And those depositors started turning a blind eye and a deaf ear to the bankers' "promise."

Certainly, if a banker in the 1990s attempted to convince people to deposit money into a bank by showing that the bank had paid an average of 10 percent (or more) interest over the previous ten or fifteen years, people would have laughed. Who cares what a bank deposit account yielded in the past? The question is what is the bank paying now and into the future?

Yet the same people who would have laughed in a banker's face for trying to pull such a spurious argument as past performance to attract their money to the bank's stewardship, then went on to drool over the performance charts of mutual funds. During the early 1990s mutual fund promoters encouraged this. Seemingly, there were people — including many financial journalists — who looked at these charts as if they presented some type of guideline for future expectations. Little consideration was given to the fact that a complex and unique set of circumstances had delivered both historically unprecedented high interest rates during the 1980s as well as nearly unprecedented high returns in stock and bond markets. The high interest rates of the 1980s were a legacy from the 1970s when the government hiked rates to battle extraordinary inflation. But while the inflation rate decreased rapidly in the 1980s, high interest rates went down relatively slowly. Yet the decline of both inflation and interest rates had a positive effect on stock and bond markets — raising speculative markets to new heights. With these unique circumstances at play during the 1980s and the earliest days of the 1990s it was difficult *not* to be successful at making money from money, no matter which avenue you turned to. But while the performance of interest-bearing bank accounts of this past period was dismissed as irrelevant (as indeed it should be), the past performance of stock and bond mutual funds was projected, compounded, twisted, and twirled to encourage people to think that these types of gains could be expected perpetually into the future.

The game of projecting financial gains into the future based on what had happened in the recent past was not a new one when it got applied to mutual funds in the 1990s. Back in the late 1970s and early 1980s, the same thing was done. But in those days it was done with bank accounts — specifically, certificates of deposit. Then, when such deposits sometimes yielded over 15 percent, the most widespread conventional wisdom being shouted from the rooftops focused on "the magic of compound interest." Investment advisers, looking back on the previous fifteen years of ever-rising interest rates, projected forward based on a continuation of about the same rates. Magazine and newspaper articles "proved" how rich you were going to be in twenty or thirty years with such great interest rates. Worst-case scenarios went like this: "Even if interest rates on CDs go all the way down to 8 percent, in twenty years you'll still have . . ."

This was a time when stock and bond mutual funds got little attention. Mutual fund salespeople of the late 1970s and early 1980s would not have been caught dead with a performance chart of stock and bond investments of the previous fifteen or twenty years. In those days the few people who put money into mutual funds went into them *despite* the experience of the previous two decades. Who would have dared show charts of bond funds with their staggering losses? For example, the value of long-term municipal bonds — which became such a panacea for low bank rates in the 1990s — went into a tailspin in the late 1970s with a decline of over 35 percent from December 1979 to December 1981. And with the stock market in the late 1970s/early 1980s standing at a point *lower* than it had fifteen years before, few charts could have convinced people of the value of stock investing as a wealth builder or even as an inflation hedge. In fact, from the late 1960s throughout all of the 1970s and into the early 1980s, stock market averages did *not* keep pace with inflation. Rather, they declined sharply relative to inflation — at a time when inflation was growing at a historically unprecedented pace and when an inflation hedge was needed the most.

And don't let anyone tell you otherwise, because stock market investing is *not* always a successful hedge against inflation. A person who started at age forty-five in 1966 to plan for retirement at age sixty-two in 1982 and followed an investment plan focused on stock or bond mutual funds ended up in the hole in real dollar terms and even worse compared to inflation. And that's the truth.

Before going any further, there is one historically consistent maxim about the human pursuit of making money from money that needs to be stated and kept in mind if you want to be a mutual fund survivalist in the 1990s: whatever somebody did five, ten, or fifteen years ago that delivered uncommonly high reward today is *never* what you can start doing today that will deliver uncommonly high reward five, ten, or fifteen years from now. Never.

Despite this inarguable truth, the happy recoveries and then sensational rises of stock and bond markets — despite a few heart-stopping moments — from the early 1980s into the early 1990s somehow were viewed in hindsight not with nostalgia (as they should have been) but as certain proof of how these markets can deliver the goods. And from that starting point these financial markets went on to become interpreted as the universal, unquestioned best ways for individuals to meet their financial future. And as in the late 1970s and early 1980s, which featured endless projection charts of how much money you were going to get in the future from high-interest, low-risk bank accounts, mutual fund promoters of the late 1980s and early 1990s — along with the popular press that enthusiastically reprinted verbatim their words and numbers — offered similar forward-looking charts, with similar-sounding worst-case scenarios: "Even if the stock market retreats during the 1990s to its historical average return of 8 or 9 percent a year, you'll still see a gain of . . ."

On top of this came the distorted perception that it had been mutual funds themselves that delivered the goods — not the overall direction of the markets. And, worse, just as the idea of mutual fund diversification became distorted from its simple purpose of offering convenient access to markets into becoming the actual reason for success, the idea of professional management of funds similarly was distorted until the people running funds personally received the credit for the positive performance of markets.

Mutual fund managers became celebrities. They were featured on magazine covers and on TV talk shows, further focusing attention on the funds themselves — as these guys hawked their own special funds — instead of the markets the funds represented. (Not everyone was taken in by this shift of focus. As famed economist John Kenneth Galbraith put it so succinctly: "Genius is a rising market.")

This elevation of the people known as money managers to near-godlike status happened even though statistical studies dating back to the 1940s consistently show that in any average year less than 20 percent of mutual funds ever deliver any "beat-the-market" performance — and over longer periods of time the percentage of superior performance to the markets themselves is even smaller.

Yet the drift of Americans' money to the obscure promise of professional management turned into a torrent. People handed money over to the managers of mutual funds as if this special fraternity of financial professionals — more than any other fraternity — somehow had taken possession of the magic key to the secret garden of financial delights. Americans chucked out one set of financial professionals (traditional bankers) because the stingy bums wouldn't pay out what people wanted. And another set of financial professionals (fee-paid money managers) was embraced even though that set didn't promise anything — except hope.

Perhaps it is not coincidental that as Americans were turning their backs on the traditional and the known as a place for their accumulated wealth, the professional gambling industry enjoyed a growth spurt in America. Less than a decade ago there were only two main casino cities in America. But by the end of 1993 every state except Utah and Hawaii had some form of legalized gambling. Gambling became one of America's few true growth industries. From 1989 to 1993 gambling operations were opened at sixty-five Indian reservations — all exempt from state laws — in seventeen states, and eighty more were on the drawing board in twelve other states. Riverboat gambling on the Mississippi River started with two operations in Iowa in 1991 and by early 1994 had expanded to over seventy similar operating or planned casinos in six other states. And the money Americans gambled away at these new centers reached $30 billion in 1992 — six times the amount spent on movie tickets. But the rush to the gaming tables, it seemed, had become something more than just entertainment. Is it a comment on how far the American Dream has deteriorated that instead of expecting future financial reward and stability from hard work and ethical behavior — making a promise to others in return for a promise from them — our last best hope is to put a quarter in a slot machine, a marker on a Bingo card, or a dollar on the nose of the latest financial magazine cover boy?

And how frustrating for the financial professionals called bankers — who were promising something specific based on their personal investment expertise — to see these other guys — who were promising only dreams and an effort to try their best to reach them — take all the money and be paid handsomely in the process.

Of course, rather than fighting this situation, the banks joined in — promising the same dreams and collecting similar no-hassle fees for making the promise. With the easing of government regulations in the mid-1980s that had largely prohibited banks and S&Ls from involvement in the mutual fund game, banks jumped into the arena with both feet. By the end of 1992, 91 percent of commercial banks offered mutual fund products — up from 46 percent in 1985. Those banks offering their own proprietary funds grew from 17 percent in 1987 to 45 percent in 1992. By 1992 banks had attracted 20 percent of the mutual fund business. And of the banks that had not already started their own funds, another 27 percent planned to do so in the future.[3]

Bank customers started changing their view of bankers. No one wanted to hear from a person marked with the stingy-bum stigma "banker." But the same person relabeled "mutual fund manager" got looked upon with dreamy-eyed wonder as the provider of future wealth. This changed view, however, fails to ask: Why is it that people who as "bankers" cannot find investment opportunities that yield high interest returns on bank accounts will as "mutual fund managers" be able to find investment opportunities that yield great wealth for the bank's customers? (The quick and brutal answer is: They won't.)

But in the early 1990s banks were promoting mutual fund products heavily against their own traditional offerings with advertising headlines like "Attractive Alternatives to CDs."[4] The ironic thing is that as Americans became dissatisfied with the returns they could receive from traditional "fixed" and guaranteed sources, the leaders of the very financial institutions that offered those traditional options didn't really *want* people's money under those terms any more — even when the interest rates promised seemed so low. It became far more appealing for the bankers to take fees and ask customers to trust the bankers to do their best — while expecting customers to continue paying fees no matter what happened.

Actually, like mutual fund promoters before them, bankers discovered the great business potential of being free to create financial "products" to satisfy customers' impressions of market opportunities with no other personal demands or responsibilities on the bankers. As the manufacturers of financial products, they have no need to promise anything specific. Also, and more important, the people who are manufacturing the financial products do not even have to reveal what they personally believe to be true about the markets — or, in fact, what they personally believe to be true about the different financial products. All they have to do is present financial wares and let the customers decide on what looks best to them. Even more realistically, all they have to do is create products that they think will appeal to customers — whether the products have any real value or not.

In the midst of all this, you want to do the wise thing with your money. You want to align yourself with other wise people. You look to leaders of our great financial institutions for truthful guidance. In the 1990s those leaders were telling you that the answer was mutual funds and that it was mutual funds, period. And since you didn't want the headaches or responsibilities of direct ownership of the types of investments reached through mutual funds — now promoted not only by investment companies but also bankers — you gladly sent your money off to the professionals. The professionals, in turn, gladly accepted your money — and the adulation, fees, and godlike status that came with it. At the same time, however, they returned every drop of risk of what they do with your money and what happens to it as a result right back to you.

By waving performance charts of speculative markets from a fifteen-year period when those markets enjoyed success almost unparalleled in history, leaders of the financial world were by the early 1990s rapidly achieving a change in expectations of what they had to deliver to maintain their roles of leadership. For most of this century and certainly for most people living today, the dominant view of the role of financial leaders was that of intermediary risk taker between the American "saver" and those people or businesses that wanted the use of that money. The financial leaders were given their position of leadership (and the rewards that went with it) by searching out investment opportunities, assessing the risk, and then taking that risk on themselves. The "little guy" — the "saver" — was largely insulated from the complexities of the financial world so that he could go on about the main business of his life without worrying much about them.

Throughout this conversion, the little guy was heralded as finally moving from a stodgy saver perspective to the more sophisticated position of "investor." This conversion, however, mostly benefited the financial world leaders who actually had the little guy's money in hand. Those leaders had successfully achieved the supreme late-twentieth-century dream job — high compensation, high status, no promises, and no ultimate personal responsibility. (And if you want to know exactly how little personal responsibility they hold, go read the tiny, tiny print of the mutual fund prospectus sitting over there in your drawer.)

As financial leaders were successfully achieving a conversion of expectations, leaders in other arenas were also retreating from past expectations of their leadership roles. One of the biggest changes was the conversion of the American worker's expectations about pensions. For most of this century, Americans enjoyed a defined-benefit style of pension that put the responsibility of pension payout on the employer. If a company's pension fund did not have enough money to pay the promised monthly payments, that was the problem of the employer. At the peak of this approach to retirement benefits in 1980 the number of Americans covered was 30.1 million. Since then, however, the number has diminished as the idea of pensions moved from the responsibility of companies who employ people to the employees themselves. The defined-contribution plan — typically encountered in companies as a 401(k) plan — became the approach increasingly favored by companies both large and small. The number of Americans covered by defined-contribution plans only went from 6.2 million in 1980 to 16.1 million in 1990. Those covered by defined-benefit plans shrank to 26.4 million by 1990.

Almost all of this new defined-contribution money, provided by the employee and directed by the employee, is concentrated in some form of mutual fund to the near exclusion of any other type of financial "savings" or "investment" option. And not only have business leaders now gotten rid of pension responsibility, new laws passed in 1993 removed a company's management liability for the performance of those mutual fund–style pension choices, as well as liability for choosing the financial institution handling the defined contribution plans.

While effectively washing their hands of all pension responsibility, business leaders did not lose any of their status or compensation with this reduced expectation. All of which probably would not have been as easy to accomplish if speculative markets as represented by mutual funds had not been so successful over the previous twenty years (again, a period of success almost unprecedented in history).

Government leaders also saw an opportunity to get rid of past assumptions of what they had to promise in regard to overseeing the financial world. One way was to call for less involvement as guarantors of the safety of money deposited in banks and S&Ls. In the past, government leaders had been willing to guarantee the safety of depositors' money by regulating how that money was invested. The regulations were designed to force the people who had control of the money to invest it in prudent ways that would have little chance of failure. And, indeed, that approach worked well for decades.

When, however, the investment regulations and limitations were removed from the "professional management" of S&L executives, the new "faith" that government regulators now had in the expertise of this group of managers proved to be unfounded. The bulk of that unfounded faith, however, had little to do with actual out-and-out crookedness. Instead, most of the billions of losses from the S&L experience was caused by simple errors of investment judgment on the part of the "professionals." A 1993 government study of the S&L debacle concluded that only about 10 to 15 percent of the billions lost came as a result of fraud. The rest was lost because the "professionals" were wrong. Yet the government reaction to this study was not to suggest further guidelines to define how "professionals" should act so that they will be more certain to be "right" than "wrong." Instead the government's conclusion from the study was to suggest removal of the government insurance program from the actions of the "professionals" and put the risk on the individual depositor — "just like a mutual fund." In other words, government leaders have decided that they are unable to identify the guidelines necessary to limit investment behavior so that it is possible to offer insurance against loss. They can't tell if something is done right or not. Instead, you, without the access to bank or S&L accounting books or the privileges, as government officials have had in the past, of questioning the people who handle the money, are now supposed to make an assessment of the risks yourself and then take those risks on personally — freeing the government and the "professionals" from such worries.

Thus, government leaders, corporate leaders, financial world leaders, all anxious to grab the goodies of leadership, and all equally anxious to play hot potato with the type of responsibility that has traditionally gone along with the role (and rewards) of leadership, have dropped the hot potato right in your lap. In all, it was an opportunistic and clever shift.

GOOD IDEA #4: Mutual funds offer more efficient access to markets than investing on your own

This is a good idea that mutual fund promoters don't tout as much as they used to.

When looked at closely, the mutual fund idea is not always more efficient — and the promoters know it. For one thing mutual funds are no longer an efficiently easy way to access markets in the sense that they save you time and effort from sorting through possible investment options. In fact, the mutual fund landscape has become much more complicated than the markets themselves. For example, it is simply *not* easier to try to go through more than 1,700 choices of equity mutual funds to find the right one for you than it would be to build a personal portfolio by sorting through the mere 500 stocks, for example, that make up the Standard & Poor's list of 500 leading American corporations. Analyzing and evaluating a stock is a far, far easier thing to do than trying to analyze a portfolio of stocks as represented by a mutual fund — particularly when the information you have about the portfolio and the investment techniques managers are using to knead that portfolio is out of date and sketchy.

Also, when it comes to the expenses of equity mutual funds, discount brokerage fees for individuals have narrowed the gap between commissions paid by big institutional investors and what the individual investor must pay. And as an individual investor there's no exposure to the expenses that a mutual fund manager can build up by churning a portfolio in an attempt to realize capital gains that can be claimed as "performance" on the next quarterly horse-race chart. Then, of course, for an individual investor who picks stocks and holds them with a long-term perspective there's the cost savings of not having to pay taxes (if the fund is not held in a tax-protected account such as a retirement plan) on all those supposed capital gains from the manager's churning of the fund portfolio — which can accumulate toward the manager's delightful "performance" even when the net asset value of the fund's shares goes *down*.

Equally, in the bond area, mutual funds are rarely "efficient" from a cost perspective. For conservative investors, for example, who are interested in the safety of government securities, there is simply no reason to pay a management fee (or, worse, a sales load) for being in a fund of U.S. Treasury bills, notes, or bonds. Buying these securities directly from the government by mail with as little as $1,000 — which doesn't even require a broker's commission (see Appendix B) — is not much more difficult than involvement with a mutual fund.

The real reason that mutual fund promoters don't flash the "efficiency" banner as much as they used to is that they don't want you to notice that costs and expenses for mutual fund shareholders have gone *up* in the last decade. As more and more people joined in on the idea, it didn't provide the economies of scale that promoters had once promised. Instead, the unquestioned popularity of funds allowed the promoters to raise prices on their products — just as any manufacturer of a product hopes to do.

In the ten years of 1982 to 1992 the percentage of mutual fund shareholders' assets scooped off by the fund promoters via expenses increased from 1.04 percent of investors' money to 1.45 percent. Moreover, the economies of scale benefited the promoters more than the shareholders with increased profit margins. For example, in 1991 the promoters of Value Line Income, Seligman Common Stock, Putnam Tax Exempt Income, and WPG Tudor enjoyed pretax profits of 55 percent, 44 percent, 36 percent, and 22 percent respectively. But by the middle of 1992, following a series of raised fees, these promoters jumped their pretax profits to even more enjoyable levels of 67 percent, 60 percent, 41 percent, and 55 percent.[5] Industry-wide the approximate profit margin has increased from about 34 percent in 1990 to about 50 percent in 1993.

The greatest efficiencies can be found in how large a mutual fund organization need be to handle ever-increasing amounts of money. For example, at mutual fund promoter T. Rowe Price, about 1,400 people handle the approximately $40 billion the promoter has under management. Compare that with the Bank of New York, which also has about $40 billion under management. At the Bank of New York it takes 14,000 people — ten times as many as at T. Rowe Price — to handle it all. Are the people at T. Rowe Price ten times smarter than at the Bank of New York? Have they figured out systems that are ten times more efficient? Maybe. But they also do not have to operate under as much regulation as the Bank of New York with its "government-insured" accounts. Further, since mutual fund promoters don't actually have ownership of the risk involved, they don't need to check, double-check, and triple-check a decision. (Don't cry for Bank of New York. Like many other banks in the early 1990s, Bank of New York moved into the mutual fund business in 1991. Perhaps it too can improve its efficiencies and better its profit of a mere 6 percent in 1992.)

GOOD IDEA #5: *Mutual funds have greater clout to achieve "shareholder rights" demands to enhance shareholder value*

The early 1990s saw a rash of announcements from mutual fund companies and other institutional investors — most notably, large pension funds — of their intentions of becoming activist shareholders. Many of the largest mutual fund companies made the move into an activist position, including T. Rowe Price, Vanguard, and Scudder, as well as many smaller funds like the highly successful Kaufmann Fund.

Fidelity Investments went further than most mutual fund companies (so far) in its proposed activist role when it removed its "no takeover" provisions from the bylaws of its equity funds to allow the funds' investments to be used "for the purpose of exercising control or management" of public companies. Fidelity's shareholder rights plans became so aggressive that the laws of Massachusetts, where Fidelity is headquartered, would not permit them. As a result, Fidelity turned to lawmakers in the state of Delaware, counseling them on law changes necessary to accommodate Fidelity's needs. And in 1991, after the Delaware laws were changed, Fidelity applied for permission to move all its funds for legal purposes to Delaware.[6]

In the early 1990s these announcements of a push by mutual funds and other institutional investors into activist roles were generally greeted with enthusiasm. One editor of a widely circulated newsletter that tracks mutual funds reacted: "If Fidelity says, 'Let's be more aggressive in enhancing shareholder values,' God bless 'em."[7]

This enthusiasm seems to rest on the conviction that the managers of American companies are belligerently holding back on reasonable strategic maneuvers that would make their companies more agreeable to the Wall Street perspective. And, therefore, shareholders (via mutual funds) are not seeing the stock prices they deserve. Or, as notable, self-styled shareholder rights champion T. Boone Pickens once brusquely claimed: "Eighty percent of America's top executives are incompetent."

Corporate executives might find that evaluation a little harsh. They might wish to point out that the incidence of incompetence tends to be spread out proportionately throughout all sectors of the population. After all, there isn't any master human resources clearinghouse that assigns all the dummies (and crooks) to corporate management and all the geniuses (and ethicists) to money management and investment advisory firms.

The pitting of institutional investors against corporate management of public companies will develop into one of the most hotly debated issues of the 1990s. The name calling that is already a feature of this conflict is not as important as the two factors that override everything else affecting these two groups: self-interest and power.

Simply put, the self-interest of fund managers is to achieve performance returns relative to other similar funds that will satisfy the expectations of current shareholders so that those shareholders will not pull money out of the fund and, to a greater extent, to achieve performance returns that will attract money from *new* shareholders. This performance is announced and measured against competing funds every three months. That quarterly time pressure is what dictates a mutual fund manager's daily life. (Don't forget: "The more you rule, the more gold you get.") Combine that time pressure with the current unprecedented financial power — a power that continues to grow — of mutual fund managers and you will begin to see how this comes into conflict with the supposed long-term interest of corporate management trying to build a business that will remain viable for years to come.

As anyone with even a nodding acquaintance with the doings of Wall Street knows, a lot can be accomplished in three months with the power of big money. And as anyone who has worked in business knows, three months of work toward fulfilling a business plan can mean nothing.

While a company's managers are effectively locked into their situation, a large, well-financed shareholder activist can move easily from one situation to another. If one company can't be pushed into action to "enhance shareholder value," another can be quickly found. And there's no standard that dictates that one target of such attention is more "deserving" than another. In fact, as we saw in the 1980s with the "corporate raider" movement, decisions about targets usually had more to do with the raider's assessment of how vulnerable the company was to insure quick success for the raider and *not* because the managements of the targets had committed greater transgressions than were committed at other companies.

One noted mutual fund manager who announced in 1990 his intention of becoming an activist shareholder was John Neff, the long-time manager of the $10 billion Windsor Fund. For the first twenty-five-plus years of his career, Neff practiced a traditional form of investment. When he lost faith in the future of an investment target, he sold his shares and walked away. The sale of those shares would have gone to a "greater fool" who, not recognizing the negative signs that Neff's astute analysis identified as gathering around a company, would have bought Neff's shares at a premium price. Considering Neff's excellent long-term performance results at the Windsor Fund, this approach apparently worked very well from the late 1960s through the 1970s and 1980s. Why, then, in the early 1990s has Neff (and other mutual fund managers) suddenly moved away from this traditional investment approach to become an activist? Is it because corporate management is now more unresponsive to the interests of shareholders than it was a few years ago? Perhaps.

But there is also the reality that Neff and other highly successful fund managers who manage billions of dollars and control large blocks of company shares are quickly painting themselves into a corner. There are far fewer opportunities to sell the shares of a company that the manager doesn't like. With elitist stock ownership of companies controlled by a few people, all the "fools" know each other. That handful of people who could sit around a small table and represent majority ownership of a company not only know each other but also know exactly what each is doing with his shares. If one of them becomes displeased with the company's future prospects and tries to sell his large stake, who would buy it? Not the rest of the people sitting around that little table. They would want to dump their shares too. But they couldn't without deflating the price of the stock and losing money. So the growing trend is for that handful of people to gang together and beat up the company to try to satisfy their self-interests through that route.

One activist fight that Neff attempted in the fall of 1991 was against New York megabank Citicorp. At that time Citicorp was experiencing huge losses and as a way of saving money was considering omitting the dividend on its common stock. Neff, whose Windsor Fund held a large stake in Citicorp common stock, knew all too well that a dividend omission would mean loss of dividend income for his fund, as well as the certainty of a sharp drop in the value of his shares after the dividend omission was officially announced. Neff fought bitterly against Citicorp management to try to halt the dividend omission move.

But Neff lost his fight. Citicorp omitted its dividend, and its stock price promptly dropped from $13 to $8½. This had a strong negative impact on the performance of Neff's fund. But by early spring of 1992, less than a year after Neff's unsuccessful activism, Citicorp's prospects had improved — in large part because of the money the bank saved by not paying a dividend. Those improved prospects raised its stock price to $19 by mid 1992 (and to $43 in late 1993). In spring 1992, a *New York Times* reporter asked Neff about his struggle with Citicorp over the dividend omission and the subsequent rebound in the bank's stock price. Neff made a gentlemanly admission about his dividend fight: "Obviously, in retrospect, I was wrong."

However gentlemanly this admission of being wrong was, it has broad implications. If Neff (or another fund manager) had been successful at Citicorp (or, more likely, at some smaller company that would not have been as strong in fending off the pressure from a big investor), there might not have been a "retrospect" opportunity for a gentlemanly admission of being wrong. The powerful fund manager would have been successful in achieving his short-term goals, while crippling the company in its efforts to achieve long-term goals.

The increasing involvement of mutual fund managers in the arena of shareholder rights and the power of the investments they control will certainly evolve into something much more in the 1990s beyond simple fights over dividend cuts. Here's a recent real-world illustration of where this trend is probably leading and the types of activities that mutual fund industry leaders seem willing to engage in to reach their goals. Information International, Inc., is a California-based NASDAQ-listed company that develops computer systems used in newspaper and magazine composition and production. In 1987 an investment group controlled by Fidelity Management & Research, the parent organization of the mutual fund company, started accumulating a large shareholder stake in Information International. This investment group was *not* a Fidelity public mutual fund (although for a few years the management of Information International was given the impression that it *was* a Fidelity public mutual fund). This Fidelity-controlled group was, instead, a *private* pool that included the personal investment dollars of Fidelity executives, including Fidelity chairman Edward C. Johnson 3d. The private pool was organized through Fidelity's offshore operation based in Bermuda and included the money of several deep-pocket individual foreign investors. This group has been active in dozens of situations since the early 1980s.

The management of Information International was very happy to get this investment attention from Fidelity and cooperated with the investment group's special information requests.[8] By early 1990 the Fidelity-controlled group had acquired over 30 percent of the shares of Information International. Then, at the 1990 shareholders meeting, the manager of the Fidelity-controlled group shocked Information International's management with angry accusations of management incompetence and in the name of "shareholder rights" demanded that the company be liquidated and the cash paid out to the shareholders. The management of Information International was startled by this action because before this meeting the manager of the Fidelity-controlled group had always been friendly and had never expressed any dissatisfaction with management or with the company's business plans.

Ironically, Information International's pension fund was being managed by Fidelity. The company's managers came to view that pension money as actually helping to finance the effort to dissolve their company (and their jobs). The pension fund was hotly removed from Fidelity management with an accompanying sharp letter from Information International's president to Fidelity chairman Johnson accusing him of being personally involved in "penny-ante corporate raiding."

The real point here is not to assess the appropriateness of the actions of the Fidelity-controlled investment group. Although the action was certainly hardball, the group's push to liquidate Information International may have been a fully responsible reading of the potential alternatives concerning the company's prospects in the years ahead. The fact that the Fidelity-controlled group would have achieved substantial cash returns on its investment with the liquidation of the company may simply have been a coincidental result of a weighing of the alternatives. (Another possible irony in this situation was that the Fidelity group went by the name of the Integrity Fund.)

The significant point, instead, is that the people at Information International never investigated or questioned the investment tactics used by Fidelity until they came to view themselves as victims of those tactics. Before the personal experience of potentially being thrown out on the street as a result of the investment power of the Fidelity-controlled group, the company's management was apparently concerned only with the percentage return that Fidelity managers could deliver for their pension fund. And if that return was achieved through shareholder rights activity at the expense of other people's jobs or businesses . . . well, so what?

You may be equally unconcerned about the tactics used by the managers of your funds as the people at Information International initially were. (When one is focused entirely on the return that an investment can deliver toward a personal goal of wealth achievement, all other considerations can be easily dismissed as merely philosophical.) But the growing trend toward greater involvement of mutual fund operators in the arena of shareholder rights can be viewed from another perspective that directly affects your wallet. The costs associated with shareholder rights activity — such as proxy fights and legal fees — can be expensive. And those costs will come out of your fund — above and beyond the management fees you are already paying. The fine print of the prospectus of one mutual fund company that announced plans in the early 1990s to become actively involved in exercising "its rights as a shareholder" puts it this way: "This area of corporate activity is increasingly prone to litigation and it is possible that a Fund could be involved in lawsuits related to such activities." The prospectus goes on to say that the fund operator would try to avoid such risk of litigation, but then says: "No guarantee can be made, however, that litigation against a Fund will not be undertaken or liabilities incurred."

There also is no guarantee that the shareholder rights activity will be successful. In 1990, for example, there were 120 proxy proposals sponsored by institutional investors. (There were only twenty-eight such proxy proposals in 1988.) Of the 120 proxy proposals, twenty-three were successful. These 120 proposals carried varying degrees of expense charged back to the funds the institutional investors represented. And 80 percent of them failed.

Moreover, corporate America is very aware of the trend for institutional investors to flex their investment muscle, and it is very threatened by it. The battle lines are being drawn, just as similar battle lines were drawn in the 1980s against so-called corporate raiders. As corporate managers become more aggressive in the 1990s in protecting their personal self-interests and fund managers become more aggressive in searching out ways of achieving *their* self-interests, the costs (and bloodiness) of these battles will likely increase. An alternative scenario to blood-drenched battles, however, is potentially more troubling. Instead of fighting the powerful institutional managers, a company's management team may decide to focus on the reality of keeping their high-paid jobs by easily acquiescing to the Wall Street perspective — no matter how it may affect the long-term prospects of the company. Whatever way things go, you, as a mutual fund shareholder, will be paying for it. You can't be the bemused bystander you may have been during the corporate raider frolics of the 1980s because now your money is the central character in the drama.

In the 1990s one of the decisions you'll have to make in choosing mutual fund alternatives is whether you want to put your cash at risk to finance these shareholder rights forays. You will have to make that decision *before* you commit your money, because by the time you have evidence in hand that the returns have *not* outweighed the costs, it will be too late to withdraw your money from the fund without loss.

You may also want to assess whether you want your money to finance this type of activity at all. Eventually, as this trend snowballs (as all such trends tend to do), the financial power rapidly being concentrated in the hands of institutional investors will most likely personally touch your life or the lives of people you know, perhaps in a way similar to the experience of the people at Information International.

As it turned out at Information International, the company was not liquidated. Instead, the Fidelity-controlled group took a seat on the company's board of directors. Other seats on the board were then filled with Fidelity sympathizers. The company's president, who had written the sharp letter to Johnson, retired from the company. A new management team was brought in. An aggressive expansion program was started. The company purchased other companies in related businesses — expanding capabilities to include nationwide communication systems linking a publication's editorial center to distant printing and production centers. With these added capabilities, the company took on new clients, including the *New York Times, Investors Business Daily, Fortune, Time, Money,* the *Wall Street Journal,* and other Dow Jones publications. By mid 1993, therefore, the people who effectively controlled the largest investment company in the world also effectively controlled the company that in turn effectively controlled the communication systems of nearly every major investment/ business publication in America. (Fidelity's interest in Information International builds on its interest in other publishing and investment/business information services. At the same time as the Information International investment, the Fidelity group also controlled a director spot and a large stock position at Primark, a Virginia-based company that during the early 1990s redefined itself from a utilities company into an information services company offering, for example, an on-line financial data service for investment professionals and news publications. Also controlled by Fidelity executives are forty-six community newspapers covering almost all of eastern Massachusetts. In addition, in 1992 Fidelity started publishing a high-gloss "investment" magazine called *Worth.* The fact that Fidelity is the publisher of the magazine is not mentioned anywhere on its pages. Instead, the magazine is published under the name of a Fidelity subsidiary.)

The action Fidelity executives took in the Information International situation as a *private* pool was not fully legally permitted by Fidelity *public* mutual funds until 1993. One of Fidelity's first targets that year was photography giant Eastman Kodak. Beginning in early 1993, various Fidelity funds collectively amassed over 6.5 million shares in the company. Fidelity quickly became the largest holder of Eastman Kodak stock and also quickly became frustrated with Eastman Kodak's chief executive's lack of willingness to follow Fidelity's "advice" concerning steps for enhancing shareholder value by streamlining operations. At the beginning of August 1993, following Fidelity's prodding, the uncooperative chief executive had been forced to resign.[9] Within a few weeks after the chief executive's ouster, Eastman Kodak announced its plans, which, not surprisingly, closely matched Fidelity's "advice." Those plans included the elimination of 10,000 jobs. What is unknown is how many of the 10,000 people slated for removal from the Eastman Kodak payroll had previously sent money into Fidelity funds and thereby empowered Fidelity management to take such shareholder activist steps. Also unknown is whether the productivity gains from those eliminated jobs will be reflected in an increase in the price of Eastman Kodak stock sufficiently to counteract the loss of income from those jobs for the individuals involved as well as the communities where those jobs had been located. What is known, however, is that there will be no opportunity for a John Neff–style retrospection.

Clearly, mutual funds and other institutional investors have the power to reshape the face of American business. Increasingly clear is their inclination to do so. So far, they have declined to define what their vision may be for that reshaping — if, in fact, they have a vision beyond next quarter's horse-race performance chart. Nonetheless, every time you send a dollar into a fund that has announced its intentions of shareholder activism, you are sending a positive vote for that undeclared vision.

All Good Ideas, but None New

The good ideas offered by the mutual fund concept — from diversification to professional management to efficiency to God-bless-'em shareholder activism — are not, of course, *new* ideas. The basic concept and all the good ideas that it encompasses have been around for over a hundred years.

Moreover, the elevation of the basic concept (and all its accompanying good ideas) to a status of unquestioned popularity is not new either. There have been two periods in this century when Americans lifted the idea to mania status. Once in a massive way during the 1920s; once in a somewhat less massive way in the 1960s. And during the last century,

British investors did the same thing in a massive way in the late 1880s. And, as always happens with manias, these three periods ended in disasters: twice in massive ways — at the end of the 1920s in America and in the early 1890s in Great Britain — and once in a somewhat less massive way in America at the end of the 1960s.

CHAPTER 2

■ ■ ■

How It Happened Before

History never repeats itself exactly. But when new generations choose to ignore the broad forces as well as the specific details that shaped past epochs, history has an ugly tendency to return with only slightly different features. When it comes to lessons of financial history, you are probably tired of hearing about the 1920s, the financial collapse beginning in 1929, and the following Great Depression. But just as we should never forget how Nazism developed and exerted itself during the 1930s and 1940s, we should never forget what happened in the 1920s. The financial dynamics of the 1920s brought out the worst in human nature and crowd frenzy, and as a result the lives of countless people suffered immeasurable damage.

It was during the 1920s that the idea of large investment pools created out of money gathered from the general investing public — as opposed to pools created by small groups of wealthy people who knew one another — first achieved what an article in *Barron's* at the time called "universal favor." It all really started during the 1924 presidential election year when the Federal Reserve Board, fearing looming signs of a recession, eased credit and lowered interest rates. At the time, confidence in America's future was low. Faith in leadership following the Teapot Dome Scandal of 1922 was shaken. Americans were just beginning to recover from a sharp stock market drop in 1921 and a following deep economic slump that lasted into 1923. With these volatile swings in the economy and with memories of the recent Communist takeover of Russia fresh in mind, there was no interest in letting anyone think that capitalism "didn't work," particularly since third-party presidential candidate Robert LaFollette of the Progressive Party was spreading unsettling statistical evidence about the widening discrepancy of wealth distribution among

Americans. But the Federal Reserve Board's action pepped things up and Coolidge won.

The Fed's action also had the effect of lowering interest rates paid on bank savings accounts to below 4 percent. Historically, the inability to get a 4 percent return from "safe" instruments like bank savings accounts and government bonds has had a strong psychological impact on people. It frequently has sparked periods of speculative investment activity as waves of small savers increased their risk exposure in pursuit of better returns on their money through "investments" in speculative instruments like securities and nongovernment bonds. This happened in 1822, 1825, and 1888, as well as during the 1920s. It would happen again in the 1960s (and, apparently, once again in the 1990s). Each of these past periods of varying degrees of speculation ended in varying degrees of collapse.

In the 1920s many former small savers exercised their speculative pursuit of high returns on their money through "professionally managed" public investment pools known as *investment trusts*. These were the forerunners of today's mutual funds.

The Era of the Investment Trusts

Although the basic idea of the investment trust had been used in Great Britain since about 1860 and had been available to Americans since at least 1908, investment trusts didn't catch on in popularity in America until the 1920s. But then the investment trusts became *very* popular. In 1924 there were fewer than fifty investment trusts with only a few thousand investors. By the October 1929 crash there were 755 investment trusts. And about 10 percent of American households had money in at least one of them by that time.

The speculative period that began in 1924 and reached its peak in early 1929 and its ending in October 1929 had a lot of crazy elements to it. But the investment trusts ended up being the craziest of them all — with almost all the shareholders losing everything.

Several important factors converged during the 1920s that made people go seemingly crazy overnight and made them ripe for the "promises" of investment trust promoters. The drop in interest rates was certainly one of them. But there were others.

Perhaps the single most important factor was the government's 1924 redemption of Liberty Bonds, which were sold during World War I. Before the government aggressively sold these bonds to help finance the war effort, few Americans had any exposure to the financial world and its language. Stocks and bonds were rarely owned by anyone except the very wealthy. Most people with small amounts of extra cash didn't even have bank accounts. People literally kept cash under the mattress or buried in the backyard. But the promotion of the Liberty Bonds — most of which paid 4.25 percent interest — pulled that money out of hiding and introduced millions of Americans to the concept of "bonds." Then suddenly in 1924, when interest rates dropped and the government redeemed the bonds, people who were forced to sell their bonds back to the government had money that they had to put somewhere else. And because they had had such a good experience with the government bond, they started viewing *all* bonds — including what we would now call junk bonds — with equal faith. It was then a short leap from the concept of getting fixed income from bonds to the glamour of chasing after capital appreciation via rising prices of common stocks.

Another factor prompting the investment fever of the 1920s was simply the growing size and wealth of the American middle class. The United States had become the industrial and agricultural giant of the world — achieved to a degree by default because of the chaos in Europe following the war. Incomes rose, particularly among new classes of middle and upper management white-collar workers.

During the first part of the decade, people used this new wealth to go on a buying spree of shop-till-you-drop consumerism. Part of that consumerism was touched off by the pent-up need to begin lives that had been delayed by the war. This shopping spree was also set off by the introduction of a dazzling array of attractive mass-produced products that were priced within the buying range of most working people — products like cars, radios, and phonographs.

After a while this heavy consumerism slowed. (Everybody can't buy a new car or new model radio *every* year.) And then people with money decided it was time to grow up and stop the mindless buying and put the money to good use to make it increase. The compulsion to buy was replaced with a compulsion to use excess wealth to accumulate even more wealth — particularly for retirement years.

The thought of spending one's later years in healthy, idle retirement was a new idea for most Americans in the 1920s. Until this period people expected to work until they died or were too sick to go on. But with wealth increasing among new groups of people, the thought of retirement became a realistic expectation. Retirement, however, was not considered a "right" and certainly not a right to be guaranteed by the government as later generations would come to expect after the creation of Social Security in the 1930s and Medicare in the 1960s. The idea in the 1920s, therefore, of "investing for the future" became embedded in the general consciousness as a mandatory personal responsibility. (In 1929 only about 10 percent of Americans were covered by any type of corporate or union pension plan. And, of course, there wasn't any Social Security.) A typical magazine article of the time would be headlined "Starting at Age 40 On the Road to Financial Independence"[1] and would paint a grim picture of old-age poverty if an aggressive investment program was not begun immediately. For many people it was this fear of the future — the fear of becoming an abandoned pauper in old age — that made them fearless about the investments they made in the present. The great irony, of course, is that this fearless attitude actually made many of them paupers long before they reached old age.

Yet another factor that would become extremely important as the decade developed was the widespread acceptance of the new idea of buying things "on time" in monthly payments. The concept of paying for all those cars, radios, and phonographs over a long period of time was then applied to buying bonds and stocks as well as shares of investment trusts. People were so certain about the successful outcome of these investment products that they were willing to borrow money to get in on the action more fully. This, of course, is what buying on margin is all about. Once you had an established account of stocks or bonds (or shares of investment trusts) you could borrow against the value of that portfolio to further expand your holdings with only a small down payment of cash — which in the 1920s was as low as 5 percent.

During the 1920s buying on margin was not considered a risky thing to do. Instead, it was the solution that allowed the "little guy" with only a few dollars to put aside every month to make his nest egg grow quickly. Interest rates were so low that it made sense to borrow and put the money into investments that from all available evidence (up until October 1929, that is) were delivering far better returns than the margin loan interest. It wasn't until the 1930s, when people looked back and tried to figure out what had happened, that excessive margin buying was identified as one of the culprits. Margin buying, which was considered the *answer* by people during the 1920s, has since become viewed as the dirty word of that decade's particular insanity. (Don't forget, however, that every period of history has its own particular insanity that is almost never identified until years later.)

The role of the investment trust in all of this became very significant. The reason that it became significant is that it allowed large groups of people who otherwise would not have participated in the direct owner-ship of bonds and stocks or been involved in more esoteric investment techniques, such as short selling and dealing in puts and calls, to join in on what became a financial free-for-all. If a general obsession during the 1920s in making money via bond and stock investments fueled those speculative markets with more money than could be prudently put to good use, then the essential appealing "promise" of the investment trusts — professional management of a diversified portfolio — fueled those markets even more by bringing in the money of the unwitting.

From Theory to Craze

The incredible thing was that the investment trust, which was an obscure and theoretical idea in 1924, grew to become a true national craze in less than six years. It's not surprising to find that, because of its theoretical nature, the earliest supporters of the idea were college and university professors. This academic support provided credibility and was quickly exploited by the people who actually made money from the idea — the investment trust promoters of Wall Street. Dozens of professors from the top schools (and many from some not-so-top schools) lectured and wrote countless books and articles about the idea. They also served (lucratively) on the boards of the investment trusts.

The preeminent academic supporter was a then well-respected (and in some circles *still* well-respected today) professor in the economics depart-ment of Yale University named Dr. Irving Fisher. Fisher, one of the most prolific writers and lecturers on finance of his day (as well as being a well-paid investment trust director), was a true believer. "The investment trust principle," he declared, "acts to reduce risks by utilizing the special knowledge of expert investment counsel, and by diversifying investments among many kinds of common and preferred stocks and bonds, foreign and domestic. It also operates to shift risks from those who lack invest-ment knowledge to those who possess it. As a consequence normally speculative properties gravitate into the hands of these skilled agencies better able to forecast their true future value. . . . Investment trusts buy when there is real anticipation of a rise, due to underlying causes, and sell when there is a real anticipation of a fall. . . . They buy at prices less than the true worth of the securities purchased, taking advantage of their superior knowledge of industrial and trading conditions."[2]

Among the many errors of Fisher's claims, the most important perhaps was that the risks did *not* shift from "those who lack investment knowledge to those who possess it." Instead, the risks stayed firmly behind with "those who lack investment knowledge" while the money alone got shifted with full faith and few strings attached. But at the time Fisher's confidence in the expertise of investment trust managers was categorical and unswerving. (Many managers of the investment trusts were Fisher's own former students, so from Fisher's perspective how could they have been anything less than infallible experts?)

Today's mutual fund promoters never go as far as Fisher did when making promises. They may try to imply that what they do matches Fisher's promises. They may wish that you believe that Fisher's promises are the same today as they had seemed to be so many decades ago. They may encourage others — such as financial journalists — to say such things about them. But they never claim these things directly themselves, because they know these assumptions are not true. And there's plenty of evidence to prove that they are not true — not true in the past, and — because of the huge factor of human limitation and its companion human error that is inherent in investment activity — never to be true in the future.

Unlike those of us living today, however, the people of the 1920s did not have the benefit of statistical evidence to temper their expectations about the value of "professional management." All they had was the word of Fisher and other investment oracles. And what mere mortal could question the words delivered by Fisher from such a lofty mount as the economics department of Yale University?

The words of Fisher and the many other then-credible academic theoreticians were picked up and altered only slightly as their ideas were spread like wildfire through the financial press and then in increasingly simplified terms on to the popular press to satisfy the information needs of newly cash-rich, investment-hungry Americans. The early magazine and newspaper articles on investment trusts displayed a skeptical perspective as they introduced the new idea. The articles had titles like "New

Investment Fields," "Something New for Your Money," "What to Ask Before Investing," "What Investors Should Know About Investment Trusts," "Investment Trusts — Investment or Speculation?," "Investment Trusts, A Caution."

The later ones lost their skeptical edge and showed full faith: "Endorsing the Investment Trust," "Investment Trusts for the Poor Man," "Buying Investment Trust Stocks for Profit," "Investment Trust, A New Money Power," "Investing Where One Trusts."[3]

By the end of the decade it was difficult to pick up a newspaper or magazine without finding some article about the easy road to financial security via investment trusts — and all supported by pages and pages of ads for investment trusts. All of this reached a pinnacle of sorts in August 1929, when the *Ladies' Home Journal* ran an article titled "Everybody Ought to be Rich" that promoted not only the easy wonders of investment trusts for the smallest of small investors but also the power to be gained in buying shares of investment trusts on margin. Not to be outdone by a competitor, *Good Housekeeping* promptly started a service that invited its readers to send in their lists of bond and stock holdings for personalized appraisal.[4]

As the decade developed, the "proof" of the success of the investment trusts became so compelling that anyone still clinging to bank savings accounts or government bonds paying piddling interest rates compared to the annual returns of 20, 30, 40 percent and more via investment trusts was considered a complete fool. And as the investment trust became more popular, the popularity itself was presented as proof of its appropriateness for all. If everybody was doing it, the reasoning went, then it must be right. And, certainly, how could it be wrong? The few nay-sayers of the day were drowned out by all this proof.

Even in 1929, when many voices were publicly expressing concern about the ever-rising stock market, investment trust promoters continued to ballyhoo their idea as being immune to such worries. In the middle of October 1929, Irving Fisher uttered his then widely reported and now legendary pronouncement that stock prices had reached "what looks like a permanently high plateau." In addition, Fisher claimed, there was even further opportunity through investment trust involvement: "Largely through the influence of the investment trust movement, the public has been waking up to the superior attraction of stocks over bonds. . . . The operation of the investment trusts . . . has acted to stabilize the stock market rather than to make its fluctuations more violent. . . . [The investment trusts] are safeguarding the public."[5]

What Fisher didn't know was that a few weeks earlier — on September 3, 1929, to be exact — the Dow Jones Industrial Average had reached its high of the 1920s bull market. It would not reach this level again until 1954 — twenty-five years later. In other words, those investors who went into a diversified portfolio of stocks during the heady days of 1929 (whether "professionally managed" or not) had to wait twenty-five years to break even — that is, if they had the patience or longevity to hold on that long. Fisher himself died in 1947 and therefore was unable to experience directly exactly what "long-term" meant in his promise to others of the value of common stocks as long-term investments.

But before that day of reckoning in 1929, American investors thought they had found the easy answer, and they embraced the investment trust — described at the time as "the department store of finance"[6] — as a riskless way to be involved in the broad world of investments. It is important to remember that the people who put their money into investment trusts during the 1920s did not think they were doing anything risky. Fisher and many, many others continually assured them that it was not risky. It was the small individual investor who tried to invest directly into bond and stock markets who, according to the conventional wisdom of the time, was the gambling speculator, not the investment trust shareholder. Today when an image of the late 1920s is conjured up, it usually includes a vision of some cab driver or messenger boy frantically speculating on the hot stock tips of the day. While this image may have some validity, shareholders of investment trusts were not considered part of that speculative scene. Instead, they had professionals "safeguarding" them.

The number of investment trust shareholders grew from a few thousand in 1924 to over 50,000 in 1927. Then things started really to heat up. By late 1929 there were about 525,000 investment trust shareholders — a tenfold increase in less than two years.[7] The amount of money involved went from about $350 million in early 1927[8] to about $8.5 billion in 1929.

Later these hapless shareholders would learn painfully that just because ten times as many people with twenty-five times as much money wanted to do the same thing at the same time didn't mean that there was suddenly a similar increase in the amount of good investment opportunities available or enough of Irving Fisher's beloved "professionals" to manage it all effectively (and honestly).

Actually, the decade's shift of attention from consumerism to savings and investment activity slowed the potential for investment return. It had been unusually heavy consumerism that had delivered much of the tremendous rate of industrial growth (and accompanying investment returns) earlier in the decade. And when people changed their use of money from unusually heavy buying to unusually heavy "investing," there went the fast growth (as well as the potential of making fast-growth investment return).

But there was no absence of growth of the investment trust industry to scoop in all the money and keep the bullish publicity machinery churning. From 1927 through 1929, about six hundred new investment trusts were formed. In 1929 new trusts were created at a rate of about one a day. It seemed that any business with any type of connection to money formed one or more investment trusts — investment banks, brokers, trust companies, investment consultants, commercial banks and their affiliates, and on and on.

By late 1929, half of the two hundred New York banks ran investment trusts. As in the early 1990s, bankers of the 1920s found it very appealing to make money through the collection of fees from their customers by selling them shares of investment trusts, as well as securities and bonds, instead of trying to make money via the actual investment expertise that is demanded by traditional banking.

Today we would recognize the investment trusts that got everybody so excited during the 1920s as direct progenitors of *closed-end* funds — the funds that issue a limited number of shares that are bought and sold among investors via the stock exchange.

The *open-end* fund, which continually issues new shares and redeems them directly from the fund company to investors depending on the amount of investor demand, traces its origins to the 1924 founding of the Massachusetts Investors Trust. Still operating today, the Massachusetts Investors Trust featured many of the characteristics that we normally associate with today's modern mutual fund. This includes the ability to sell shares back to the fund company — to redeem them — at full asset value. To sell shares of closed-end funds, a shareholder must go to the stock market and sell the shares to another investor at whatever price can be obtained — whether that price matches the actual asset value or not.

The open-end form of investment trust was not very popular in the 1920s. In fact, by the October 1929 crash there were only nineteen of them with assets of barely $140 million.[9] One reason for this lack of popularity was that the open-end funds were not as aggressively sold as the closed-end. The potential for commissions for brokers and others selling investment trusts was smaller for the open-end trusts than for the closed-end.

Another reason that the open-end trusts didn't spark much excitement was that most of them followed the practice of publicly revealing where the shareholders' money was actually being invested. At almost all the closed-end funds the specific nature of the investments was a carefully guarded secret. They were truly "mystery stocks." People sent their money into what were essentially *blind* pools based on their full, unquestioned faith in the abilities of the professionals. The trusts justified this secrecy on the grounds that if others knew how they were investing it would compromise their investing effectiveness. And small investors at the time bought that mystery — and the mystique that went with it. The open-end trusts, with their policy of full disclosure, lacked this appealing ingredient of mystery.

Before the sobering days of reality hit in the 1930s, the closed-end investment trusts had quite a moment in the sun. Since investors didn't know where the professionals were investing the money, they could only imagine the moneymaking adventures going on behind closed doors. And if the stock market was going through the roof, the mystique dictated, then the investment trust professionals would make the future value of the shares of the trusts go sky high. As a result, the small investor was willing to pay a hefty premium for each share of an investment trust (bought on margin, of course) over the actual asset value per share. By 1929, shares of many of the most popular investment trusts traded on the stock exchange at prices double or more their actual asset value.

Hidden Agenda

It would take a few years before shareholders found out the full truth, but the secrecy that the investment trusts operated under and the mystique that surrounded them hid a lot of business shenanigans. Part of the shenanigans was pure thievery: sales of the investment trust managers' worthless securities at high prices to the trusts they ran; no-interest "loans" to managers and their cronies that were never repaid; simple theft of the money without investing it at all; or, in short, the usual set of shenanigans that goes on when the unscrupulous come in contact with other people's money.

But more serious than the effects of bald fraud were the investment trust managers' secret forays into far-flung, high-risk, speculative arenas. The investments went far beyond the "many kinds of common and preferred stocks and bonds, foreign and domestic" that Irving Fisher had promised. It also went into direct ownership of real estate (sometimes purchased from the investment trust managers themselves at inflated prices) and direct investment into highly speculative oil, gas, and mineral-exploration projects. And when competition for the "many kinds of common and preferred stocks" became fierce, a number of the trusts took on the profile of venture capital pools, pumping money into "unseasoned" new companies (often set up quickly by the investment trust managers or their friends) and the day's equivalent of junk bonds. Other so-called investments included nonproducing orange groves in California, a subway line in Buenos Aires (which, at the time of its bankruptcy, made up 70 percent of the portfolio of one trust), a Mississippi River barge line, and swampland in Florida.

Without the knowledge of their shareholders, the investment trust managers threw money at everything with little regard — or, more accurately, with total contempt — for the principles of investment prudence that were already well established by this time. But those principles were considered old-fashioned, stodgy, and out of touch with what was being touted as "New Era Economics" and its accompanying set of new rules.

The cruel ruse of the investment trust movement was to attract the money of the most risk-averse type of people — those too afraid, or those who had insufficient amounts of money, to do any type of investing on their own — and then secretly expose that money to the most risky types of investments and investment techniques (such as short selling) imaginable. For investment trust managers it seemed that other people's money was fair game for anything once they got control of it. Perhaps more accurately, however, other people's money became the equipment for the investment trusts managers' pursuit of exciting sport and their own dangerous game of one-upmanship among themselves.

Moreover, the trusts became convenient vehicles for self-serving behavior that at the time was legal. For brokerage companies, for example, running their own investment trusts became an easy way to dump shares of new issues that the brokerages were underwriting. (The brokerages would get a fee for underwriting the new issue. Then they would get a management fee for selecting the stock for their own investment trust's portfolio!) As the fever for anything called "securities" reached a boiling point in 1929, there was a rush of companies going public to satisfy the demand. Just about any harebrained idea could be guaranteed a welcome stock sale at high prices, particularly from brokerage-controlled investment trusts. It was only later that it was discovered that there really was no market — and therefore no value — for most of the shares of these harebrained new companies.

Another shocker revealed to investment trust shareholders in the early 1930s was that several trusts had only masqueraded as general investment pools. In reality they were organized purely for controlling or influencing the management of certain public companies. Although this was unknown to most trust shareholders, these trusts were really more like holding companies with concentrated power over specific industries rather than investment entities with diversified portfolios.[10] For the people who controlled the money of these trusts, it provided financing for their own power trips over public companies and their personal moneymaking schemes — and all without the nuisance of having to put up any of their own money to achieve it.

But those revelations would come later. Meanwhile, during the last two years of the decade, everybody was getting rich — or at least they thought so. By 1929 the investment trusts had become an end in themselves. In fact, investment trusts became the fastest-growing industry in America. In 1929, the formation of new investment trusts accounted for nearly one-third of all new stock issues coming to market.

Why bother setting up a business that had to make a tangible product or deliver some personal service when it was easier to make money from money by managing investments via investment trusts? And as a small investor why bother trying to search out the hot companies of tomorrow or even to use your financial resources to set up your own business when it was so easy just to give your money over to professionals who knew for certain where to put it?

After a while some investment trusts were formed for the sole purpose of investing in other investment trusts. This idea was said to help investors get multiple layers of diversification. It wasn't good enough to have one set of professionals taking care of your interests (and, incidentally, collecting the management fees for doing so), you needed many sets (collecting multiple layers of management fees). Small investors got so confused about the number of complicated choices of trusts that they needed to hire professionals to sort out the professionals. Thus the investment idea that had promised to make things easier for small investors got beyond the understanding of the very people it was originally meant to serve.

Actually, the phenomenon of trusts buying trusts was a classic sign of the peak of a financial mania — that is, when a financial idea takes on the characteristics of financial cannibalism — a self-consumption that has nothing to do with the actual underlying investments supposedly being represented. These trusts of trusts were the first to tumble like fragile houses of cards in the early 1930s.

Later in the 1960s, when Americans exhibited their second mania of the century for large public investment pools (by then restructured and named mutual funds), this idea was revived in a form called "fund of funds," which came to similar grief. Just as the forming of trusts of trusts marked the nearing conclusion of the era of the investment trusts, the fund-of-funds idea came near the end of the popularity of mutual funds in the late 1960s. All these funds of funds had disappeared by the late 1970s. Not to be discredited by the facts and meanings of history, this idea was revived again in the early 1990s with new names: "multifund funds" and as some versions of "wrap-account" and "asset-allocation" funds.

Added to the investment frenzy of the late 1920s was the ingredient of margin buying. Small investors bought shares of investment trusts on margin. Those investment trusts bought their investments, including shares of other investment trusts, on margin, and the other investment trusts bought their investments on margin — including shares of the first investment trusts that had bought their shares. Thus there was margin upon margin upon margin upon margin upon margin.

Then, in 1929, the margin craziness got even crazier. At the beginning of the year the Federal Reserve Board, now worried about the rising wave of speculation that was taking over the investment world, raised interest rates. Supposedly, this would raise interest rates on margin loans to make them less attractive and thereby slow the speculative fever. The Fed's action also raised interest rates paid on bank savings accounts to above 5 percent. But this didn't slow borrowing for margin buying. Even when the money was lent at 20 percent interest, it didn't matter to the borrowers, who, based on past market performance, were expecting even greater annual returns. In addition, getting a mere 5 percent return on your money was simply no longer tolerable — even for those people who would have been more than happy with such a return just six years earlier.

The interest rate increase, however, became a boon for the investment trusts. It gave them the opportunity to *lend* money at high interest rates to people looking for margin loans. Lending this money became one of the best methods for making certain money in 1929. After all, those loans weren't speculative. The lenders *knew* what they would get in return for their money. The investment trusts ended up lending money to small investors who then turned around and used it to buy shares of the same trusts. After a while some investment trusts became less of investment pools putting money into many different types of investments and took on more of the characteristics of a recirculating fountain — with the money being churned repeatedly within the trust itself or among the different trusts in the same company's "family" of trusts.

All this made sense to the people involved. They had the proof that everybody was getting rich. It didn't seem to matter that the returns they were enjoying did not reflect the underlying companies — the businesses — that the investments were supposed to represent. Apparently, very few people questioned how it was possible for so many investors to enjoy 20 percent or more annual returns on their money when very few businesses (except investment trusts) were growing at a similar pace.

The Unraveling

Of course, it was only an illusion. When this illusion began unraveling in October 1929 and investors started finding out exactly what the professionals had been doing with the money, the idea of "professionally managed" took a nosedive. The first stage of disillusionment with professional management came shortly after the 1929 crash when people found out how the managers reacted. Far from "safeguarding the public," the investment trust managers turned out to be among the most panic-prone of anybody. First, they privately dumped their own shares of their trusts while publicly touting their abilities to make everything right. Then, instead of using cash reserves to stabilize the market — as Irving Fisher and others had promised would happen — the managers used the money to buy back shares of their own trusts to maintain their price levels while ignoring (or selling) the stocks in the trusts' portfolios. When tested, the managers revealed that primal instinct of self-preservation. Lofty ideals and theories evaporated.

Then there was the devastating effect of leverage — the investment trick of margin buying that had promised to be the magic bullet to make everybody rich. When the market tumbled, leverage went into reverse and forced investors to sell shares of investment trusts and other stocks in order to raise cash to pay back margin loans. Leverage dealt the final blow. The dizzying heights turned around to become grim lows. One investment trust group — the Founders Group — that had used the powers of leverage especially deftly delivered to shareholders the thrill of watching a $1,000 investment in 1925 explode to a $10,500 peak value in 1929 and then the equal thrill of sorts of watching it plunge to a 1932 low of $25. (Unfortunately, almost half of the investors in this trust latched onto its star at or near its peak price.)

Looking back at the investment trust mania of the late 1920s from as close as May 19, 1930, *Barron's* observed: "Obtaining the necessary funds with which to operate an investment trust was easy. It was not so easy for a management with well-balanced investment judgment to know what to do with the money in its hands." Unfortunately, that observation was a little too late. It would have been more helpful about a year earlier. But a year earlier *Barron's* was busy reassuring its readers about the investment trusts' stabilizing effect on markets: "With the support of investment trust buying and the confidence of big interests, the market hardly seems likely to enter any sudden liquidating movement."[11]

At the bottom of the market in 1932, following three years of feeble rallies and increasingly deeper declines, the Dow Jones Industrial Average had lost 89 percent of its value at its 1929 high. But the investment trusts had done even worse. One dollar invested in an average closed-end investment trust in July 1929 was worth 2 cents in June 1932. That performance, however, was for those trusts still in existence in 1932. Fewer than two hundred remained.

While some of the trusts vanished or collapsed simply because of fraud by the investment trust promoters, it wasn't the fraud and accompanying shareholder abuse that caused the movement to collapse so completely. What truly did it in was the realization that trust managers were not infallible, along with the revelation that managers had secretly spread the money into a hodgepodge of speculative arenas from real estate to oil well prospecting and that the high-risk investment tricks like leverage and short selling when actually tested were uncontrollable.

The investment trust mania of the 1920s and its subsequent collapse, although unprecedented in America, was not unprecedented in history. Forty years earlier, Scottish and English investors experienced their own investment trust mania. This mania lasted from 1888 through early 1890. Then the inevitable collapse started and things deteriorated until reaching rock bottom in 1893.

The British Precedent

The British experience closely paralleled what Americans would go through just forty years later. During the 1920s the many similarities between the earlier British phenomenon and the growing American phenomenon were noticed and discussed.[12] But they were largely ignored. Whenever the British experience was brought up, American investors were told that things were different, people had changed, investing was now a science, and that the leaders of the modern American investment trusts were university-trained in a well-defined and experienced profession. Subsequent events would prove otherwise, and the similarities with the earlier experience became painfully clear.

The origins of the nineteenth-century British investment trust mania can be traced to events in the Scottish city of Dundee beginning in 1873. At that time Dundee was, like many other British cities of the nineteenth century, when Great Britain was the unchallenged industrial leader of the world, a wealthy manufacturing town. Looking for a way to get a better return on their money at a time when interest rates were dropping, the moneyed people of Dundee latched onto an idea created by twenty-eight-year-old Robert Fleming that would become the first real investment trust. Fleming had great success investing in the American railroad expansion and development of newly opened lands of the West.

Over the next fifteen years Fleming's investment trust idea spread. More than a dozen investment trusts were formed during that period. Steady performance and a prudent investment approach practiced by the investment trusts during this relatively "calm" world economic period gained widespread awareness.

Then in early 1888, in a turn of events that perfectly presaged the redemption of Liberty Bonds in 1924, the British government redeemed its debt securities, called *consols,* that had been yielding 3 percent interest for new ones paying 2½ percent. British "savers" were incensed. Three percent was bad enough, but 2½ percent was intolerable.

The "savers" looked around for an alternative, and many of them found Fleming's idea very attractive. Here was fifteen years of proof that "investment" wasn't all that risky. And the potential returns would certainly have to be better than a mere 2½ percent. As well, these investment trusts were run by the professionals who could keep pace with the fast-moving global investment world created by the newfangled instantaneous communication technology of the telegraph and telephone.

The investment trust suddenly became very popular. From 1888 through 1890, thirty new investment trusts were formed. And the British people moved millions of pounds into them out of their old safe "savings" instruments.[13] The people of Dundee were particularly enthusiastic. By 1890 the amount of money Dundee residents had committed to investment trusts was over three million pounds or an amount equal to the savings of the entire population for twenty years. This money also represented an amount that was about ten times the value of every building and foot of ground in the city.[14]

But then, in 1890, the problems started. They stemmed from the same situation that affected American investors in the 1920s: too many people trying to squeeze through the same door. The doorkeepers didn't close the door, of course. Nor did they warn anyone of what could be on the other side of the door. Instead, they made the doors wider. And why not? The doorkeepers themselves had the "proof" of their own success and expertise from the previous fifteen years. If they had been so consistently right before, how could their next moves possibly be wrong? Thus, for example, since investment into the developing United States had proved to be generally successful, investment into other developing economies would probably prove to be successful as well — countries like Australia, New Zealand, South Africa, and Argentina. And since people were finally going to allow the professionals to put money to aggressive good use instead of insisting on the stodgy ways of the past, investment trust managers snapped up floods of shares from a rush of private companies going public — providing an ever-widening fresh supply of securities for the professionals to play with. (Brewery companies achieved the greatest amount of speculative attention during this period of obsession with new public companies.)

And for a while it all looked good. Everybody was making money. That is, until November 1890. Then, kaboom.

This particular kaboom was called the Baring Crisis after Baring Brothers & Co., a highly respected brokerage firm that had started several investment trusts and loaded them up with foreign bonds paying high interest. The crisis occurred when the Argentine government defaulted on much of those bond holdings. (Default on loans to South American countries has been a recurring story of incredible consistency throughout financial history.) The Baring Crisis and the accompanying collapse of the Baring investment trusts, however, was just the beginning of a three-year downward spiral. Next, the investment companies that had underwritten the shares of newly public companies and then placed the shares in their own investment trusts at artificially high prices went down in flames. By February 1893 the *Economist* was chastising the investment trusts for their reckless investments: "Of many of the trust companies which were formed in such rapid succession a few years ago, when the mania for this form of joint-stock enterprise was rampant, it may be said with truth that, having sown the wind, they are now reaping the whirlwind." Worse would come in May 1893, when the American stock market crashed, followed by other crashes in South Africa and Australia.[15] These collapsing markets, whose previous spectacular rises had been achieved in large part by the money pumped into them by the British investment trusts, brought down so many investment trusts — with a total loss of investment of about two-thirds — that British investors generally avoided the idea for almost thirty years. This investment trust episode was a significant wealth destroyer of nineteenth-century Great Britain, particularly among middle-class people with small amounts of money to put at risk. The country never recovered its role of world financial dominance. It quickly deteriorated in status from a lender nation to a debtor nation.

Robert Fleming himself and his Dundee investors, however, survived all this. Interestingly, when the investment atmosphere was heating up in the late 1880s as other investment trust managers were cranking up the high-risk machine, Fleming became more and more conservative. (There is an important lesson here that should be noted.)

Following the 1890 crisis, the British investment trusts went through a period of reform that resulted in a retreat of investment temperament to one of extreme conservatism that limited investments almost exclusively to income-producing bonds and preferred stocks. But by the time in the 1920s when Americans took on the basic idea of the British investment trust, the lesson the British had learned was ignored so thoroughly that the only thing the American version had in common with the British was the name. Then, when the American trusts lost their own "test under fire," they went into a period of the same type of reform as had their British antecedents.

Reform

The first result of the devastating experience of the 1929 crash was the immediate turnaround of investor attitude toward the closed-end investment trusts. While during the 1920s the stocks of these investment trusts usually sold for more than their asset value, now they sold for large discounts from their asset value — often more than 30 percent. No new closed-end trust would be started for over a decade. (To this day the prices of shares of closed-end funds are usually below actual asset value. To a large extent this is a carryover from the early 1930s.)

While the closed-end trust idea all but disappeared, people noticed that the open-end "mutual" investment trusts had all survived. Their portfolio values had been clobbered mercilessly, but because none of them had engaged in margin buying or most of the other investment tricks that the closed-end trusts had, the open-end trusts still maintained some reasonable values — including a few that declined by less than half their 1929 highs. (As strange as it may seem, investors of the late 1920s who survived into the early 1930s by losing only half their money were considered the winners of the day.)

Unfortunately, the tricksters who had done so much to sully the name of the closed-end trusts just moved over to the open-end business and started a new round of shenanigans. In the 1930s most of the shenanigans involved the way the "mutual" trusts were sold. The actual investments of the trusts of this period tended to be conservative, but as they became more popular some of them reverted to the old tricks of the 1920s.

The selling was aggressive and supported by sales charges (or *loads*) that were negotiated to as high as a customer would pay. During this period an average load was 10 percent. Since there was actually little interest in stock market investing, the trust salespeople had to beat a lot of bushes to find anyone to send money into a trust. And they had no compunction about saying *anything* to sell. Since there was no regulation of the advertising messages or promises that could be made potential investors, the "mutual" trust salespeople and the advertising that supported their efforts did indeed say anything. The trusts, advertising promised, were the way to certain wealth. People literally were promised wealth as great as J. P. Morgan's and John D. Rockefeller's via trust investment.

As the 1930s advanced, more people began to rethink the possibilities of stock market investing and the concept of professional management. That revived some optimism. And beginning in 1932, the stock market embarked on one of the biggest bull advances in history, with the Dow going from 41 at its low in 1932 to 195 in 1937 — but still far below its 1929 peak of 381. But then another setback in the economy and another stock market crash, on March 19, 1937, caused yet another reassessment of what professional money managers were doing with the money of small investors.

To investors' dismay, the professionals turned out to be up to the same old tricks. Politicians finally reacted and congressional hearings followed. For the next three years, the public heard a seemingly endless series of horror stories of investor abuse. On the verge of near total disintegration, leaders of the "mutual" investment trust industry finally decided to cooperate with the government to come up with regulations to restore investor faith. (At the time there was a strong and almost successful movement among lawmakers to completely outlaw all forms of investment trusts.)

Industry leaders huddled with SEC rule makers and hammered out what became the Investment Company Act of 1940. It was at this time that the tarnished term "investment trust" was changed to "investment company." (The label "mutual fund" wouldn't come into popular use until the 1950s.) The Investment Company Act of 1940 was the document that set out rules for mutual fund management behavior: rules such as investment limitations to protect the interests of investors as well as the smooth running of markets, and rules against misleading advertising as well as regulation requiring disclosure of investment holdings and policies to do away with the secrecy that had been the root of so much of the problem of investment company management in the 1920s and 1930s. It was a strict and apparently stringent document. And, thus, a happy ending? Not quite.

The Next Round

Today when people working in mutual funds talk about the history of their industry — at least those few who know that their industry has a history that predates current ten-year performance charts — they occasionally acknowledge the unscrupulous behavior of the 1920s investment trusts and the raucous congressional hearings leading up to the passage of the Investment Company Act of 1940.

But when it comes to what happened in the 1960s, they try to scoot right over it, because what happened then shouldn't have happened. Regulations were in place. And, of course, people were different, times had changed, investing was a "science," and modern money managers were university-trained and were now assisted by number-crunching computers capable of superhuman calculations and projections.

The seeds of the story of the 1960s probably can best be summarized by a message you most likely remember hearing in 1993: "Today's interest rates are the lowest in 30 years." That 1993 message was absolutely true. While interest rates on "safe" savings instruments were on the rise in the late 1950s, they had fallen in the early 1960s to below that magic level of 4 percent. What the message you heard in 1993 didn't tell you, however, was what happened afterward because of those low interest rates of 1963. For many people who looked to the mutual fund concept for financial answers, it wasn't very pretty.

As in the 1920s and 1880s, the factors that sparked the mania for mutual funds in the mid 1960s — a mania that peaked in 1969 before the inevitable collapse pushed the mutual fund idea into almost total extinction by 1975 — were more complicated than just low interest rates.

As in the period following World War I, the United States had emerged from the chaos of World War II as the industrial and agricultural leader of the world. This sparked another period of wealth, achieved with relative ease by the lack of global competition. A new period of heavy consumerism followed. Again, pent-up demand, following the austerity of war, for housing and all the furniture, appliances, cars, TVs, and other goodies that went along with it (and all "Made in America" in those days) delivered even greater wealth. Then, like their parents in the 1920s, after accumulating the goodies, people with money decided to grow up and start making money from their money. Consumerism slowed and "investing" became an obsession.

By the early 1960s the stock market was on a roll. Over the previous fifteen years common stock investment had delivered generally good returns as a reflection of the revival and growth of the American economy. And by this time people had started to forgive and forget the abuses of the 1920s. In fact, Wall Street in general and mutual funds in particular had been on good behavior since the early 1940s and had been working hard to regain investor trust.

Throughout this period the rule of the day at mutual funds was conservative investment policy. (It should be remembered that the successful rebuilding of America following the depression and the war and the successful investment returns of the time were *not* achieved through fancy financial tricks like junk bonds, margin investing, short selling, and so on. It was, instead, a period of relatively calm markets and a stodgy — if not downright dull — approach to financing.) For the small investor of the early 1960s — now ready, with money in hand, to try a new generation's version of investing — here was nearly twenty years of positive mutual fund performance "proof" that had been delivered by people who could now be trusted.

Along with this accumulating "proof" of the certainty of reward via mutual fund investment, there also was a massive growth in the business of high-pressure mutual fund selling. At a time when mutual funds sold with an average 8.5 percent sales charge, selling mutual funds and collecting the commissions became a good way for people to make money — particularly on a part-time basis. And it seemed that all kinds of people tried their hand at it: teachers, soldiers, social workers, junior executives, civil service employees — all selling mutual funds to friends and neighbors. By the end of the 1960s there were about 200,000 full- and part-time mutual fund salespeople.[16]

The sales effort was made even easier in the early 1960s when the recovery from the stock market crash of May 28, 1962 — the biggest since the October 1929 crash — was credited to mutual funds. At the time, mutual funds had large cash reserves, which they used to buy heavily following the crash. This activity had a positive stabilizing effect on the market. And the mutual fund managers' image as cool-headed and dependable caretakers of the interests of small investors became cemented, finally wiping away the negative memories of the old investment trusts.

But just as the mutual fund industry was regaining much of the hard-fought-for faith, a few large funds threw out the old conservative rules that had been so critical for reestablishing this faith and began a new period of sophisticated speculation. Before it ended in the early 1970s, that period became almost as overheated as the 1920s.

Gunslingers and Go-Go

As the 1920s had been the era of "Jazz Age Economics" the 1960s became the "Go-Go Years," with go-go and yeh-yeh mutual funds to match. As they became more and more popular, investing in mutual funds was considered "mod" and made you "with it."

The leading funds of the period — many of which are no longer around today — that epitomized the new speculative approach included Manhattan, Fidelity Trend, Fidelity Capital, Mates, Oppenheimer, Invest, Channing Growth, Enterprise, and Fletcher. The changing investment policies of these funds, which initially delivered success, were later copied by other smaller funds.[17]

At the same time as funds started to walk away from "old-fashioned" investment policies, the phenomenon of the money manager as superstar emerged. Just as you can probably rattle off the names of a few outstanding mutual fund celebrities of today, the 1960s had its own crop. Today, however, most of those names of a generation ago are obscured by the dustheap of disappointments and embarrassments of financial history. There were, for example, the "Three Freds" — Fred Carr of Enterprise Growth Fund, Fred Mates of Mates Investment Fund, and Fred Alger of Security Equity Fund. As the decade developed there would be many, many more as their activities became as closely followed as those of sports figures and movie stars.

Most important of all the money manager superstars of the 1960s was Gerald Tsai (pronounced sigh). Tsai became the embodiment of the ideal mutual fund manager of the decade. It was his image as a youthful, bold investment genius that investors seemed willing to apply to all people who called themselves money managers.

Tsai was the manager of the Fidelity Capital Fund. This was the first of the so-called go-go funds that by the mid 1960s became a national passion. Although Tsai's investment techniques were viewed skeptically at first, his performance record of double-digit annual returns in the early 1960s was outstanding. Fidelity promoted the results aggressively, attracting huge amounts of money to its management and making Tsai famous in the process. But Tsai left Fidelity in 1966 to start his own independent fund after he was told plainly that the reins of control of the Fidelity organization would not pass to him from Fidelity's head, Edward C. Johnson 2d, but would instead go to Johnson's son, Edward C. Johnson 3d.

Tsai's new fund was called the Manhattan Fund and, based on Tsai's reputation, was an instant success with investors. Tsai hoped to start his fund off with $25 million, but investors had sent him $250 million by opening day — which, at the time, was a record for a new fund. Within a year of operation people had sent Tsai an additional $250 million. The success of this new-fund launch did not go unnoticed by Wall Street. This was big money with juicy fees to match. Copying Tsai's apparent formula for success, nearly one hundred new funds closely patterned after Tsai's were launched in the next two years. As in the late 1920s, investors thought they had found the easy road to riches. And mutual fund leaders made every effort to encourage them to believe it more fully and to send in increasing amounts of money to test that belief. By the end of the 1960s it was estimated that about 60 percent of mutual funds were of the old-style and the other 40 percent were fashioned after Tsai's go-go approach.[18] The competition among these funds and the armchair thrills that they gave American investors as each tried to outdo the other (in a revival of the dangerous 1920s game of one-upmanship) bred what became known as the "Performance Cult."

The excitement generated by the bold risk-taking mutual fund managers of the 1960s earned them nicknames like "gunslinger." The boldness of their investing, however, depended on a few tricks. The tricks were different from the margin buying that had been the magic bullet of the 1920s, but they were tricks nonetheless — and produced a similar outcome: success for a while, and then disaster.

One trick that was popularized by Tsai and copied by others was to concentrate the shareholders' money in a small number of stocks rather than the old-fashioned path of broad diversification. By concentrating on only a few stocks — a few dozen, for example, instead of a couple hundred — you can make more money — if you are correct, that is. And when this concept was first tried, Tsai and others were indeed correct. With the selection of a few pinpointed "winners," the funds enjoyed the full power of advancing prices on those stocks without having to be weighed down by stocks that were there just to provide balanced diversification across industry lines or within industries.

The stocks that the go-go managers selected for these small portfolios were often those of obscure companies. The obscurity was itself the appeal, as managers sought out the next Polaroid or Xerox, which had been incredible performers in the late 1950s. Unfortunately, the fund managers — and, more painfully, the fund shareholders — eventually found out that there weren't enough Polaroids and Xeroxes to go around. But before they found it out, the fund managers, like their investment trust forebears of the 1920s and 1880s, ended the decade latching onto any harebrained new company possible — running up the prices of their stocks to unbelievable heights.

Another favorite trick was the buying of large amounts of "letter stock" of public companies. (Letter stock is unregistered shares not being publicly traded via the stock market. A company sells shares directly to an investor with an accompanying "letter" stating that the shares cannot be sold to the public unless certain requirements are met — usually a holding period of three to five years.) The go-go fund managers routinely used letter stock to inflate artificially the performance they announced to the world. Here's how: Since letter stock can't be traded, the company would sell the shares to the funds at a price lower than the market price. For example, if the stock was selling in the marketplace for $10, the fund might buy the letter stock for $6 a share. But then, the fund would immediately show the same shares on its books as being worth $10 a share. With this gimmick the fund could claim that it had made a 67 percent capital gain virtually instantaneously. As with the gimmicks of the 1920s, the real value of the letter stock — or rather, lack of value — didn't become evident until later.

And as in the 1920s, few mutual fund shareholders had a full understanding of what was being done with their money. Fund companies became adept at covering up the actual nature of investments in prospectuses and other literature while remaining within legal guidelines. Also, there was no knowing what the throngs of fund salespeople were saying behind closed doors to prospects. And, of course, as long as people thought they were making money, few of them looked too closely at what was going on.

Also, as in the 1920s, media coverage of mutual funds during the 1960s reflected the accumulating "proof" of performance and the growth of mutual fund popularity — going from skepticism to full, unquestioned faith. In the early 1960s typical headlines would wonder "How Good Are Mutual Funds?"[19] But by 1968 the general view had become so positive that even *Better Homes and Gardens* was passing out advice touting the certainty of mutual fund investment: "Mutual funds are less risky than most investments because of their combination of diversification and professional management. . . . There is virtually no possibility that you'll lose your shirt."[20] Financial and popular media featured the money managers as celebrated heroes, adding credibility to the managers' claim that what they were doing with other people's money was "right." Confidence in the certainness of mutual fund investment perhaps reached its height in the late 1960s when the *Reader's Digest* announced plans to become a mutual fund sales agency — selling load funds directly to its millions of subscribers and collecting the sales charges as compensation.[21]

Mutual funds of the 1960s, however, did have their critics. It was in the 1960s that it was first observed that few mutual funds over the previous twenty years had ever "beaten the market" on a consistent basis. Also, critics were showing how the high cost of front-load charges — averaging about 8 ½ percent during this period — and high management fees ate away at the shareholders' investments.

Another criticism directed specifically at the go-go funds was that big-money targeting of small companies with thinly traded stocks contained the element of self-fulfilling prophecy by pushing prices up dramatically and artificially. These stocks — called "glamour stocks" at the time, but proving later how such glamour can be skin deep — typically traded from one go-go fund to another at prices 30 to 80 times earnings.

The absurdity of this practice wouldn't be identified until it was too late. In the mid 1960s mutual fund critics were effectively brushed aside. The tricks were working. In fact, 84 percent of mutual funds beat the Dow in 1968. Mutual fund promoters were riding high. With performance returns looking so great, critics were cheerfully razzed with the simplicity of: "Cost [of sales charges and management fees] is relevant only when measured against results; it is performance that counts." And: "Let the record speak for itself." And: "The proof is in the pudding." These frisky words would come back to haunt their speakers, because the pudding actually turned out to be a soufflé that began to collapse in late 1968.

Some financial historians date the beginning of the end of the go-go era as December 20, 1968. On that day it was announced that the Mates Fund — one of the most spectacular performers of the go-go funds — suspended share redemption. The reason for this halt was that the fund held a large chunk of a company's letter stock that became obviously worthless when the company went under. By that time 40 percent of the portfolio of the Mates Fund was illiquid. The net asset value that Mates had claimed to shareholders was nearly a complete fantasy.

This was shocking news to mutual fund shareholders. It prompted the beginning of a reassessment of what the fund managers were doing. Actually, mutual fund shareholders of the period got lucky with this event. It opened their eyes before a true catastrophe happened, because by this time mutual fund industry leaders were starting to promote aggressively the ideas of margin buying, short selling, and all the other crazy things that brought down the investment trusts a generation earlier. Then a stock market drop in 1969 showed that the mutual fund managers — now working under a different set of standards than just a few years before — turned out *not* to have a stabilizing effect, but instead increased volatility with their panic-prone trading. At first, small investors viewed the market drop as an opportunity to put *more* money into mutual funds, and 1969 saw the greatest influx of new money in mutual fund history. But then heavy fund redemptions started as revelations of high-risk shenanigans and raw fraud started to crop up over the following few years. The amount of new money going into stock mutual funds in 1969 would not be seen again until 1981.

By early 1973, *Business Week* was ready to summarize what had happened to the mutual fund idea during the 1960s: "A safe place for small investors became a playground for speculators." And since the funds had sold themselves to shareholders based on hot performance and touted their managers as special beings to achieve it, "the funds had to keep running, so they took greater and greater risks in a frantic chase after performance: half-baked franchising stocks, flaky computer leasing and software companies, 'letter stock' that could only be sold when — and if — it was registered."[22]

The highfliers of the 1960s went down in flames. Many of them liquidated or were folded into other funds. As horror stories of market manipulation and fund shareholder abuse unfolded in the late 1960s and early 1970s, the stock market entered a zigzagging bearish period beginning in early 1969 that despite a few strong rallies would last until 1982. (On an inflation-adjusted basis, the stock market peaked in 1966 and then started a seventeen-year decline, giving a new generation an idea of what "long-term" meant.) This took another devastating toll on the concept of professional management — particularly the caretakers of the go-go idea. Like the little bag of tricks of the hotshot investment trust managers of the 1920s, the gunslingers' bag of tricks that might have worked when the market was on the rise did nothing to halt a fast shift into reverse on the way down. The funds once again delivered far worse than the market itself.

Somewhat typical of the period was Gerald Tsai's own Manhattan Fund. One of the best performers of 1967 (when the go-go tricks were still working) with an advance of 39 percent, it was one of the poorest performers of 1968 with a decline of 6.9 percent. The Manhattan Fund then continued to fall steadily, losing 73 percent of its value from September 1969 to September 1974. (That's about the same as having four stocks in a portfolio and having three of them go under. So much for the certain value of diversification via mutual funds.) During the same period the Dow was down 25 percent.

Other eagerly purchased funds of the 1960s turned in similarly disappointing performances. For example, the Fidelity Capital Fund, Tsai's first experiment with the go-go idea, lost 43 percent of its value over the same time frame. Fidelity Trend was down 42 percent. Channing Growth, down 48 percent. Invest Fund, down 50 percent. Enterprise Fund, down 51 percent. Neuwirth Fund, down 52 percent. Eaton & Howard, down 62 percent. American Investors, down 63 percent. Keystone S-4, down 63 percent. Value Line Special Situations, down 74 percent.

During this bloodbath, however, Tsai, who may have lost his touch for making money for others, did not lose sight of his own pocket. By 1974 Tsai had sold his fund (for a personal profit of about $35 million) and had left the industry.

And the small investors who had put so much unquestioned faith into the promises and abilities of Tsai and the other managers of the 1960s? They learned much the same lesson their parents had with the investment trusts of the 1920s and a previous generation had in Great Britain in the 1890s.

CHAPTER 3

■ ■ ■

What's Happening Now

The story goes that when Gerald Tsai presented his idea for a new type of mutual fund to Fidelity head Edward C. Johnson 2d, Johnson gave his nod of approval after less than half an hour of consideration with the words "Here's your rope. Go ahead and hang yourself with it."[1] The rope that Johnson so blithely handed to Tsai was, of course, other people's money.

When, in the late 1960s, the other people got around to forming a posse to hang Tsai and the other gunslingers, the lynching lasted about seven years. Past mutual fund enthusiasts became acrimonious critics. In May 1970, for example, syndicated financial columnist Sylvia Porter, who had been one of the mutual fund industry's most influential supporters for nearly twenty years, publicly apologized to her readers for her previous unquestioned recommendation of mutual fund investment. She "condemned" mutual fund industry leaders, saying that she "couldn't anticipate — nor could you — that respected, trusted professional managers of money would become so emotional and erratic."[2]

Not all mutual funds, however, were taken to the gallows. For example, the Massachusetts Investors Trust — the fund that during the 1920s had clung to "old-fashioned" investment policies and gone on as a survivor of the 1929 debacle to become a model for the modern idea of the mutual fund — once again had stuck to its conservative investment principles during the go-go years to emerge anew as a model of a prudent investment approach appropriate for public pools.

But just as a few rotten apples spoil the barrel, investors, who only a few years before embraced all things called mutual fund, reacted to the scandals of a few and became almost as universally distrustful of the financial idea as they previously had been universally trustful. Investors, fearful of losing more of their money to high-risk investment tricks that they didn't understand and even more fearful of widening revelations of raw fraud that emerged in the early 1970s, pulled out of the funds.

In 1970 there were, for the first time in decades, more mutual fund redemptions than purchases. The bear market of 1968–70 with a Dow loss of 36 percent didn't help matters. But the 1970–73 bull market with its 66 percent rise didn't bring investors back into mutual funds either. Investor disillusionment was with mutual funds and not with the vagaries of the stock market.

Today, mutual fund promoters would like you to believe that it was unwarranted fears about the stock market that caused the near-demise of the mutual fund idea during those years, but that is a rewriting of history. Instead, the stampede out of mutual funds was caused by disillusionment with the mutual fund idea itself. Media coverage of mutual funds reflected the change in attitude. Books about mutual funds, for example, that during the 1960s had titles like *How to Get Rich Through Mutual Funds* were replaced during the early 1970s with titles like *If They're So Smart, Why Aren't You Rich?*, *The Mutual Fund Trap*, and *Fleecing the Lambs*. Then, as in the late 1930s, Americans watched the spectacle of a new round of congressional hearings uncovering mutual fund abuse of shareholders and markets. And magazine articles of those years typically blared: "How the Fund Managers Let You Down" and "The Year the Go-Go Funds Went into Reverse."

Reprieve

But the invention of the money market fund in 1972 (and its introduction to the general public in 1974) saved the mutual fund industry from total extinction. In the early 1970s interest rates were on the rise, but because of government limitations at the time on how much banks and S&Ls could pay out in interest, people couldn't get more than a 5.25 percent yield on savings accounts. In fact, interest rates on U.S. Treasury bills became *higher* than what you could get at a bank or an S&L. At the same time, however, the government raised the minimum denomination of T-bills from $1,000 to $10,000. That effectively locked out the small saver from easy access to realistic interest rates. The money market fund idea solved the problem. In its original form, money market funds pooled money from small savers to buy T-bills. Mutual fund companies then used this feature of virtual *risk-free* yield that was higher than you could get at a government-insured bank account to attract money from people who were otherwise revulsed by the high-risk frolics of the 1960s mutual funds.

The income that mutual fund companies got from managing the new money market funds allowed most — but not all — of them to survive. For example, the Fidelity Capital Fund, the first of the true go-go funds and perhaps the single most famous fund of the period, limped along until the late 1970s, when it was quietly put out of business and folded into the Fidelity Trend Fund. A few years later Fidelity took the name of this past-glorious fund out of mothballs and changed it only slightly to create the Fidelity Capital Appreciation Fund in 1986. Similarly, Fred Carr's Enterprise Fund, which followed stellar success in the 1960s with death in the 1970s, got a resurrection in name with the 1993 launch of the Janus Enterprise Fund. The Manhattan Fund passed through the hands of different promoters until it found a permanent home in the late 1970s with an adviser that changed the investment approach to a more standard mutual fund profile. Throughout this period of industry contraction and redefinition it was the money market fund idea that gave it a reprieve. And industry leaders used the reprieve as a period of reform in an all-out effort to regain investor trust. The emphasis on raw performance was shunted off to a secondary position. Now fund promoters were tripping all over themselves to prove how prudent, if not "conservative," they were. New investment limitations were adopted (or re-adopted by those who had thrown them out during the previous decade). Much was made of the new conservative investment policies. In addition, most fund companies fired their vast sales forces, implying that it had been uncontrollable salespeople in the field who had misled small investors into expecting too much (when in reality these salespeople had been doing only what they had been trained to do by the fund companies). Government regulators also added some new restrictions. As is typical, however, regulators practiced a closing-the-door-after-the-horse-is-out approach to protecting investors. For example, it took nearly a year after the grisly Mates Fund experience with "letter stock" for government regulators to limit mutual fund ownership of these illiquid securities to no more than 10 percent of the value of a fund.

By the mid 1970s, the punishment of the mutual fund industry started to abate. People began to believe that the industry had cleaned up its act. But the conventional wisdom of the day was to proceed with *extreme* caution. Sylvia Porter, in her 1975 best-selling investment-advice book *Sylvia Porter's Money Book,* once again suggested mutual funds to her readers, but now with forewarning: "There is far more to the purchase of mutual funds than a simple decision that this is the prudent way for you to invest. There is much more to the wise selection of a fund than a cursory comparison of records and a quick look at a fund's portfolio of investments."[3]

The reform period of the 1970s that ultimately brought Porter and others back into the fold (although with a somewhat widened skeptical eye) matched the type of reform the British investment trust movement went through following the Baring Crisis of 1890 and the American investment trusts went through following that movement's collapse in the early 1930s. It was, therefore, the third time in less than one hundred years that the basic idea of professionally managed public investment pools had to go through a process of reform following a period of reckless excess by the leaders of the idea. And, as during the previous periods of reform, two central issues surfaced as most critical:

1. **High-risk investment policy.** Exposing the money of risk-averse people to investment techniques or policies known to be high-risk as well as techniques untested in the real world — while at the same time professing to be manageable — was viewed as an unacceptable business practice.

2. **Secrecy.** Attempts to camouflage, withhold information, or mislead fund shareholders about the actual nature of investments as well as the risk profile of investments also became viewed as an abuse of trust. Moreover, no institution alleging to deliver "democratic" access to the investment world could itself practice secret dictatorship over the very people who "vote" by sending in money and who actually carry all the risk.

During each past period of reform, it has been the resolution of these two issues — prudent investment policy and full, honest disclosure — that created the cornerstone that revived trust in the idea. Yet, in the 1920s, when Wall Street borrowed the British investment trust idea, it seized on the part it liked (namely, gathering up lots of other people's money) and took the cornerstone of disclosure and prudent investment policy that had been so important for the rebuilding of the British industry since the 1890 collapse and threw it out the window.

After the collapse of the American investment trust movement in the early 1930s, the cornerstone was rediscovered during a period of reform that lasted through the 1950s. But leaders of the investment idea of the 1960s, while again enjoying a period of unquestioned popularity, threw the cornerstone out the window again. And during another painful period of reform the cornerstone had to be rediscovered afresh.

Then, ominously but perhaps not surprisingly, in the early 1990s, as the mutual fund idea was enjoying another period of maniacal popularity, leaders of the mutual fund industry grabbed up that cornerstone and heaved it out the window yet again.

Beyond Go-Go

It's not clear how it all started or who started it. There are different opinions. Maybe some financial historian of the future will be able to trace the specific sequence of events and name the names. But by the middle of 1990 there was an obvious growing groundswell among mutual fund companies to get rid of long-held investment limitations and expand their investment powers. And by 1993 the mutual fund industry was well along in reshaping itself into a speculative force greater than any seen during the go-go years and one approaching a freewheeling investment profile on a scale unmatched in the experience of American finance since the days of the investment trusts of the 1920s.

Throughout the early 1990s many mutual fund companies — both large and small — started stuffing their shareholders' mailboxes with lengthy proxy statements asking for permission to invest shareholders' money with greater "flexibilities," with more investment "freedom," and with less future permission needed from fund shareholders to change investment policies further. These new "freedoms" — while always legally permitted under the Investment Company Act of 1940 but used by only a small number of funds since the reform days of the 1970s — included wider adoption of leverage techniques — such as margin buying and short selling — and expanded entry into higher-percentage ownership of high-risk investments — such as the type of illiquid securities that brought down the Mates Fund and others during the 1960s.

And while mutual fund operators were doing away with as many of these investment policies as possible, industry leaders also successfully lobbied the Securities and Exchange Commission to review the Investment Company Act of 1940 to see where regulations could be "modernized." This resulted in a 1992 government report calling for sweeping changes, some of which were enacted immediately, in restrictions and laws governing what mutual fund managers could do with other people's money.

There was also a movement to convince state legislators to relax mutual fund regulations in those states that historically have been more stringent than federal regulations. These more-stringent restrictions, usually referred to as "blue sky" laws, were enacted by several states, primarily concentrated in the Midwest, long before the passage of the federal Investment Company Act of 1940. The blue-sky laws were an attempt by state politicians at the time to protect the populace of their largely rural states from getting roped into pie-in-the-sky, high-risk schemes by city slickers from the east. The restrictions, therefore, reflected the perception that people need to be protected. In contrast, the basic premise of federal securities laws begins with the assumption that people can judge for themselves what is best as long as they have the information to know what they are getting into. Therefore, federal securities laws emphasize disclosure, not restrictions. For example, federal restrictions allow a mutual fund to call itself "diversified" as long as 75 percent of its holdings are diversified among stocks so that no more than 5 percent of that portion of assets of the fund are in the securities of one company. The other 25 percent of the fund's money could be concentrated in one company. Securities regulators of several states, however, viewed this liberal interpretation of "diversified" as too high risk and therefore unacceptable to their states' citizens. Those states had a more restrictive profile that permitted no more than 5 percent of assets in one company as it applied to 100 percent of the fund's money — effectively disallowing a high concentration of 25 percent in one company as permitted by federal guidelines. The more restrictive blue-sky laws of a few states have since the 1930s generally defined what the mutual fund industry did with people's money. If a fund would not abide by these restrictions, then the fund couldn't sell its shares to people living in the states covered by the blue-sky laws. For the fund promoter the decision was either to go along with the blue-sky restrictions completely or not sell the fund in the blue-sky states — which is why some funds were not available in some states. In the early 1990s, however, fund promoters — with the help of the federal government — successfully got most of the blue-sky laws removed, arguing, in part, that federal laws should supersede state laws. (Incidentally, European securities law generally follows the idea of the blue-sky laws that assume that people need some protection as opposed to depending on the mechanics of disclosure alone to do the job.)

The radical changes in the early 1990s all took place with little fuss or notice. Fund promoters had reestablished themselves over the previous fifteen years in a new position of unquestioned faith. Few fund shareholders paid much attention to their requests for "new" investment freedoms. Fewer shareholders resisted the changes. Many didn't understand what the rules changes meant or didn't know the historical reasons why the rules had been put there in the first place. Still others didn't care even when they knew that the greater flexibilities and freedoms meant greater risk. They were the people who during the high-inflation/high-interest days of the 1980s had become used to being treated as pampered Little Lord Fauntleroys by being paid historically unprecedented high interest rates on no-risk instruments, but who, when interest rates dropped, had become a collective embodiment of a starving Oliver Twist with hands outstretched to the mutual fund industry in a plea for "More." As in past periods when the plea for "More" was heard, leaders of mutual funds (and, formerly, investment trusts) didn't bother explaining that "More" carried an extremely high risk. Instead, they just encouraged the starving to send in their money in greater quantities — and not to look too closely at what was being done with it or ask any questions. In addition, by the early 1990s a new Performance Cult had, after nearly a decade of regeneration, developed (as it had in the 1960s and 1920s) and was judging everything by a quick and simple look at the bottom line every quarter. Like Performance Cultists of the past, they had little regard for the actions that delivered a fund to its "winner" position or the types of special risks that shareholders — past or future — were exposed to while the fund managers were furiously sowing the wind.

Although neither the SEC nor the mutual fund industry's professional organization, Investment Company Institute, kept a running tally of the number of funds changing their investment profiles, some Wall Streeters estimated that during the early years of the 1990s between 40 and 60 percent of established mutual funds removed significant limitations against high-risk investment policies. In addition, fewer and fewer of the multitude of newly created funds adopted what had been for nearly two decades the boilerplate description of appropriate mutual fund investment procedures. The "old-fashioned" investment limitations that were removed by existing funds or omitted by new funds included not only those pertaining to margin buying and short selling, but also, at many funds, those prohibiting direct ownership of real estate, direct investment into gas, oil, and mineral-mining projects, buying the shares of other mutual funds, high-percentage ownership of the shares of one company, and concentration of ownership in one industry — and on and on.

While fund promoters embraced wider and wider investment freedoms, the prospectuses of their funds disclosing the nature of investment activity grew thicker and thicker. The more complicated the investment techniques became and the broader the involvement in previously uncharted high-risk arenas, the more there was to disclose. But few fund promoters were particularly interested in making sure that the risks involved were clearly understood by potential shareholders. When it comes to writing prospectuses, mutual fund promoters, who demonstrate such splendid talents for clear communication in explaining how to get money transferred by wire from your bank account to the fund's coffers, curiously lose those talents in describing the nature of the investment risk to which money in the fund is exposed. But it is the fund promoters' lawyers who write the prospectuses, and as the director of the Division of Investment Management of the SEC observed in 1992, "lawyers view prospectuses not so much as disclosure documents, but as liability documents."[4] As a result, the prospectuses became mired in so much indecipherable self-protecting legalese as to effectively transform them into documents of nondisclosure. Few small investors could unravel the jargon and quickly find the hidden land mines placed there by the fund promoters' staff of full-time, high-paid, and clever securities lawyers.

Not all funds, however, changed their policies and started printing thick prospectuses. For example, the Dreyfus Leverage Fund — a fund that since its creation in 1968 had practiced such speculative leverage techniques as margin buying and short selling — did not change its policies. But it did change its name in 1992 to the Dreyfus Capital Growth Fund. And why? A spokesperson for the fund company said that it was "for marketing purposes." And when pressed further, the spokesperson acknowledged that while the fund's profile as a leverage fund had had specialized appeal for a certain segment of the investing public throughout the years since 1968, the changing nature of so many other mutual funds in the early 1990s made the leverage profile of the Dreyfus fund "not as unusual as it used to be."

Indeed, among closed-end funds — those funds issuing a limited number of shares that are traded via the stock market — the number involved in some type of leverage technique increased from 39 percent in 1989 to over 50 percent in 1993. Among open-end funds, which since the investment trust days of the 1920s have always been more conservative than closed-end funds, the estimated number of funds with investment policies allowing leverage techniques increased from under 5 percent in the late 1980s to nearly 30 percent by 1993. (Added to the increased use of leverage by funds, in 1992 discount broker Charles Schwab and the discount brokerage arm of Fidelity Investments started promoting to small investors the idea of buying shares of mutual funds on margin — all poising American markets for a new round of margin piled upon margin.)

There were, however, a few funds — a very few — that actually tightened investment policies. The Strong Total Return Fund was one of those very few. The trustees of this fund decided in 1992 to limit exposure to previously practiced high-risk investments. But this action was taken because the fund had failed at its high-risk adventure and was attempting to stem shareholder redemptions caused by its losses. The Strong Total Return Fund, which is officially defined as a growth and income stock fund, had during the late 1980s invested over 30 percent of the fund's money in junk bonds. While the junk bond market was booming in the 1980s, the Strong Total Return Fund was one of the best performers of the decade. But in 1989/1990, when the junk bond market collapsed and the value of those bonds went down over 50 percent in less than six months, the Strong Total Return Fund saw its value drop by nearly 15 percent before recovering for a loss for the year of 9.5 percent. Shareholders started evacuating the fund. And the fund's management rewrote its policies to limit junk bond investment to only 5 percent of the fund's assets. While the Strong Total Return Fund had been one of the few funds in the 1980s to hold such a high percentage of junk bonds in its portfolio, in the early 1990s more and more funds reached to the outer legal limits of junk bond ownership. (Government regulations are very liberal about holding junk bonds. For example, a fund calling itself an "investment grade" bond fund may hold up to 35 percent of its value in bonds rated below "investment grade.") The increased appetite for low-rated bonds helped the junk bond market rebound in the early 1990s. Ironically, the Strong Total Return Fund became one of the most conservative funds while others, apparently unconcerned that a fate similar to the Strong Fund experience of 1990 could befall them, waded merrily with their shareholders' money into the same treacherous waters.

The Strong Fund experience underscores an important point about the long-held investment policies that so many mutual fund promoters casually threw out the window in the early 1990s. These policies — these investment limitations — had not been put there originally because someone had plucked them from thin air as a guard against theoretical or hypothetical possibilities. Instead, those policies were written into the "laws" for mutual fund management because of the explicit horrific experiences of real people and their real money.

But these realities of the past seemed not to matter to fund promoters who were anxious (as were their predecessors at the peaks of previous periods of mutual fund/investment trust manias) to shrug off restrictions and open the investment floodgates wider for the increasing amounts of money they were successfully shoveling in from small investors. In the spring of 1992, their efforts in getting rid of restrictions and attracting even more money with even greater ease got a special boost from the SEC when it released a report recommending a host of relaxed rules and changed regulations.

The Big Red Book

The SEC's analysis of the mutual fund industry and the agency's recommendations for "modernization" of the Investment Company Act of 1940 filled an oversize book of 560 tightly printed and footnoted pages. Titled a self-congratulatory *Protecting Investors: A Half Century of Investment Company Regulation* (a title apparently bestowed by someone with amnesia who was unwilling to consider how regulatory inadequacies had victimized so many small investors during the mutual fund mania of the 1960s), the report's bright red cover and hefty weight (just under three pounds) prompted its quick dubbing on Wall Street as "the big red book."

As soon as the big red book hit the streets, mutual fund securities lawyers began running a fine-tooth comb through its pages to snag the loopholes. As is common with any industry that reviews a new set of government regulations, the game of finding ways to circumvent the intention of the changes or to use them to the industry's best self-interests was pursued in split-second earnest. It is the simple act of making regulation changes and new laws that creates the ability to find new loopholes. (And since there hadn't been a major rethinking of the Investment Company Act since the early 1970s, the mutual fund industry hadn't had much chance for such fun and games in nearly two decades. Moreover, the changes made in the 1970s were done in the restrictive atmosphere of reform, not the expansive mood of back-patting celebration of the early 1990s.) It often takes years before the effect of new loopholes prompted by regulation changes — changes that at the time may have been well meaning and seemingly innocuous — can surface with harmful repercussions. Then, as in the recent example of the S&L debacle, there is a new round of reregulation — but not, of course, until the damage is done.

The full impact of possible loopholes lurking in the big red book (damaging or otherwise) wasn't, of course, readily obvious — and probably won't be for a few years. But there were enough obvious immediate changes and recommendations for further changes to make it clear that the mutual fund industry had gotten from the SEC pretty much what it wanted. (In fact, some mutual fund companies appeared to be so certain of what the SEC would do that fund bylaws were changed months before the actual content of the report was released to the general public.)

Packed among the changes were eased rules on how funds had to communicate with existing shareholders and removal of some of the duties and obligations of a fund's trustees. New guidelines on charging shareholders fees included the freedom for fund promoters to charge different shareholders different fees for participation in the same fund. Other changes included relaxation of advertising restrictions — including for the first time since the 1930s a proposal to permit funds to solicit money directly from prospective investors via coupons printed in newspaper and magazine ads or from a direct mail brochure, without the necessity of first delivering a prospectus to investors. Still other relaxed rules would allow American investors easier access to foreign mutual funds.

Beyond eased restrictions and changed rules that the big red book outlined, the SEC went even further and actually encouraged mutual fund companies to take on greater investment risks. In March 1992 the commission members — people who are unelected government officials named to the commission's board as political appointees — raised the amount of illiquid, high-risk securities that mutual funds are permitted to hold from the 10 percent that had been put in place following the "letter stock" horror stories of the 1960s to 15 percent. Happily, this particular restriction was reinstated in 1994.

In addition, the commission recommended that a new type of mutual fund be created that would limit shareholders' redemption privileges to certain intervals — weekly, monthly, or quarterly. These "interval funds" would, the commission promised, allow mutual fund managers to invest money into less liquid securities — such as the stocks of small, new companies that are thinly traded — and more stocks of foreign companies whose stocks are traded only on foreign exchanges, which are not as active as American markets and therefore are less liquid. By not requiring mutual funds to redeem shares every day, fund promoters could be freed of having to set their fund prices every day — a task that isn't easily accomplished when a portfolio is concentrated in illiquid securities.

Like so many ideas that were presented as "new" in the early 1990s, the interval fund idea wasn't new either. In fact, the Massachusetts Investors Trust — the open-end investment trust founded in 1924 that later served as a model for the modern idea of the mutual fund — was originally structured as an interval fund and remained so for many years. When the fund was first formed its net asset value was set only once a month, and shareholders were allowed redemption privileges only once a month (on the 15th with a 1 percent redemption charge) and had to request a redemption weeks in advance. Later, mutual fund shareholders started demanding as much liquidity from their fund investments as they could get with investments made directly in the market. With an interval fund, as mutual fund shareholders of the past discovered, the risks of illiquidity — the inability to sell when selling looked like the best course to take or the money was needed — far outweighed the rewards that the interval fund delivered. There was also the risk — a risk discovered during the investment trust days as well as the 1960s, when the go-go managers got so much artificial mileage out of inflating the value of "letter stock" — of overly optimistic fund managers putting high values on the assets in their illiquid pools in order to announce performance that had little to do with reality when it actually came time to liquidate the pool. (An earlier generation in Great Britain saw the same thing, of course, when the investment trust managers in the years leading up to the Baring Crisis of 1890 loaded the trusts up with overpriced, unmarketable securities, which turned out to be completely worthless scraps of paper. A revival of such an experience in the 1990s won't even leave a residue of scraps of paper — it will just be beheld as disappearing blips on a computer screen.)

Yet, like the mutual fund industry leaders who decided to ignore the lessons of financial history in the early 1990s as they threw out the "rules" of the past, the SEC apparently decided that these past experiences were irrelevant as well.

But apparently there was another agenda afoot. Government officials had decided it was time to tap into the growing stash of small investors' cash committed to mutual funds to help finance small and new businesses — whatever the risk to those investors. Political leaders during the summer recession months of 1992 just prior to the presidential election of that year blamed a slow economic recovery on bankers for not making enough business loans. They also claimed that the pool of private venture capital money was not enough to take up the slack. The result was a hastily prepared program from the SEC called Small Business Initiatives (created just days before the Republican Convention in August 1992) that emphasized new liberalized investment opportunities for mutual funds. The program also outlined a slew of reduced regulations for new and small companies that wanted to raise money by selling securities.[5]

The decisions about these radical changes — changes that both increase the intrinsic risk of those mutual funds that take them on and remove many of the safeguards of new securities registration — were personal ones made by politically appointed, unelected government officials. Those officials soon went on to something else after the election, but the rule changes have stayed.

But the SEC's push to make it easier for mutual funds to spread the money around and for small companies to raise money by selling securities — rather than having to bother bankers or venture capitalists for money to start or expand their businesses — was actually one part of a much larger shift in American finance that paralleled, and in large measure was made possible by, the increasing popularity of mutual funds.

The New "Answer"

Just as leverage had been such an appealing "answer" for people of the 1920s (and later the dirty word) and creative debt products had been the appealing "answer" in the 1980s (and later that decade's dirty word), the "answer" for the 1990s surfaced early in the decade in the form of "securitization."

Securitization is one of those buzzword terms that can mean many things to many people, including the people who are supposed to be experts on the subject. But as the idea of securitization developed in the 1980s and on into the 1990s to become the financial idea to nearly dominate all other financial ideas, it primarily came to mean the ability to turn mortgages, credit card receivables, boat loans, or just about any other loan-type financial product into a marketable security. Or, in other words, instead of the originator of a loan (a bank, for example) holding the loan to collect the interest, the loan is pooled with other similar loans and sold as a security, usually to institutional investors, including mutual funds. In simple terms, once these assets get pooled to represent a security, the security is traded from one investor to another in the same way as an interest-paying bond is traded.

The first version of this type of pooled security was introduced in 1970 with the creation of the Government National Mortgage Association (GNMA) — or Ginnie Mae. This pool was made up of the safest types of mortgages possible — government-backed Federal Housing Administration (FHA) and Veterans Administration (VA) mortgages. "Ginnie Mae" quickly entered the financial vocabulary as a rock-solid investment/savings option that delivered impeccable creditworthiness and fairly predictable returns. Ginnie Mae went on to spawn the other now well-known government-backed versions of securitized loans: "Freddie Mac" (Federal Home Loan Mortgage Association), "Fanny Mae" (Federal National Mortgage Association), and "Sallie Mae" (Student Loan Marketing Association).

It wasn't until the mid 1980s that Wall Street started flirting with this method of manufacturing new types of securities. In 1985, for example, automobile loan receivables were bundled together and sold as securities for the first time. Since then Wall Street's special creative abilities for turning the unimaginable into something salable have been well exercised. By 1993 securitization offered up such diverse pools as motorcycle loans, computer leases, commercial real estate loans, railcar leases, and aircraft leases, with plans on the drawing board for pools of hospital receivables, loans of bankrupt companies, U.S. receivables of European and Japanese companies, and car-dealer receivables.[6]

The securitization movement got its big push in the late 1980s when savings and loan companies were looking for a way to get their burdensome and illiquid mortgages off their balance sheets. So their mortgages — like the Ginnie Maes before — got bundled together and sold off to mutual funds and others. The new securities were snapped up — particularly after the junk bond market fell through the floor in 1990 and institutional investors went looking for other interest-bearing alternatives.

The securitization setup seemed to make everybody happy and quickly turned into a boom. The total amount of these securitization pools in 1987 came to $10 billion, but during 1993 the figure had exploded to nearly $500 billion. The banks and insurance companies that originated the loans liked the idea because they could get the loans off their balance sheets and not have to worry so much about holding illiquid loans in the hope that the loans would be paid off in a timely manner and at a high enough return to give them a profit above the interest rates they were offering their depositors. Wall Street liked the idea because of the hefty fees for bundling the pools and creating the securities. The buyers of the securities (mutual funds and other institutional investors) liked them because it gave them a new place to put the burgeoning loads of money that the former bank depositors were handing over. In addition, these buyers liked them because they were marketable securities that could be traded to satisfy whatever strategy the institutional investor was following at the moment.

And perhaps most of all, the government liked these securitized pools. With more loans off banks' balance sheets, there was less to cover with government deposit insurance! The former savers who used to put their money in banks to get interest returns from the bankers' loan of that money to others (a system that the government guaranteed through deposit insurance and monitored through regulation) had now become investors in mutual funds getting paid interest from those same bank loans, but now without any government deposit insurance guarantees.

It's no wonder, then, that the SEC's "modernization" plans for mutual funds as revealed in the agency's 1992 big red book removed as many barriers as possible between mutual funds and the rapidly growing field of asset- (or loan-) backed securitization. The report encouraged as much securitization as possible — exempting all asset-backed securities from all mutual fund rules. The SEC also encouraged law changes to allow banks and others to securitize small business loans — an effort seen as relieving bankers from the risks of making such loans so that more money could get into circulation. The congressional legislation needed to make this possible was introduced in 1993, and a new government agency that was proposed to handle it was nicknamed "Velda Sue" (Venture Enhancement and Loan Development Administration for Small, Undercapitalized Enterprises).

With further securitization and further encouragement of the mutual fund idea, the government solves a big problem — namely, avoiding having to pay for a bailout of some future 1980s-style S&L debacle. If in the future enough of the "professionals" running this idea of securitization make "mistakes" on the scale of the mistakes made by the "professionals" who ran the S&Ls of the 1980s, the government isn't left holding the bag to pay for them. The "professionals" who originated the loans, of course, won't be left holding the bag either, since they will have already gotten rid of the loans. And the managers who choose the securities for fund investment — as the funds' increasingly thick prospectuses make abundantly clear — won't be holding the bag either. Moreover, with this system of securitization, the leaders of various financial institutions, as well as the government agencies that watch over them, achieve a goal of circulating money without personal ownership or any particular personal responsibility for the ultimate outcome. And, best of all, the full burden of risk for any mistakes they may make is put in your hands.

Era of Securitization

As this "modern" idea of securitization was exploding in the early 1990s, a more standard version of securitization exploded as well — that is, the proliferation of new bonds of all types of quality and new issues of stocks — from both established companies and, to an even greater degree, newly public companies. More and more companies found it easier to raise capital by going to the bond and stock markets rather than going to banks for loans.

This aspect of securitization was easily absorbed by mutual funds in the early 1990s. As new issues of stock reached record proportions year after year in the early 1990s, mutual funds snapped up about 70 percent of everything that was new. Other institutional investors — pension funds and insurance companies — made up the smaller, less enthusiastic portion of the buyers of these generally higher-risk new issues.

Nineteen ninety-three became Wall Street's first trillion-dollar year in the sale of new stocks and bonds. By early December of 1993 there had been a record 6,652 completed U.S. stock and bond deals. The $1 trillion mark was up 30 percent from the $6.8 billion figure for 1992.

Despite the staggering figures of the early 1990s, this type of securitization is nothing new. Such obsessions with stocks and bonds (particularly exotic bonds, such as junk bonds) come and go with the rising and falling tide of speculative fever. At peak times of speculative fever — for example, the late 1960s, the late 1880s in Great Britain, and, of course, around the world in the 1920s — securitization is thought to provide ever-widening opportunity for everybody to achieve great (and easy) wealth. And this is exactly how it is sold. Remember, it may be the crowd in its mad frenzy to get rich that actually buys things at the height of manias, but the crowd is sold on the idea of it by leaders. (A footnote to the 1993 banner year for securities sales, providing a possible macabre visitation from the ghost of the Baring Brothers investment trust crisis in Great Britain in 1890, was that the precise $1 trillion mark was reached when U.S. investors bought $500 million of global bonds issued by Argentina.)[7]

As the era of heightened securitization was ushered in during the early 1990s, government agencies were actually encouraging the fever with lowered standards for new issues, widened embracement of asset-backed securitization as an alternative to loans held by banks, and expanded opportunities for mutual funds and other institutional investors to broaden out into arenas avoided for decades as too risky. But the push to securitization didn't stop there.

Just as banks were rushing to get into the mutual fund business in the early 1990s (as laws that had prohibited them from doing so since the nightmare days of the 1920s investment trusts got reversed) and getting out of the loan business (by securitizing as much of their loans as possible), they also were trying to get into the securities business. Outlawed since the 1930s when securities laws separated commercial banking (to make loans) from investment banking (to underwrite and trade securities), banks had been sneaking back into the business by getting lawmakers and regulators to rethink the depression-era laws.

Beginning in 1991, government regulators had begun to allow commercial banks to underwrite the sale of securities. By 1993 seven bank companies, including New York's Chemical Bank and Chase Manhattan, had been given special permission by banking regulators to underwrite and sell securities. The special permission limited the underwriting business the banks could do to 10 percent of their total revenues. While commercial banks were anxious to get into the investment banking arena, there was little interest on the part of investment bankers in getting in on the traditional playing field of commercial banks by pressing for greater freedom to make loans. The natural inclination of the financial world is toward securities — financial products that generate fees and allow fast, liquid opportunities to make profits without the long-term obligation of ownership.

The argument used by commercial bankers and other financial institutions that have successfully lobbied to get old regulations changed is that the separated powers, which had been so important for people of the 1930s as they looked back with personal experience on the horrors of the 1920s, had now become inefficient, cumbersome, unfair, costly, slow, and simply nonsensical. But, of course, they were all those things in the 1930s as well. And, indeed, those arguments were used in the 1930s by opponents of the regulations that went on to separate the financial world into different elements. But for the people with firsthand knowledge of the abuses that occurred during the 1920s, it didn't matter. It was more important not to let any group or financial institution get too much concentrated power. In addition, the 1920s had taught them that financial institutions could not properly serve the best interests of too many different types of customers — that it wasn't possible to perform all roles perfectly. It was better, they determined, to have separated competition to provide checks and balances so that no one financial idea could dominate all others. (To put the concerns of the people of the 1930s in some perspective, the domination of securitization as the financing idea of the 1920s delivered not only the famous stock market debacle beginning in 1929 but also a 50 percent default on all foreign government bonds issued between 1925 and 1929, as well as default on 28 percent of domestic corporate bond issues and 21 percent of home mortgage loans.)

In the 1990s, the concept of separated financial powers was considered hogwash. And the principal piece of 1930s legislation that defined that concept — the Glass-Steagall Act of 1933 — was continually brought up for repeal. While as of this writing Glass-Steagall remains on the books, Wall Streeters, with the help of sympathetic regulatory agencies, have become increasingly successful in circumventing it. One circumvention was the entry by commercial banks into the mutual fund business and securities underwriting. Another was the de facto underwriting powers given to mutual funds and other institutional investors in 1990. This was accomplished via an SEC directive called Rule 144a. Under Rule 144a, large institutional investors, including large mutual fund companies, can buy unregistered bonds and stocks — issued by domestic or foreign companies — and trade the securities among themselves. The first buyer of a Rule 144a security is therefore its effective underwriter. But the only further market for these securities is other institutions. The greatest use of Rule 144a securities has been by foreign issuers trying to get easy access to American capital markets. In less than three years the market for these nearly unregulated securities went from zero to nearly $60 billion.

Anointed Guardians

As the SEC and other regulatory agencies were busy changing the rules to encourage the growing appetite for securitization, there was also a push to allow big holders of those securities to have a larger, more vocal say in the internal workings of the companies whose shares they held. As "owners" of a company, shareholders can expect the company to act in their self-interests — not the convenient self-interests of the managers who happen to be running the company.

Companies that choose to raise money for their businesses by selling stock are of course beholden to the stockholders in a different way than if the money is raised by borrowing from a bank. With a bank loan, as long as you keep up the payments, the bank has no business asking you anything. And, in fact, if you have difficulty in repaying, you can always try to renegotiate the debt. When stock is sold, however, the company is then liable to the foot-tapping scrutiny of shareholders. Raising money through the sale of shares of stock may have the appeal of never having to pay the money back, but it brings other, often more onerous, burdens.

The issue of corporate accountability is not an easy one. There is no doubt that the managements of corporations have wide abilities to abuse their positions. And there is equally no question that shareholders — particularly large shareholders — can act as watchdogs to make sure that corporate management fulfills its obligations to shareholders with limited pursuit of self-interest. Accommodating the two views of management and shareholder involves a delicate balancing of power. Perhaps that balance has never been perfect, but in the early 1990s it was tipping dramatically toward the perspective of big shareholders — mutual funds and other institutional investors — to satisfy the Wall Street view of how companies should be run and the type of corporate "performance" required to maintain "shareholder value."

Although activism was touted as the new force that (finally) had pushed big shareholders into the arena of protecting their rights against lazy and transgressing corporate managers, it was *not* a new idea. Actually, a call for shareholder activism on the part of big investors had been a hallmark of the peak of the previous mutual fund/investment trust manias.

Here's how Dr. Irving Fisher, Yale University's preeminent promoter of the investment trust theory, characterized in 1929 the investment trust manager's watchdog role over the potential misdeeds of leaders of American industry of the 1920s: "Industrial captains may prove incompetent, or may betray the confidence reposed in them. They may throw the burden of risks on those whom they pretend to shield. The analysts, statisticians, and counsel of investment trusts guard against such betrayals of confidence, or incompetence, by the constant scrutiny of the conduct of corporations."[8]

The fatal error of assumption made by Fisher and others who held the investment trust managers in such high regard — a fatal error that could be made by *anyone* who puts unquestioned faith in the actions and motives of *any* group of people — was that the investment trust managers were immune to the human frailties that Fisher saw so clearly as corrupting the actions of "industrial captains." Actually, as revealed later, the "betrayals of confidence" that investment trust shareholders suffered at the hands of the trust managers were far greater than those inflicted by "industrial captains." Many trust shareholders were surprised to discover in the early 1930s that many trust managers had used shareholders' money to take control of companies — and in a few cases entire industries — stripping them for the managers' own profit or manipulating the businesses toward their own financial self-interests — and ultimately leaving the trust shareholders with little value.

Moreover, in the early 1930s investment trust managers and other large shareholders of American companies who had been hurt in the 1929 crash went looking for a way to recoup some of those losses and started putting pressure on the companies to increase dividends, to declare special dividends, and to increase corporate profitability through greater efficiencies and productivity. Heavy layoffs followed; valuable corporate assets were liquidated; wages were cut. By 1932 the average income of a working American was half of what it was in 1929 (and there was 25 percent unemployment). In the early 1930s the widening inequalities in the distribution of wealth — now concentrated in fewer and fewer hands — were justified by a "trickle-down" concept that postulated eventual reemployment of the less fortunate. The call early in the decade was for more investment to get things going. Later in the decade it became clear that greater consumerism was needed, not more investment. The introduction of the minimum wage law was in part an action to halt companies from continually lowering wages so that higher profits could be paid out as higher and higher dividends to a few large shareholders.

The perceived villains of the 1920s and 1930s — rightly or wrongly — became those who lorded over vast industries with concentrations of control. Lost jobs and lower wages were blamed on them. For example, at the peak of its power in the 1920s and 1930s the banking firm of J. P. Morgan controlled, either directly or indirectly through affiliates, directorships of corporations representing one-fourth of the entire corporate wealth of the country. It was the exposure of this and other examples of cozy and intricate intertwining investment "relationships" that prompted much of the securities regulation of the 1930s. Financial powers were split so that no one group could have such concentrated control over any broad financial arena.

The role of the investment trusts in corporate governance matters was particularly repugnant to people who had witnessed the abuses during the 1920s. And by the time the original Investment Company Act of 1940 was drafted, the idea of shareholder activism on the part of investment trust managers was widely considered an inappropriate "diversion from their normal channels of diversified investment to abnormal channels of control of industry."[9] And little was heard from mutual fund managers about the internal workings of corporations during the 1940s and 1950s.

But in the late 1960s, the idea of mutual fund shareholder activism became a hot issue. As the popularity of mutual funds grew, promoted in those days as a way for everyone to get democratic access to ownership of American companies (and publicized using the catchphrase "People's Capitalism"), fund managers once again heard the call to shake up corporate board rooms to "enhance shareholder value" in ways reminiscent of Irving Fisher's injunction of the 1920s and presaging the movement of the early 1990s.

In 1966, for example, *Business Week* reported on developments in a way that could have been picked up word-for-word from the 1920s or reprinted verbatim in the early 1990s: "Institutions traditionally have avoided using their stock holdings as a weapon against managements; they prefer to sell a stock rather than fight to get management to change its ways. Last week [at a conference of institutional investors], however, there were predictions that mutual funds and other institutional investors are going to be forced to take a more active role in the companies whose stock they hold."[10] (Curiously, when *Business Week* reported in 1993 on the latest revival of this activist approach, the magazine called it a "provocative new investment idea.")[11] By May 1967 the movement had gathered enough steam so that *Fortune* could declare in the title of a detailed article on the subject: "Mutual Funds Have the Votes: And some of them are starting to lean on management." The movement then grew so quickly during the last days of the 1960s mutual fund mania that by July 1968 *Dun's Review* was asking on its cover: "Will the Funds Run Companies?" and answered in its article that "fund managers, with their multimillions, their analytical expertise and their interest in performance, are now becoming a clear and present danger to many a complacent man in the executive suite."[12]

But after revelations of mutual fund excesses of the 1960s started unfolding (beginning in late 1968 with the "letter stock" scandal surrounding the Mates Fund), it became evident what this activism meant in the real terms of Wall Street. And it showed a pattern of self-dealing and hypocrisy similar to the shenanigans of the 1920s and early 1930s.

One area of shareholder activism of the 1960s that started out as a good idea and then deteriorated into scandal was the managers' declared right to vote for takeover offers that would benefit the fund's shareholders. Since these were the days of active merger and takeover activity to satisfy the then-popular concept of "conglomerates" (also referred to in those days as "diversified growth companies"), getting top dollar for shares held in a fund's portfolio meant big performance returns. As the takeover/merger fever built, however, some funds became friendly warehouses for large blocks of stock, with the managers conspiring with investment bankers looking to put together takeover deals. When this activity was uncovered, attitudes changed. Now mutual funds had to clean up their own act before anyone could take them seriously about their right to dictate the actions of others.

The current revival of the idea of institutional investor shareholder activism surfaced at the end of the 1980s with the disappearance of the corporate raider. There wasn't anyone around to shake things up. In addition, there were fewer big takeover deals going on to capture periodic big-dollar hits. When the institutional investors decided to take up the slack, they preferred to make the activity look more gentle in keeping with the New Age 1990s and to continue attracting the money of aging flower children. Shareholder activism became known as "Relational Investing" and "New Capitalism."

Growing out of the activist movement was the creation of funds specifically designed to go after transgressing companies. For example, Allied Investment Partners, an investment fund run by investment company Dillon Read, started raising money in 1991 for the express purpose of taking large stock positions in public companies in order to capture board representation to advance the fund manager's view of how the company should be managed. Other investment companies, including Lazard Frères and Brown Brothers Harriman, started similar funds with similar goals.[13]

While the creation of these funds was greeted with enthusiasm and attracted billions of investment dollars, other such aggressive investment pools were not as happily received. For example, one fund started in early 1993 — a limited partnership based in Delaware called AmeriMex Maquiladora Fund, L.P. — came under attack for its specific stated intention of buying American manufacturing companies to move to Mexico. As the prospectus for the fund put it: "The fund anticipates that moving the manufacturing operations to Mexico will significantly reduce the labor costs of production and enhance the profitability of these companies." One of the principal investors in the fund was the Mexican government's main development bank. Revelations about the fund came just before the start of voting on the controversial North American Free Trade Agreement to remove trade barriers among the United States, Mexico, and Canada. Under pressure from opponents of NAFTA, who feared precisely the type of systematic planning to move jobs to Mexico as this fund openly declared, the Mexican bank withdrew its support of the fund, although the fund continued to operate.[14] (The big mistake made here was that the fund's management had been too direct and honest about its true "intentions." U.S. securities laws rarely require such specific declarations of reality, and when they do there are far more artful ways to word a prospectus than with such harsh clarity.)

In the early 1990s the most popular issue for justifying activist moves was excessive compensation of the top management of companies. Indeed, during the 1980s, corporate officers had become clever in hiding the ways they could compensate themselves. Activist shareholders found this compensation — once uncovered — to be a good way of measuring the officers' actual worth compared to the company's performance.

(The executive compensation issue raised persistently by institutional investors as a toehold entree into the shareholder activism door has in at least one case come back to bedevil the institutional investor. In 1993, the Teachers Insurance Annuity Association and College Retirement Equities Fund, a nonprofit organization handling some $52 billion and with a history of pressing companies on the compensation question, was itself a focus of protest by one of its shareholders on the $1 million annual compensation of the fund's chairman. The fund tried to block the shareholder's attempt to question the salary as a proxy motion in the fund's annual proxy statement. But after appealing to the SEC, the shareholder was able to force the fund to present his motion to other shareholders.)[15]

In 1992, the SEC, in answer to the outcry about excessive executive compensation, issued new guidelines and expanded disclosure requirements for officers of public companies. When the rule changes went into effect, then-SEC head Richard Breeden declared that the changes "will do away with impenetrable legalistic narratives that hide the bottom line of" executive compensation.[16] But at virtually the same moment that Breeden was patting himself and the commission on the back for solving this corporate management abuse of shareholder interests, mutual fund executives were coming up with their own impenetrable legalistic narratives to hide the bottom line of *their* activities.

Part of this was done with help of the SEC itself. At the same time in late 1992 when new disclosure rules went into effect to expand the amount of information that public companies had to provide, the SEC was busy removing long-held disclosure rules governing mutual funds and other institutional investors. An important one that relates directly to the issue of corporate governance was the ending of the SEC's requirement for shareholders of a company to disclose communications among themselves concerning the company.

The SEC's decision to remove this regulation was presented as a way of helping small shareholders bring their "grass-roots" grievances forward without first going through costly filing procedures. Coincidental to the timing of this decision, however, was the exact moment when institutional investors had just gone over the 50 percent ownership level of all shares of American companies. In reality, this regulation did little to help small shareholders. Instead, the appealing grass-roots image was exploited to benefit big-money powers, just as it had been in the 1920s and 1960s.

Before this disclosure requirement was removed, when eleven or more shareholders were actively communicating either by oral or written means, they had to disclose in a filing with the SEC that they were talking among themselves as well as the nature of the communication. This disclosure requirement grew out of the abuses of the 1920s and 1930s (and was reinforced in the early 1970s following the games of the 1960s) when investment trust managers, bankers, and other big shareholders secretly joined forces to pull the rug out from under a company without the company's management knowing what was going on. But like so many of the regulations that got discarded in the 1980s and 1990s, this one was shrugged off as some worthless bit of "depression-era legislation." That depression, we should not forget, was thought by many people who lived through it to have been caused in large part by secret concentrations of power. That concentrated power was achieved by collecting little sums of money from many people and then actually used against those people in the name of greater efficiency and productivity as companies were forced to raise dividends, streamline workforces, and liquidate assets to appease the immediate interests of big shareholders.

The idea of disclosure in those reform-minded days recognized that shareholders could have legitimate complaints about the way that a company was being run, but it was also felt that complaints should be made in the full sunlight of democratic expression so that the players could be identified and no "special deals" could be made in secret. But in the much different days of the early 1990s, when the push was on to make money from money, such considerations as secret deals mattered little if the end result was delivery of a "beat-the-market" performance.

While the SEC was offering special dispensation from long-held disclosure rules to institutional investors, many mutual fund promoters were removing traditional disclosure procedures of their own. Shareholder voting privileges on possible changes in a fund's investment policies were removed. This was justified, the funds said, because whenever changes were requested the shareholders always voted yes anyway. While that may be true, the process of voting is a way of alerting interested shareholders that the profile of the fund is changing. Without the voting process, shareholders are told of changes only with the printing of a new prospectus — requiring a nearly impossible comparison of the old and the new to discover the changes and the possible new risk profile of the fund as defined by its investment policies. Some fund promoters stopped requiring trustees of the funds to attend shareholder meetings to answer shareholder questions. Other funds simply wouldn't identify the names and backgrounds of the managers actually running the fund. And, of course, they certainly wouldn't tell shareholders the exact nature of the costs of running the fund, the compensation given the management of the fund company, or the level of profitability of the fund to help shareholders determine if the expenses and fees were fair or justified. It was all behavior that fund managers professing to be shareholder activists would never abide on the part of the managers of public companies.

Weird Instruments

Layered on top of a burgeoning era of securitization unmatched since the 1920s and a push by fund managers to throw away historical safeguards of prudent investment policy is a truly new idea: derivatives. By the middle of 1994 this new form of security already was hurting mutual fund shareholders.

Virtually unregulated and complex enough to make the most sophisticated version of an asset-backed security look like a sand-box toy, derivatives, which quite literally are financial products that are derived from other financial products, take the idea of securitization to the extreme. These are securities made up of slices of other securities and then repackaged into a new derivative security. It's all done via complex computer models and massive mathematical calculations, and it's all overseen by Wall Street's newest savior, the "rocket scientist."

A simple example of one of these derivatives is the slicing of mortgage-backed securities into two parts. One part represents the interest-paying portion of the mortgage security; the other part represents the principal of the mortgage. Big investors — institutions, including mutual funds — could choose through such slicing only that part of the security that they believe fits their investment strategy. For example, if you're running an income fund, you may want to hold the derivative representing only the interest part of the mortgage security. It gets more complicated, of course, if the home owners whose mortgages are actually the underlying reality of the derivative start paying their mortgages off early, causing the value of the derivative to plunge. (This experience actually tripped a number of mutual funds — causing big losses — in the early 1990s when home owners refinanced homes at lower interest rates and paid off earlier mortgages. This early warning of derivative dangers was ignored.)

The use of derivatives by mutual fund managers has increased dramatically since 1990. Derivatives — and their equally complex companion, "synthetics" — have grown into such a global phenomenon that an estimated $30 trillion was committed to them worldwide. They have become the investment trick of choice for the money managers of the 1990s. But the dangerous use of derivatives wasn't caused by the derivatives themselves. Instead, the managers used this "new" idea in the old ways that had proved so disastrous in the past. Namely, as the vehicle for high-risk leverage and hedging tricks.

For mutual fund shareholders, the risks of these new and extremely complex financial products are immeasurable. Although completely untested in the reality of any major downdraft in markets, they promise to be the successful hedging devices to save the global financial world from the unthinkable. Wouldn't that be nice? But it is a claim that has been made before. Every generation seems to have found one — until it actually was tested. There's no proof that the derivatives or synthetics — financial products more divorced from the reality of the underlying investment than any previously invented financial idea — will be able to overcome the human factor that ultimately drives all markets.

Actually, the evidence that derivatives could not overcome the human factor started piling up in 1994. Dozens of mutual funds were caught in the downdraft of high-risk forays with derivatives — including supposedly low-risk money market funds and government bond funds. These incidents, affecting some of the best-known names in the mutual fund industry, brought widespread awareness of the dangers, as did the collapse of the investment pool of California's Orange County via reckless use of derivatives. The securities industry, however, generally shrugged it all off as isolated experiences — caring little for the individuals who were affected by the calamities.

Then in early 1995, in one of the greatest ironic turn of events in financial history, the giant investment bank Barings P.L.C., the same British company that was the cause of the Barings Crisis of 1890, went bankrupt after a billion-dollar derivatives currency play backfired. Unlike the experience a hundred years before, this time the Bank of England decided not to bail out the company — giving the world a clear message that bailout days were likely coming to an end. It also sent a clear message that governments would no longer automatically back up financial institutions that people had come to believe were "too big to fail."

CHAPTER 4

■ ■ ■

The People Handling
Your Money

One classic characteristic of periods of financial mania is the emergence of infallibly expert heroes. Everybody loves a hero, particularly when it comes to the search for simple, attractive answers to complex and disagreeable problems. Leaders of the mutual fund industry have always been more than willing to assume that role. And by the early 1990s an unprecedented number of Americans had decided to go along with this fantasy.

Specifically, the fantasy at work here is that anonymous people in a distant office are laboring — expertly and infallibly — in speculative markets to make you rich while you stroll the golf course carefree and without even an inkling of what they are doing with your money. (This precise image was used repeatedly by different mutual fund promoters in the early 1990s in TV commercials and newspaper and magazine ads. The image of someone caring for your money while you stroll the golf course can be traced back to Robert Fleming's first investment trust in the 1870s, when he promised to manage the finances of the moneyed classes of Dundee, Scotland, so that they could go off to the nearby town of St. Andrews, where the game of golf was invented.)

In the early 1990s the heroes who were to take us out of the financial morass of the 1980s and into a financially secure future had been labeled fund managers, financial consultants, investment executives, financial managers, money managers, investment advisers, and "rocket scientists."

But this crop of financial-world heroes is not some new species that has been beamed down from another planet. Instead, they are the same people we met recently under different — but now largely discredited — labels: junk bond dealers, arbitrageurs, stockbrokers, S&L executives, customer's men, investment bankers, registered representatives, and even corporate raiders. All that has happened is that they have changed hats and printed up new business cards. Those who believe that Americans were led down a financial garden path in the 1980s will find in the 1990s that the path may be different but that many of the tour guides are the same.

That is not to say that these tour guides are crooks. Not at all. There are very few true crooks among them (although as the mutual fund crisis moves toward its conclusion, crooks will certainly surface). Like most of the rest of us, the people managing your money and the people who are trying to sell you on the idea of sending your money in to be managed are working hard to make an honest dollar. One problem we face today, however, is that the definition of "honest" recently has been expanded and continues to be expanded further. Activity that a few years ago would have been considered brushing up against the concept of fraud has now been largely decriminalized through government deregulation and the removal of long-held investment limitations by mutual fund promoters.

The people handling your money now have more control over it and fewer controls over what they can do with it. In addition, as the people running our era of securitization they are providing absolutely no guarantee that what they do with your money will be successful. Leaders of pooled funds have all the control, and they are compensated solely for their "best efforts." You carry all the risk, with almost no say in how the money is invested and, in fact, an increasingly limited opportunity to find out how it is being invested.

"Golden Age of Investment Management"

The 1990s has already been dubbed the "Golden Age of Investment Management."[1] But the very term "golden age" is a time-limiting one. There has never been a golden age that lasted forever. If during this golden age, which is a golden age not only of investment management but also of securitization, you are able to achieve positive and lasting financial return on your money, it will be a happy, coincidental by-product of the actions of the golden age's leaders as they pursue their own financial self-interests.

The financial self-interests of the people running our current era of securitization — which, again, is matched in scale only by the 1920s — is evident on every level of the process from getting the fees by making the "deal" that defines securitization to selling you on the idea of handing over your money to them to back the "deal." Or, in other words, not only do you assume the risk for their "deal," you are also expected to pay a premium fee for the privilege.

Consider one small part of the push to securitization and the potential impact of the actions of the individuals running that part as they pursue their self-interests: the securitization of mortgages, both home and commercial. In 1980, banks and savings and loan companies owned about 80 percent of the mortgages they originated. The mortgages were held in the companies' portfolios and profits were made via collecting on those mortgages. The other 20 percent was securitized through "sale" of the mortgages to investment pools — mutual funds, pension funds, and so on.

By 1992, however, nearly 80 percent of all mortgages had been securitized (mainly into pension funds), while banks and S&Ls retained ownership of only about 20 percent of the mortgages they originated.

This dramatic change, which began in the late 1980s as banks and S&Ls looked for ways to dig out from under massive mortgage defaults, has been great for banks. Now, instead of having to worry about mortgages turning sour, the banks are compensated primarily through the fees for originating the mortgages. And the shift reduced the assets and liabilities of their now much smaller portfolios. They don't have to put as much capital aside, for example, as provisions against mortgage losses because they don't own the mortgages. And they don't have to pay as much of a contribution to the Federal Deposit Insurance program, because their activities now are not covered by this insurance program. (This shift has also been a boon for the government, because now it doesn't have to insure against the mistakes of bankers. The risks have been privatized through ownership of these mortgages by pension funds and mutual funds.)

With that in mind, however, ask yourself this question: Will the people who showed so little prudence in signing up mortgages in the 1980s, when they had ownership of those mortgages, now show *greater* prudence after the burden of risk has been passed off to someone else's shoulders, namely, yours? Not bloody likely.

Today, people signing up mortgages have far less accountability than they had just a few years ago. They don't have as many headaches worrying about what might happen three or five years from now. They can, instead, focus on their real daily business — generating as many deals as possible to obtain immediate fees. That daily "honest" pressure drives all the work of securitization: the bigger the deal, the bigger the fee and the greater the profit.

By the time the mortgages (and other securitized deals) turn to dust, the people who had originally made the deals will have been long gone. Those who had been most successful in signing up the deals — the ones who made the greatest immediate profits for their companies — will have been promoted to the status of hero. Those who had not been as successful — perhaps showing too much dogged prudence — will have been punished with banishment from the industry. And when the "mistakes" from this system become evident, there will not be any government bailout as there was for the "mistakes" of the 1980s. You will pay for it personally through your mutual fund and pension fund involvement.

There is nothing that can be done to avoid the probable results of the collective actions of individuals acting legally and "honestly" as they run our era of securitization. The course is already set. Your likelihood of coming through this era of securitization relatively unscathed, particularly as a mutual fund shareholder, begins with healthy skepticism about what the people in charge of the awesome mutual fund sales and marketing efforts are directing your way.

The New Legions

The mutual fund industry has always been primarily a sales-oriented industry rather than an investment-oriented one. The old adage is "funds are sold, not bought." More than banks or even brokerages, mutual fund companies have closely paralleled the sales techniques of the insurance industry to sell financial products. Like insurance promoters, mutual fund promoters depended for many years on large full-time and part-time sales forces — which in the 1960s reached a peak of over 200,000 salespeople. But unlike the insurance industry, the mutual fund industry has been an innovator in the use of advertising and direct mail.

Insurance industry people used to bristle at being compared to the mutual fund industry. In fact, they used to sell against mutual funds by pointing out that insurance products promised something definite — namely, the death benefit — while the returns from mutual fund involvement were uncertain.

This bickering isn't as intense as it once was. With the invention of universal life insurance, variable life, single-premium life, and other mutual fund–type products, the insurance industry view has changed. And it has brought with it an army of new (and effective) salespeople who now not only sell the insurance versions of mutual funds but also sell mutual funds themselves. With the introduction of mutual fund–style products at brokerages and banks, these industries too have joined the sales effort, until by 1993 an estimated multitude of 450,000 Americans — including stockbrokers — were registered to sell mutual funds to other Americans.

Actually, the cross-fertilization of the mutual fund business and the insurance game was sparked in part by a renegade from the 1960s go-go mutual funds who moved over to the insurance world in the 1970s — taking some of the mutual fund tricks with him. The fellow's name was Fred Carr. In the 1960s, Carr headed the highly successful Enterprise Fund. This was one of the leading go-go funds and a big winner for much of that period's mutual fund mania. Carr, however, made a timely exit from the Enterprise Fund in 1969 just before the go-go era and the Enterprise Fund itself tanked and the go-go funds collapsed around the ears of those not so fortunate to have exited in such a timely manner — both managers and shareholders.

By 1974 Carr had taken up residence in an insurance company called First Executive. Remember that, in the early 1970s, as people reacted to the disastrous results of the high-flying tricks of the go-go funds, they turned to the perceived safety of banks, S&Ls, and the "guarantees" of insurance companies.

At First Executive, Carr combined the "guaranteed" appeal of insurance with the "performance cult" appeal of the 1960s mutual funds. Using the idea of single-premium deferred annuities (or SPDAs), Carr sent his sales force out in the late 1970s and throughout the 1980s to sell First Executive's version of this rather stodgy insurance company product with the special twist that First Executive would pay two or three percentage points more of annual yield on the money than anyone else. He offered this high yield by loading up the annuities with junk bonds. Then, the same approach, which hundreds of thousands of people clamored for, was adopted by the company's "guaranteed investment contracts" (or GICs), which promised a fixed rate of interest for a period of time — usually one to three years — that was higher than anyone else's rate. Again, people rushed in. Why not? Look at the appeal: "guaranteed" and higher yield than anywhere else. This appeal looked so good that Carr's products were widely adopted for 401(k) plans as well as corporate savings plans and the pension programs of states and municipalities.

But the guarantee, as with any such insurance company product, is backed only by the insurance company. If the insurance company goes under, there goes the guarantee. And, indeed, First Executive went under. First Executive had, in fact, been one of Mike Milken's best and least discerning customers for junk bonds. The collapse of the junk bond market in the early 1990s brought down First Executive in 1991. Pensioners and holders of First Executive policies lost 30 percent of the value of their money overnight. Eventually, most of those people got most of the money back via a complicated arrangement put together by leaders of the insurance company industry in their attempt to deflect bad publicity — as justifiable as that bad publicity may have been.

Carr's legacy for the insurance industry, however, was similar to the legacy that he had helped create during the 1960s with mutual funds; that is, as he cranked up the high-risk machinery while giving "investors" the idea that the high yields promised were not high-risk, other companies, now losing customers to such promises, had to try to match the high yields. That meant, of course, a chase after the same high-risk tricks. Why sit around trying to uphold the grand standards of long-term prudent handling of the financial interests of customers, when the customers are rushing over to some other guy and giving him all the money?

The customers themselves, however, had little idea that all this risky one-upmanship was going on to attract their money. All they saw was respectable-looking companies and respectable-sounding insurance salesmen telling them that the ultimate nostrum had been found. It was, after all, "guaranteed."

The bad publicity may have slowed things for a while and even raised eyebrows about the assumed safety of insurance industry products. But markets recovering in the early 1990s from setbacks in the late 1980s — particularly the junk bond market that collapsed in 1990 only to dramatically rebound by 1993 — took the heat off. In addition, the general clamor for anything resembling mutual funds made life easier for insurance salespeople with mutual fund–type products under their arms.

Added to this aggressive crew was the growing presence of mutual fund salespeople in banks and S&Ls. In the 1990s in-bank mutual fund sales was becoming big money. And banks and mutual fund promoters made agreements with each other to widen the sales presence at banks.

For example, New York-based Chemical Bank, the fourth largest in the country, made a 1993 agreement with Boston's mutual fund company Liberty Financial Companies to sell fund shares to Chemical's 2.5 million customers in its four hundred New York area branches — with a new sales force of 230 "investment advisers" to do it. At NationsBank a similar agreement with Dean Witter Financial Services brought over four hundred "investment advisers" into the branch offices of that bank's sprawling empire.[2] And at the end of 1993, Pittsburgh's Mellon Bank acquired Dreyfus Corporation, the country's sixth-largest mutual fund company, in a deal worth $1.85 billion.

Officially, the government agencies overseeing bank activities have "strongly recommended" that mutual fund sales activities be physically separated from the "normal" bank activity so that bank customers don't get the wrong idea that the mutual fund products are as safe as the insured bank products. Also, the government "strongly discourages" allowing employees who take insured deposits to sell uninsured investment products. It's unclear whether in the 1990s the banks themselves wanted customers to make a sharp distinction between the bank's traditional products and the mutual funds. For example, despite criticism of the practice, banks like calling their mutual fund products by a name similar to, although perhaps not exactly the same as, the bank's name.

The last time this experiment was attempted — back in the 1920s — bank customers later complained that they did not realize the difference between securities speculation as promoted by bank employees with one hand and the process of "saving" via bank products as sold by banks with the other hand. A 1993 study conducted by the Securities and Exchange Commission indicates that it's not much different this time around. The survey showed that 28 percent of bank customers thought that mutual funds sold by banks were insured like all bank products and 30 percent said that funds sold through banks were safer than other mutual funds. The survey also found that 66 percent of respondents thought that money market funds sold through banks were federally insured. (The misunderstanding about the safety of mutual funds doesn't stop at the bank's door. The same survey revealed that 36 percent of the people questioned thought that mutual funds purchased from a stockbroker were federally insured. And of those people in the survey who were actual mutual fund shareholders, a whopping 49 percent believed that mutual funds bought through a broker were insured against loss by the government.)

How many retired, fixed-income people, in fact, walked up to bank counters in the early 1990s to renew their CDs and after complaining about the low interest rates got subtly gestured across the lobby to the mutual fund counter? By early 1995 we were already finding out how many, as a flurry of class action suits were brought against several banks by customers who felt victimized by misleading marketing practices.

While insurance salespeople, stockbrokers, and banks were expanding the mutual fund sales network, other people adopted official-sounding titles — such as "financial consultant" or "financial planner" — to help them earn commissions as fund sales representatives. The growth in interest in becoming a fund salesperson even spawned a home-study correspondence school called the Institute of Certified Fund Specialists, which issues a C.F.S. degree (short for Certified Fund Specialist, of course).

But as thousands of people were added to the ranks of fund peddlers, government control and guidelines covering those who call themselves "financial planners" or "investment advisers" remained nearly non-existent. Although registration requirements differ widely from state to state, most states do not have any guidelines at all. And federal requirements make the whole idea of regulation a farce. A "registered investment adviser" — a person who is officially "registered" as such with the federal government — was becoming by the early 1990s not only a joke, but a big and dangerous one. To obtain this distinction from the government you need only be twenty-one years old with no felony convictions. That's it. To "register" costs a once-in-a-lifetime fee of $150. There's no test and no educational or investment experience required. In fact, it is estimated that about 15 percent of those registered in 1992 did not finish high school. However, with such an official-sounding label as "registered investment adviser" you can prowl the countryside touting any old mutual fund or any other "investment" product you want — from gold mines to real estate limited partnerships. And many people have done so. The number of "registered investment advisers" has grown from 8,000 in 1984 to over 20,000 in 1993. The amount of money that these people manage accounts for more than $500 billion. Moreover, there is little likelihood that anyone will ever look into what these "registered investment advisers" are doing. The SEC has about fifty examiners inspecting what "registered investment advisers" are up to. That averages out to about one inspection every twenty-five to thirty years per adviser. Not that the examiners would have to examine much anyway. There's very little that the "registered investment adviser" has to do to keep within government guidelines. The adviser doesn't have to determine, for example, that the investments are in any way appropriate for customers. Nor, in fact, are the advisers even required to send statements of the status of accounts to the people whose money they control. At least, stockbrokers are required to make decisions about investment appropriateness and to deliver timely statements about accounts. And if they don't, a customer financially hurt in such ways by a broker has defined legal recourse to recoup money. No such restraints need immobilize a "registered investment adviser."

High Commissions, Low Credibility

The proliferation of personal selling efforts — delivered under the guise of "financial planning" — is paid for, of course, via commissions from mutual fund manufacturers. It has also not made it any easier to determine whether or not you're receiving unbiased help. Quite simply, you *can't* determine it, and therefore it is better just to avoid all these people who are so personally anxious to map your road to certain future wealth.

Not only are you vulnerable to the cross-fertilized sales techniques of insurance, mutual funds, and banking, but increasingly the types of selling gimmicks that had once been closely associated with unscrupulous stockbrokers have now been absorbed into the mutual fund selling game. In fact, full-service brokerages, anxious now after years of selling against mutual funds to get in on the action, are the worst. While brokerages still have the image of advising investors on individual investments, by the early 1990s they were making nearly 60 percent of their income from selling mutual fund products and other commission products like annuities. Moreover, the brokerages are particularly interested in selling their own proprietary funds rather than those of other promoters and, typically, pay their salespeople extra to sell "house specials." (Special for the house, perhaps, but rarely for anyone else — dogs, in other words, that no one would buy unless fast-talked into it. The extra broker bonuses are called "spiff" or "push money.") According to one study, mutual funds owned by brokerage firms underperformed competitors by an average of 20 percent.[3]

Also emerging in the early 1990s was a noticeable increase in the number of mutual fund "churning" cases involving various types of "financial consultants," including stockbrokers, who had been given full control over other people's money. A typical case told of the eighty-eight-year-old Tucson woman whose stockbroker churned her money among one hundred different mutual funds over an eight-year period, generating at least $100,000 in fees for the stockbroker. While legal guidelines are well established against such practices on the part of stockbrokers who control someone else's stock portfolio, the laws are very vague and undefined vis-à-vis a similar mutual fund portfolio. The churning of funds is difficult to track.[4] But the fees earned for placing someone's money in a mutual fund can be a lot higher than commissions on stock sales. Typically, a broker can clear 2 to 4 percent commission on average with a fund sale, while commission on a stock sale is one-half of 1 percent.

Even those "financial planners" who charge clients a fee may not be "fee-only" advisers. One little trick is to try to charge a fee and then put fee-paying customers into funds with high sales charges — with the "planner" collecting the sales load on top of the fee. And if a customer happens to notice this bit of double dipping and kicks over the arrangement — and only if the customer kicks — the "planner" may lower or eliminate the fee but not the sales charge.

According to a 1993 survey by the Institute of Certified Financial Planners, a trade group, only 10 percent of its members were fee-only planners. And among the full-time members of the International Association for Financial Planning, another trade group, only 8.2 percent were fee-only.[5]

Drawing on the services of such a "planner" is no easy thing. You first have to assess the planner — the planner's self-interests and competence — and then you will still have to assess the financial suggestions he gives you. Unfortunately, the whole situation involving "financial planners" — a field quickly filling up with unsavory characters — is far worse than it was just a few years ago. It is actually easier to do the whole thing yourself. As you'll see in later chapters, it isn't really that difficult, and you can be sure that it will be a *lot* safer and cheaper.

The "Seminar" Gambit

While a one-on-one encounter with a "financial consultant" — whether connected with a brokerage or fund promoter or acting as an independent agent — can be fraught with land mines, attending a "seminar" sponsored by a fund promoter or brokerage can be equally dangerous. These seminars are, of course, simply sales events that use group sales techniques instead of those designed to work on individuals. You cannot expect anything more than the standard sales pitch that favors the products offered by the sponsor of the seminar (although sometimes you might get a few pieces of cheese with some crackers and maybe even a full meal). You will *never* be given a balanced perspective on other savings or investment options at such a seminar. Perhaps if you are already a shareholder of a fund of the seminar's sponsor or if you are already seriously considering the use of the sponsor's products, you might want to attend as an opportunity to ask some tough questions about actual investment policies and risks involved with the specific products. Otherwise, attending these seminars just opens you up to sales manipulation that will have nothing to do with your best interests. After an hour or so of looking at all those cleverly designed charts and listening to seemingly informed people paint your certain stable financial future with their products, you'll be too dazzled to think straight.

Unfortunately, the seminar format also is often used to "educate" employees about 401(k) plans or some other type of defined-contribution program a company may have. Typically, the seminar is run by a representative of the insurance company or mutual fund promoter that handles the plan or even brokers and "financial planners." But all these people, even when not working solely on commissions, bring a bias toward the financial products they have been trained to sell. Even more unfortunate is the fact that since the "seminars" are held under the auspices of the company itself, the seminar leader receives instant credibility from employees because the employees think that the company has already thoroughly screened and approved the presentation as valuable and in the employees' best interests. Don't assume that. The "education" seminar, along with the defined-contribution plan itself, is simply another way for employers to get the pension monkey off their backs.

In fact, it is not likely that the managers of the company who invite the seminar leaders into the office are in any better position to judge the appropriateness of the seminar advice than the employees themselves. Just because someone may have a certain level of expertise to manage some type of business doesn't mean that person is also able to assess financial products. And if you want proof, just ask the people whose employers chose Fred Carr's First Executive to handle their retirement plans.

Mutual fund promoters have become increasingly successful selling packaged "turnkey" retirement plans to small — and even large — companies. Such plans promise to alleviate the employers' worries about government regulations concerning the way a retirement program is structured. But the regulations on what a financial services company must offer in these "self-directed" plans are minimal. A "bill of goods" sold to an employer as an easy package to solve the retirement problem can be easily (and, to be fair, unwittingly) sold to employees by the employer. For example, a plan can have as few as three investment options with different risk/reward characteristics to be legal. (A 1993 survey of employers with 401(k) plans showed that 48 percent had four or five options and 25 percent had only three.)[6] But the definitions of those risk/reward characteristics are very wide and are open to broad interpretation by both the companies sponsoring the plans and the mutual fund promoters or other financial services companies that may be actually handling them. As we've seen, an insurance company's "Guaranteed Income Contract," which, from a quick glance, could be considered a low-risk option, could also be a quick wealth destroyer instead of the "safe" savings instrument it was promoted to be.

The whole area of defined-contribution plans, where employees are responsible for their own retirement "investment" planning, is new. There has not been an experiment of this scale and kind since the 1920s, when many people turned with full faith to the investment trust concept to fulfill their retirement hopes. The fact that today's retirement hopes are once again focused on mutual funds representing speculative markets is unsettling. As of the end of 1993, those speculative markets have not been tested against the widespread use of 401(k)-type retirement plans with, for example, such market atmospheres as were experienced in the 1970s or 1930s.

This situation has come about in large part because of government regulation favoring the mutual fund structure over nearly all other savings/investment options. The extent of this favoritism was revealed when the Labor Department ruled in 1993 that as of January 1, 1994, employers offering 401(k) plans had absolutely no legal responsibility for the outcome of the retirement plan investments as long as employees were given three broad, diversified investment options. As of that date, employers no longer had any liability for the investment options offered employees or for the selection of the financial services company running the plan.

That's nice for the employer. It's also nice for the government, since the government doesn't have to come up with many guidelines to define what is appropriate or not. But it's not nice for those who want to be mutual fund survivalists. For you, if you are involved in a defined-contribution plan, in this area of your financial life, as with all areas of mutual fund contact in the 1990s, the decision to join in on the plan should have more to do with the nature of the risk the options represent than the fact that the plan has been offered by your employer — even if your employer is matching any part of the money you contribute with additional money. What options are available? How are they managed? Who manages them? What is the exact nature of the investment policies followed by the managers of the investment pools? Are any investment "tricks" — such as junk bonds — being used?

And if the options are *not* acceptable, then you have a problem that can be dealt with in only three ways: (1) don't participate; (2) get your employer to come up with something better; or (3) consider your future seriously and look for a new employer.

Learn a lesson from the people who got burned with First Executive. When the insurance company went under, people who were faced with a loss of money complained to their employers, who had chosen First Executive to serve the retirement plan. The employers simply replied that the employees had made the investment decision to put their money into First Executive's products and that the nature of the junk bond investment in the retirement accounts had been disclosed to the employees in annual reports from the insurance company — which, indeed, it had, although questionably obscured in small print and technical jargon. It was the employees' problem, therefore, that they had not recognized the investment risk or had ignored it. The employing companies had no liability. And when some employees tried to sue their employers over this issue, the courts agreed with the employers.

This story provides a glimpse of the future. Just as there is wide misunderstanding of whether or not mutual funds sold at banks and through stockbrokers are guaranteed by the government, the precise nature of risk for those in defined-contribution plans may not be fully understood. How many people who put money from their paychecks every week into company-sponsored 401(k) plans mistakenly believe that these personal contributions going into mutual fund–style investment options are immune to fluctuation or, indeed, loss? The popularity of these plans is still relatively new, and as of this writing, the plans have not been tested in declining speculative markets, and, therefore, the answer to any question about what people believe or expect from their defined-contribution plans is unclear. One clear thing, however, is that now, more than at any time in the last sixty years, you, as one member of the new breed of American worker, are completely on your own.

Time-Honored Sales Pitches

With about 450,000 people personally trying to sell you on putting your money into mutual funds added to the full-page ads in newspapers and magazines and the TV and radio commercials bombarding you, along with the government's embracement of the mutual fund concept as the nearly exclusive option for defined-contribution retirement plans, you are faced with some formidable forces trying to shove this financial idea down your throat — and all panting over the portion of your money that they can keep for themselves while at the same time thrilling to the prospect of hoisting the full burden of investment risk of these financial products off onto you.

Not only are you up against the magnitude of the marketing effort focused your way, you are also up against a carefully presented sales pitch that has been artfully honed over the last one hundred years. In fact, the precise sales technique — including most of the exact wording you hear today — has remained virtually unchanged since the idea of the mutual fund was first introduced in this country under the name "investment trust." If you were to look back at the ads and newspaper and magazine articles of the 1920s and 1960s, you need only insert new fund names and you won't be able to tell the difference. There is *nothing* new about the basic pitch. All the forward-projecting charts showing how speculative markets will be able to help you overcome inflation, for example, or to build wealth toward retirement goals are exactly the same.

Typically, risks are shown to be minimal by demonstrating the benefit of a long-term perspective. In the late 1920s, proponents of the value of common stocks as long-term investments liked to show charts of their steady growth — despite a few temporary setbacks — starting from 1865, the end of the Civil War. That was a sixty-year performance chart that people of the 1920s looked on with confidence. The 1920s investment trust promoters also saw the sales value of showing a twenty-year performance chart that conveniently started its measurement from the stock market's low point following the Panic of 1907. Today, similar charts showing a sixty-year-plus time span, typically dating to 1926 (and carefully avoiding measurements from the peak of the market in 1929), depict the steady growth of the stock market. And, conveniently, there is a twenty-year performance chart starting at the market's low point of December 1974. During the late 1960s, the same idea was used. Then the mutual fund sales forces could measure a twenty-year period starting with 1946, the beginning year of the postwar boom.

When viewing such charts today, remember that bull markets of any sort — whether in stocks or gold or real estate or orange juice futures or anything else — always come to an end. For the people of the 1920s, the 1929–32 bear market wiped out all the stock market's gains of the previous thirty-three years. A generation later witnessed a bear market of 1973–74 that wiped out all the spectacular gains of the 1960s to take the market back to the level of 1958. (It would not be until 1982 that the market recovered in real terms. And on an inflation-adjusted basis, a recovery from the market's peak in 1966 has yet to be achieved as of this writing.)

Also remember, when looking at the sixty-year-plus charts, that realistically your investment time frame may not accommodate such an extended view — no matter how long ago you quit smoking or how low your cholesterol level is. As shown in later chapters, there are times when you want to be in the stock market and times when you do not. Equally, there are times when you may want to be in other investment markets — either via mutual funds or directly — and there are times when you may not want to be anywhere near them.

These considerations are of little interest to a mutual fund promoter. The promoter sells only what are perceived by potential customers as desirable financial products. Period. The time-honored sales pitches are presented ad infinitum. They may seem new and intriguing to you when you encounter them for the first time, but they are old hat for the mutual fund guys. The only thing that changes from year to year is the ease with which the sales pitch brings in the money. During the early 1990s the pitch was very successful.

Here, from a 1959 book called *What Every Salesman Should Know About Mutual Investment Funds,* is a backstage peek at a time-honored approach to mutual fund sales:

> *We all have that instinct of acquisitiveness or greed. That is what causes us to buy securities for profit. When that appetite is aroused in a large number of people, we work into a bull market. This instinct is what controls the profit motive. When that instinct is aroused, you can sell any kind of securities to anybody. It is no trick at all. Bull markets make great salesmen.*[7]

As this perky writer from the dawning days of the great mutual fund mania of the 1960s suggests, success as a mutual fund salesperson is often the ability to seize the moment. For such salesmen, the early 1990s became a once-in-a-lifetime opportunity. As we've seen, all the ingredients came together to make the sales effort easier than at any time since at least the late 1960s — and possibly the late 1920s.

Perhaps it is the job of the mutual fund promoter — as well as the job of other people who want to sell speculative investment products — to get other people to accept the outer limits of their risk tolerance. But it is your job, particularly during a period when speculative financial ideas reach popular heights, to skeptically question and investigate the risk of all that is presented to you.

The promoters will try to paint high-risk investment options — the ones that usually also happen to be the most profitable for them to run — as if the reward that comes with such risk is certain. Or, more typically, they will present the presumed reward in great detail while making you forget the danger — to make it seem so remote as to have no influence on any decision you may make. While selling these high-risk products, they will try to belittle anything that they don't sell. They will come up with carefully drawn charts, which are often filled with half-truths, to prove how urgent it is for you to take on more risk — immediately — to "put your money to work" in their products.

Often they will use the word "aggressive" to camouflage the high-risk nature of the investment product. At the same time the sales implication will be that you can do whatever you want to do, but if you don't go along with their aggressive investment product, you are a wimp. And, as a wimp, you will end up in the discarded dust as others more willing to accept "just a little more risk" gallop forward into the sunset of secure and easy wealth.

Don't believe it. All those expensive ads, full-color brochures, high-pressure salespeople, and glad-handing seminar leaders are not interested in you because of their desire to make your life easier and richer. They just want your money.

So don't be afraid of being a wimp when it comes to doing what you believe is best for you with your money. Even if you have the slightest uneasy twinge about something or don't feel that you know enough about something, you are *right* not to do it. Don't be afraid of erring on the side of caution. The single most important thought you can keep in mind as a mutual fund survivalist is this: whatever you do, don't ever do anything you don't feel comfortable with. Don't be dissuaded from that feeling by salespeople, a full-color mutual fund ad, a performance chart of someone else's theoretical mile-high experience from the past, logical-sounding words from somebody on TV, a respected financial adviser, your spouse, your neighbor, your employer, or, above all, your own lust for easy wealth.

Your secure future as a mutual fund survivalist will depend on assessing your tolerance for the risks of the different options of where to put your money — which, indeed, may include mutual funds — rather than contemplating all the gains others tell you can be yours by handing your money over to them. That means that you won't do anything with your money because you think it is going to make you rich. Only losers anticipate such gains.

While it is possible to make money from money — and that's what saving and investing is all about — few people of real wealth ever achieved that wealth by taking a small amount of money and making it into a fortune by playing the stock market or any other speculative market. And *nobody* ever achieved real wealth by handing money over to somebody else to play with. Certainly, wealthy people such as Fidelity Investments' Edward C. Johnson 3d and Peter Lynch, and Mario Gabelli of the Gabelli group of mutual funds, and John Templeton, former head of the Templeton group of mutual funds, and John Bogle, head of the Vanguard group of mutual funds, and Howard Stein, head of the Dreyfus group of funds, did *not* accumulate the bulk of their wealth by playing speculative markets. Instead, they made their wealth by playing on the dreams of people who play speculative markets and collecting fees from those people. Similarly, Michael Milken did not get rich by buying junk bonds and holding them to collect the interest. He got rich by selling the junk bonds.

And once wealthy, do these and other people profiting from the mutual fund idea turn to their own products as a place for their excess wealth? The figures needed to answer this question are difficult to find. The actual investment involvement of people working within the mutual fund indus-try is a closely held secret. Unlike corporate officers and directors of pub-lic companies who must publicly disclose all of their stock holdings in their own companies, mutual fund company officers and trustees do not live under such government requirements. Instead, they need only dis-close ownership of fund shares if the ownership is 5 percent or more of the fund's shares. And since most mutual funds easily top $100 million in assets it is unlikely that any one individual holds $5 million in a single fund — no matter how wealthy he or she may be.

When asked directly whether or not they have money in their own funds, the managers' answers are cagey. When a manager is heavily invested in a fund, there is full disclosure. But other times such a question would be greeted with a sharp "It's irrelevant." Generally, however, most mutual fund managers — as well as mutual fund company officers and trustees — do *not* turn to their own funds as the place for their own money. A 1991 survey of fund managers found that only 27 percent of the managers committed money to their funds as the place for their single largest investment. For the other managers in the survey, 19 percent did not own any shares of their funds, and the other 54 percent, while owning some shares of their own funds, chose another investment or savings instrument as the place for their single largest investment.[8]

The issue of whether or not mutual fund managers held shares of their own funds took on particular importance in the earliest days of 1994 when questions were raised about managers trading in stocks for their own private portfolios that were also being traded in the funds. Investi-gations began to see if some mutual fund managers had returned to the age-old practice of "front running" — that is, buying shares of a company for a personal account just prior to a fund's large purchase of a block of shares that would have the effect of raising the price of the stock. While such practice is illegal, investigations centered on uncovering whether or not fund managers were using information for their own personal benefit to the disadvantage of their fund shareholders.

The bigger question, of course, is why fund managers would need to have active personal portfolios if the mutual fund products they promote to other people are as desirable as their promotions claim them to be. Different fund promoters had different answers. Some claimed that man-agers who traded for their own accounts kept their trading skills sharp-ened, and that it actually encouraged their managers to build their own portfolios. Other promoters prohibited their managers from trading for personal accounts. Regardless of the point of view, it is clear that the people who are closest to the widest information about their own products and have the greatest understanding of the mutual fund concept as an investment idea have *not* embraced it as the exclusive answer to their personal savings/investment needs.

This doesn't mean to suggest that there aren't reasonable investment possibilities with mutual funds. There are many, many very good choices among them and good reasons to use them — if, as shown in following chapters, you are careful. But just as mutual funds are not the sole investment panacea for mutual fund leaders, they are not the panacea for you, either.

Paying Them Their Due

While dazzling you with promises of riches and egging you on into high-risk investment arenas that you would never willingly or knowingly venture into, the promoters will also attempt to transfer as much money as possible from your pocket to their pockets in the form of fees and charges made on the fund. Here again, to be a mutual fund survivalist, you must be prepared to resist their techniques to get you to pay more for their products than necessary.

The cost of being in one fund compared to other similar funds is primarily determined by the success of the fund promoter's sales effort. There are funds that do poorly for their shareholders that are expensive to be part of. There are funds that do well that charge low fees. But the cost associated with a fund is not determined by value or performance or via any bidding marketplace. The price charged is directly related to the sales effort: how much the promoter can get for the product even if it is no better or, in fact, inferior to others that cost less.

Innumerable statistical studies over the years repeatedly have proven that there is no correlation between mutual fund costs and their performance. It is just not true that funds with high management fees, for example, do better than those with low management fees. Equally, however, the lowest-cost funds are not necessarily the best performers or the safest type of fund. For the mutual fund survivalist, therefore, it is not so much that you need to search out the cheapest fund, but that you should avoid exorbitantly priced funds and, more important, not pay more than the going rate for what you get. You can't expect the service that you get from a mutual fund to be free, of course, but if you're not on your toes, you can be easily gouged.

Fees and charges are much more complicated than they were a few years ago. Fee confusion is one of the things that mutual fund promoters spend a lot of time trying to create. They don't really want you to notice how much everything is costing or how much of a bite the costs are taking out of your investment — particularly at a time when they are trying to raise prices (and profits), not lower them to achieve the shareholder economies of scale that had once been such an idealistic rallying cry among mutual fund floggers. According to an early 1993 reckoning by Forbes, there were nine different ways of getting fees from shareholders.[9] It seems that just as people start to understand how one type of fee or charge works and affects their fund returns, another is invented to keep the confusion ball rolling.

The most obvious and offensive cost is the sales charge or front load. A dominant tradition in the mutual fund world since the early 1930s, when the open-end fund idea supplanted the stock-market-traded closed-end idea, the front load was, until the mid-1970s, a necessary evil that compensated salespeople for selling the funds. As with insurance, going through a salesperson was almost exclusively the only way to get access to mutual funds. In the 1930s the typical load was 10 percent. By the 1950s this had gone down to an average 8 1/2 percent, and by the early 1990s it was more typically 5 1/2 percent. For survivalists, all such loads are unacceptable. In the first place, a load, even as low as 5 1/2 percent, takes an immediate chunk out of your money. You would need a return of 5.8 percent to get your original total investment back up to the break-even point. (On an 8 1/2 percent load, you need a 9.8 percent return to break even.) And getting a 5.8 percent return (and certainly a 9.8 percent return) is not always easily or quickly achieved. Also, when you pay such a front load it means that you have encountered some type of commission-backed salesperson. (The sales charge does not go to the fund, of course. It goes to the salesperson.) And you want to avoid these commission people, because the higher the load the more attractive it is to the commission person to sell it to you and, by simple logical extension, the less attractive to you. Result: conflict of self-interests.

The alternative, of course, is the no-load fund. The no-loads, although they had been around since the 1920s, didn't start getting their share of mutual fund attention until the 1970s, when the load funds got most of the (deserving) blame and bad publicity for the reckless go-go years of the 1960s. Commission salespeople like to belittle the no-loads by referring to them, for example, as the choice for "blue-collar workers." The high sales charges levied by the load funds, you are to believe, are buying you premium, personalized attention worthy of the status of a "white-collar professional." Baloney. All the load does is make you that much poorer right from the start.

Since no-loads make up about half of current mutual fund choices, you shouldn't have much trouble finding the right one for you to fulfill the Mutual Fund Survival Rules identified at the end of this chapter and in other chapters. No-load funds are usually clearly identified as such in almost every newspaper or magazine list of funds. Also, you can find fairly comprehensive and up-to-date lists of them in *The Individual Investor's Guide to No-Load Mutual Funds* (American Association of Individual Investors, 625 North Michigan Avenue, Chicago, IL 60611), *The Handbook for No-Load Fund Investors* (P.O. Box 318, Irvington, NY 10533), "No-Load Directory" (100% No-Load Council, 1501 Broadway, New York, NY 10036), and *Mutual Fund Sourcebook* (Morningstar, Inc., 225 West Wacker Drive, Chicago, IL 60606). Most large public libraries carry one or more of these directories.

Many no-load fund promoters, however, also sell "low-loads." Avoid these funds as you would a full load. These low-load funds, typically charging 2, 3, or 4 percent instead of the more standard 5.5 percent load, are usually imposed on the promoter's most popular funds. The popularity of these funds — sometimes temporary — can be based on the fund's recent past performance or something even less tangible, such as a particular fund manager's current fame. When the promoter finds that the popularity of a low-load begins to wane, then you will often see great hoopla made about a "limited time offer" of a waiving of the sales charge. Often this limited time is extended forever. There is usually no need to rush to send your money in, although rushing is what the promoter wants you to do.

For those who have already paid a sales charge to get into a fund, there is no advantage to leave it now as long as it fulfills other standards for meeting investment objectives and for safety. But there is no reason to continue putting *more* money into such a fund. There are other funds just as good and less expensive. And that's a promise.

Avoiding the sales charge, unfortunately, is only the beginning. Some fund promoters, while calling themselves "no-load," then go on to try to charge an "account opening fee" of $50 or more. Others try to charge "annual account maintenance fees" of $10 or more. These fees, which can seem insignificant, even petty, can add up. They certainly add up for the fund promoter, who hopes that fund shareholders will view the fees as some type of standardized industry practice. They are not. You can find many funds that do not have these types of charges. And if you are in a fund that currently tries to get these types of extras from you, you should be particularly careful to look for other cost tricks.

Beyond these charges can come a "redemption fee" that is charged for exiting a fund. While these types of charges often feature a sliding scale of percentages charged — sometimes from as high as 6 percent down to 1 percent — for shareholders who hold the fund for longer periods of time, redemption fees also are not standardized industry practice. In fact, they are unusual, and funds that attempt to hold you hostage with such a fee should be avoided. One of the supposed attractions of a mutual fund is its liquidity. A redemption fee puts an onerous limitation on your ability to liquidate the fund's shares when you want to (because you have changed your investment outlook) or when you are compelled to (because the management of the fund has let you down for one reason or another). The fund managers don't get punished when they change their minds about the make-up of the fund's portfolio, so why should you be punished for changing your mind about a fund in your portfolio? You shouldn't. And a mutual fund survivalist cannot accept the enslavement of a redemption fee.

After avoiding sales loads and any other up-front charges as well as any redemption fee or "deferred sales charge," you should also avoid funds that charge you a sales load on reinvestment of dividends that may be collected by the fund and go toward your automatic purchase of more shares of the fund. Also, funds that charge "exchange fees" to move your money from one of the promoter's funds to another are not acceptable.

All these charges are revealed in a fund's prospectus, usually found on the inside front cover under the heading "Shareholder Transaction

Expenses." The table that shows figures for these various potential charges has been standardized by government regulation. The mutual fund survivalist should make sure that each entry in this table is followed by the word "none." (See Appendix A for an example of how this should look in a fund's prospectus.)

A second table on the inside cover of a prospectus reveals the "Annual expenses" that the fund promoter charges perpetually against the money in its hands. Each category of expenses in this table is shown as a percentage figure that would be charged against your money if you were in the fund. Heading the list on this table is the annual "management fee," which can range from as low as 0.2 percent to over 4 percent. Typically, however, the management fee hovers somewhere between 0.5 percent and 1.0 percent. This is the fee that the fund promoter collects in its official role as "investment adviser" to the fund to pay for the professional services provided.

Also included on the table of "Annual expenses" is a category of charges called, vaguely enough, "Other expenses." This category of costs includes money spent out of the fund's resources for such things as printing annual reports, postage, commissions paid to brokers for portfolio transactions, and so on.

The other important annual fee found on this table is the highly controversial "12b-1 fee." This fee was first introduced in 1980 when the Securities and Exchange Commission wanted to help funds — particularly no-load funds — to pass marketing and distribution expenses on to fund shareholders — costs like advertising, promotional materials, and mailings of sales literature. Previously, such costs were paid for out of the management fee. The 12b-1 fee is commonly referred to as the "distribution fee." The original idea of the 12b-1, however, was quickly distorted by fund promoters as a way of picking up extra money unrelated to the actual costs of these marketing efforts. The biggest beneficiaries ended up being the load fund promoters. Now, instead of charging just the front load, the promoters could tack on an additional 12b-1 fee — often as high as 1 percent a year — to get even more. And since this fee was "hidden" in the depths of a prospectus, few people who had already fallen for the high front-end load would notice that there was an even more odious annual fee added onto the other annual fees. (For mutual fund promoters, once a sucker is found, he may as well be taken for as long a ride as possible — because, of course, "It's legal.") The 12b-1 fees can be big revenue builders for a fund promoter. Dean Witter, for example, took in $178 million in 12b-1 fees in the first nine months of 1992.

About half of all funds charge 12b-1 fees. About 85 percent of load funds charge them. And, again, as with all costs associated with mutual fund involvement, the size of the 12b-1 charge has nothing to do with the actual costs incurred for the types of things that the fee is supposed to cover — it relates only to the amount that the promoter can get from unsuspecting shareholders.

The 12b-1 fees can become very expensive over time. For example, a fund that levied a 1 percent annual 12b-1 fee back in the early 1980s collected 5 percent from shareholders within five years. And that is greater than a one-time 4 percent load. With more money going into supposed long-term retirement accounts, which mutual fund promoters hope you will put money into and then forget, these annual clips can be more attractive for the promoters than a sales load. Or as the magazine *Financial World* once observed, "while that's not great for investors, good marketing can obscure that fact." (Ever notice how someone else's idea of "good marketing" puts you into the hole?)

In 1993, the SEC added further complications to the 12b-1 story. SEC rules began prohibiting funds from calling themselves "no-load" if they charged over 0.25 percent in 12b-1 fees. The new rules went on to put a cap of 0.75 percent on the 12b-1 portion of expenses. But the SEC decided to allow fund promoters to add a *new* fee of another 0.25 percent as an "additional service fee." As a result of this, a fund can still charge its shareholders the same high 1.0 percent "fee" — the 0.75 percent 12b-1 fee plus the new 0.25 percent "service fee." There wasn't much accomplished here except some new, extra complications for fund share-holders to master and a few more openings for fund promoter magic tricks.

Now, therefore, there are *four* elements that make up the total amount of annual fees for a fund's total "annual expenses." For mutual fund sur-vivalists, however, all this is simplified by ignoring the four separate ele-ments and focusing instead solely on the *total annual expenses.* This is the figure shown on the inside front cover of the prospectus that adds all these costs together. It doesn't matter how the fees and expenses are divided as long as the total doesn't exceed the outer limits of reasonable-ness. This reasonableness can be identified as the "average" annual expenses charged by funds within broad fund categories. For mutual fund survivalists, therefore, the limits on total annual expenses are as follows:

- Money market funds   0.70%
- Government bond funds   0.80%
- Corporate bond funds   1.00%
- Stock funds   1.25%
- International funds   1.40%

You can find funds in each category — good funds — that charge much less. But if you own anything costing above this, you're being taken to the cleaners. A small difference in annual expenses can add up to big money. Even fund shareholders of the successful 1980s and early 1990s lost out because of fees. For example, a 1 percent annual expense difference for any fund shareholder getting a 10 percent annual return over ten years (a nice thing if it ever happens again) would have meant a reduction in returns of $2,250 on an initial $10,000 investment.

Another complication in all this fee insanity was the 1990s introduction of multiple classes of different types of shares of mutual funds. Typically, four classes were created: Class A, Class B, Class C, Class D. Each class of share was charged for expenses and other costs differently. For example, at one fund, Class A shares had a 4 percent sales charge "load," but no 12b-1 fee added to other management expenses. The fund's Class B shares had no front-end load, but carried a 0.75 percent 12b-1 fee for the first six years that the shareholder held the shares and then a lowering of the 12b-1 fee to 0.25 percent for the remaining period that the shareholder was in the fund. Class C shares carried no sales charge, but had a perpetual 0.75 percent annual 12b-1 fee, plus a perpetual 0.25 percent service fee. And Class D shares had no sales charge or 12b-1 fees, but those shares were available only to employees of the fund's company.

Supposedly, these different fee possibilities were going to give people with different investment needs more options. For example, someone who expected to be in a fund for only a year would probably choose Class B shares because the high front load could be avoided. For those who expected to be in the fund for a long period of time, paying the front load would make sense as a way of getting it all over at once. Also, if the value of the shares increased significantly, then the sales charge paid up front would represent a smaller amount than a set percentage paid every year on a higher amount of money achieved through investment return.

In reality, however, these multiple classes of shares simply add confusion to let the broker or "financial planner" who typically sells these types of load funds find various ways of closing the mutual fund sale with the least amount of resistance. For example, the fund salesperson who is primarily interested in grabbing the full fee from a front-load sales charge can start out: "This fund would be great for you. And I want to put you into the fund's Class A shares." With a simple voice inflection, the impression is conveyed that of all the possibilities within the fund there is one class of shares that is "A Number One. Better than others. Best." And if the potential buyer doesn't go for that angle because of resistance to front-load funds, then it's a simple matter to shift to the next level — Class B. For the salesperson, this isn't as appealing, because the sales fee isn't paid all at once but is spread out over many years, with the added risk of the shareholder pulling out. But it's better than nothing. As a mutual fund survivalist, you won't have to worry about a salesperson's practiced pitch because you should be avoiding all these people in the first place.

But you're *still* not off the hook completely. There are other opportunities for the people selling you funds.

For institutional fund sales efforts — brokerages, for example, or even mutual fund promoters that have their own walk-in sales offices and compensate their salespeople primarily through set salaries instead of commissions on personal sales efforts — reaping the up-front sales charge may not be as appealing as the potential of reaping a perpetual, steady 0.75 percent annual 12b-1 fee. After five years, as you may have noticed, such a steady fee amounts to more than an original 4 percent front-load charge. With this fee hidden in different classes of shares, an institutional fund sales group can advertise the fund as "no-load" and attract the interest of those who have heard of the importance of no-load funds but have not yet noticed the trickery of hidden fees. In this case, the prospective shareholder may not even be advised that there are different options. In fact, the prospect runs the risk of responding to a promotion of a "no-load" and then getting switched to another class of shares that is really more like a load fund.

All is revealed, however, in the fund's prospectus. The existence of multiple classes of shares shows up on the page with expenses. The prospectus has to tell you of the existence of multiple classes of shares and it has to tell you how all the classes are structured.

Rather than trying to figure out the most appropriate one for you, just avoid all funds with these wacky multiple classes of shares. It's an added complication, and no matter how you try to play it, you'll probably end

MUTUAL FUND SURVIVAL RULES: THE PEOPLE

1. **If it sounds too good to be true, it is.** Whether you encounter it in an ad or from the mouth of a person, getting involved with anything that sounds as if you've finally found the perfect answer to your financial problems is very likely just the beginning of your problems. That goes for dividend or interest yield claims, "guarantees," and all attempts to get you to think that by simply handing your money off to somebody else you will get rich either in the short term or over the long term.

2. **Never go into a mutual fund suggested by a full-service broker or a commission-paid "financial planner."** You just can't be sure that a commission broker or any other commission-based adviser is working on your behalf. Beware, also, of the "fee-paid" adviser who tries to put you into load funds.

3. **Use only no-load funds.** There's no reason to pay a load. There are plenty of no-load funds that will serve just as well, if not better, than any load fund you can find.

4. **Avoid broker- or fund-sponsored "seminars" — even if dinner is promised.** You can save yourself a lot of money by sticking to no-load funds that you could find on your own in the same amount of time that you would spend at a seminar and afterward treating yourself to dinner.

5. **Don't get into any telephone conversations with strangers.** Here's the fastest way to get rid of cold callers: with a confused tone in your voice, say, "But I already have an account with your company."

6. **Never take any advice from people sitting in your bank branch office.** Some funds sold at banks are good. Most, however, are load funds paying commissions to the people at the bank's counter. Make any decision about a fund sold by a bank in complete isolation from any advice from a bank-employed adviser.

7. **Don't assume that a fund in a company defined-contribution pension plan is a good one.** Your employer has absolutely no liability for the choice of financial institution handling your defined-contribution pension plan or for the performance of the options offered in that plan. The decision to put money into the plan and the selection of the options for your money are yours and yours alone, because *all* the risks are yours and yours alone.

up with the short end of the stick. You don't need it. There's a better fund available. Also, a fund promoter who likes to play these sleight-of-hand tricks is likely to play other, more dangerous tricks like pursuing investment gimmicks that put you at greater risk than you could ever begin to comprehend.

Incidentally, as you pare back on the expenses you pay to the 450,000-plus people trying to sell you mutual funds, don't worry about putting any of these people out of work. They will find their way in the world. If you've ever met any of them you know that they are usually well groomed, articulate, and in possession of considerable moxie. These are qualities that could be put to greater good use in our society than, for example, canvassing the trailer parks of Florida to separate money from yield-hungry retired folks to put into junk bond funds so that bankrupts like Donald Trump can have an easier time financing new projects of self-aggrandizement.

CHAPTER 5

■ ■ ■

The Risks You Face: The Rudiments

Never forget that in this era of securitization you are guaranteed nothing. The people handling your money via mutual funds are fully compensated through the fees you pay for their "best effort" — no matter what happens. If anything should go wrong because of that "best effort," these people will be quick to point out an obscure line in the fine print of the prospectus that you claimed to have read and understood before sending in your money and say: "See, we told you what the risks were."

All the implied promises that may have been used to attract your money to their management will be conveniently dismissed as irrelevant. This attitude permeates the mutual fund industry. It is no different, for example, from the business attitude of cigarette makers who promote the romance of smoking while printing on each package of their product the disclaimer warning that smoking causes illnesses. If you should get lung cancer (or lose your money) because of the use of their product, then it is your fault, and your fault only.

This is, of course, one of the beauty parts of running a mutual fund business — absolutely no accountability. That is why banks and every other institution that handles money want to get into the game and are so anxious to get the laws changed so that they can get into it more completely.

The only risk that they carry is the risk of being fired by you. But by the time you figure out that you *should* fire them, they very likely will have collected enough fees from you not to care too much. Also, they can usually find a fresh supply of people who won't know why you fired them.

The reason that you may fire them is that they did not live up to your expectations. As we've already seen, many of those expectations, unfortunately, have been implanted by the fund promoters themselves with the hope that you won't remember what was actually "promised" or that you will become so complacent after you send your money in that you won't do anything about it when you should. Then, of course, there's the time-honored mutual fund promoter pattern of attracting your money with a display of personal genius and when things go poorly shrugging it all off as "uncontrollable market conditions."

Fund promoters also know that small investors tend to stick with losing situations long after they should have evacuated. Small investors tend to do this because they like to hope for the best — a revival in the market or a turnaround in a disastrous fund to recoup their losses. Also, there's an unwillingness to admit even in the face of disaster that a mistake had been made in judgment about the investment idea and the people running the investment idea — particularly when those people, who are perceived as "experts," tell small investors that the best course to deal with setbacks is not only to hold tight but to send in more money.

Since everything that can go wrong with your mutual fund investment will be your fault, you must completely understand the risks involved and be comfortable with the risks you are exposed to. Then you won't have to worry so much about when to fire somebody, particularly when it gets to be too late.

New Risks

The days are over when you could go into a mutual fund with the assurance that everything other than the relative talents of different groups of professional managers was about the same among similar types of funds. With the easing of government regulations and the widespread investment limitation changes among mutual fund promoters concerning the way your money is invested, the risks you face today are far, far greater than they were just five years ago. In fact, these new risks — some of which involve investment tricks that have never been tested in the real world — take us back to at least the days of the go-go 1960s. And, as we've seen, indications during the early 1990s seem to point to a wave of recklessness that could actually take us back to a national risk exposure not too unlike that of the 1920s.

Your success as a survivor of all this will depend on how well you assess your risk exposure — starting now — and how you continue monitoring it throughout the time up to the mutual fund crisis and afterward, during our next period of investment company and banking reform.

This doesn't mean that you should attempt to avoid all risk. That goal, of course, is impossible. Everything you could do with your money (or your life in general) involves risk. And, indeed, you cannot expect reasonable gain on your money without some degree of risk.

It also doesn't mean that you must necessarily avoid the idea of mutual funds. Using mutual funds as a way of accessing various markets can be valuable — as long as you know what you're getting into. Just because a few mutual fund promoters (or perhaps *many* promoters by the time you pick this book up) have chosen to twist and distort the good ideas that make up the mutual fund concept (and then try to rip you off in the process) doesn't mean there aren't others who are maintaining an investment perspective appropriate for survivalists at a reasonable price.

To know where you stand and where you might want to go, there are four broad categories of risk that you need to assess in terms of your own tolerance:

- **Instrument risk.** What are the risks and opportunities in the three general groups of mutual funds — money market, bond, and stock — as well as in the different subclassifications within those groups? Are there any alternatives to mutual funds that could deliver similar results at lower risk, lower cost, and with little added effort on your part?

- **Market risk.** How do market forces affect the inherent risk exposure of different types of funds?

- **Portfolio risk.** What special characteristics of the make-up of a specific fund — its holdings and the investment techniques used by the manager — define its unique risk profile?

- **Institutional risk.** How likely is it that you will encounter problems with the company running the fund?

These areas of risk assessment are critical for both newcomers to the mutual fund concept and long-time mutual fund shareholders. In fact, if you're a long-time mutual fund shareholder, a careful review of the current prospectus of your fund will probably show that you are exposed to much more risk than you were a few years ago. All the changes in the way your fund is run, the investment techniques used, and the expenses charged — all the things you may have trustingly voted for via your proxy ballots — are now working against you.

Keep It Simple

Don't forget why you got interested in mutual funds in the first place — assuming you didn't jump into mutual funds with the mistaken idea that you were going to get rich quick or, in fact, rich at all. You may remember that you first focused on mutual funds as a way of avoiding a dangerous chase after some get-rich-quick scheme that could get you into trouble. Instead, you wanted to obtain easy, no-hassle access to established investment markets. You didn't want the worrisome and complicated details of direct ownership and management of the investment. Also, you didn't want to run the risk of direct ownership of having the rug pulled out from under you because you had your back turned at the wrong moment or had done something dumb or become involved in something way over your head.

Equally, now that you are in mutual funds (or, apparently, seriously considering it) you shouldn't want to be involved with anything that you wouldn't do yourself with your money. Nor should you want to be involved in anything that you don't understand. Also, you shouldn't want to be involved with something that could in its own way pull the rug out from under you because you happened to have your back turned at the wrong moment. And you certainly shouldn't want to be involved in something that is over the heads of the fund managers — even if they don't think, because their heads have gotten so big, that it is over their heads.

One of the first things you have to shake is any obsession you may have with the past-performance results of funds as revealed on those increasingly popular and frequently elaborate performance charts distributed, it seems, wherever ink hits paper. Despite the emphasis that newspapers and magazines may be currently putting on easy-to-reproduce performance charts — which conveniently help fill up the empty spaces between the mutual fund ads — you should not be depressed or envious because you didn't happen to have your money in the "winner" of last quarter's horse race. And you absolutely shouldn't jump unquestioningly on the back of the horse that "won" that race, because you can be pretty sure without much further examination that the horse that won (and probably by a fractional nose anyway) was either lucky or pumped up on the steroids of some currently fashionable investment trick.

Rather than getting pulled down the rat hole as a member of the 1990s revival of the mutual fund "Performance Cult" by trying to chase down tomorrow's hot fund (with the likely result of latching onto *yesterday's* hot fund and tomorrow's dog), focus on how much risk you are exposed to. And assess that risk in terms of *your* perspective of the world and its risks and opportunities, ignoring the TV analysts and the full-color charts mailed to you by fund promoters.

One consistent value that the past-performance rankings provide, how-ever, is that the funds at the bottom — the losers with the worst long-term records — are likely to continue along that avenue. A number of statistical studies of past performance of mutual funds shows that this is the one thing that seems to be constant. The losers are usually identified as the bottom 10 percent of funds in a broad category. The funds either continue being dogs (because the guys running them are in over their heads) or are erratic (often because they are focused on some specialized and volatile sector of the market). In either case, these are funds you want to avoid. Occasionally, some of these dogs make a comeback, but don't bet on it. Also, if you're in a fund that gets on the dog list, swallow hard and cut the leash.

Besides identifying undesirable hotshots and moribund dogs, perfor-mance charts are really useful only as a source for identifying no-load and low-expense-ratio funds in broad fund categories. This information is usually included in the charts. The charts also usually provide the toll-free phone numbers of those funds so that you can quickly call for the *real* information you need: (1) the prospectus, (2) the "additional state-ment of information," which is the expanded and detailed version of the prospectus that must be requested specially from a fund, and (3) the most recent annual or semiannual report from the fund, which also often must be requested specifically from the fund promoter.

Besides taking a skeptical view of the raw horse-race performance charts, you have to beware of a worse type of performance chart that has cropped up over the last few years. This chart attempts to rate funds from a *risk* perspective based on how they performed in different market atmo-spheres of the recent past. Supposedly, the way in which the funds performed in "down" or "up" markets — over the last five years, for example — will tell you how the funds will likely perform in the future. Don't depend on it.

For one thing, as of this writing, there have not been any major "down" markets in the last few years. The funds and their different — sometimes "new" — perspectives have not been sufficiently tested to project likely relative performance into the future. Also, these charts, which sometimes purport to foretell the relative risks of different funds with a mere single-digit ranking or single letter, do not take into consideration any changes that may have occurred at the funds over those years. And the last few years have been a period of incredible change among fund promoters as they have taken on more and more risky types of investment tricks. All past-performance bets are off when, for example, a fund's management decides it's time to play with margin buying, short selling, puts and calls — not to mention the latest sizzling derivative touted by the latest sizzling rocket scientist. Since these new tricks have not been tested on a large scale in the real world, there is no measurement of the past that could possibly give you any idea of how a particular group of people will use them in the future — successfully or not. (And early indications are — predictably — that those who have tried the tricks tend to zig when they should have zagged.) In short, once a fund promoter changes the rules on how the fund invests money, it's a new fund.

Actually, if you are able to look at past-performance charts of mutual funds and determine in any way the likely future for a fund — either in terms of its raw performance or its risk performance compared to the market or to other similar funds — you don't need a mutual fund. You could apply that talent to selecting investment components directly from the markets for a personal portfolio. And with a personal portfolio, you don't have to be sitting in the dark trying to figure out what a bunch of securities lawyers at a fund are cooking up to get around the laws to put your money at greater risk or to siphon off more of your money for themselves.

You also don't need a mutual fund if you are willing and able to go through the intellectual gymnastics of analyzing the nuances and ever-changing investment strategies of different funds. Despite the many advisory services that have popped up over the last few years that want you to focus on the workings and performances of funds, any attempt to outguess from a distance what is being done with your money today by a group of people you don't know is a waste of time and effort. The whole idea about mutual funds was that you wouldn't have to do all this type of analysis work. The fractional differential in gain that you could possibly get from this activity is not likely to be worth it. Again, if you have the interest and talent for this type of analysis, spend it by looking at possibilities directly from the market and building your own portfolio. If at the same time you don't think that you have enough money to invest directly in the markets, then use your talent and energy to increase your *real* income so that you can put more aside. And stop thinking that someone else is going to make you rich with the few dollars you have.

For others, however, who have been watching this explosion in the analysis of mutual funds as seemingly bright people are slicing and dicing them, don't think that you have to get caught up in this trend in order to succeed. Not only is it not possible to keep in mind the differentials of thousands of mutual funds, it is, again, not the point. It is the mutual fund in its simplicity that should be the focus of your attention and your investment involvement goal, not all the complexities that have been artificially created by the fund promoters themselves to keep you guessing and to maintain an aura of confusion and mystery about what they are actually doing. It is crazy, for example, for mutual fund promoters to have come up with over six hundred different categories and subcategories of funds from which you are supposed to pick the one right for you. The reason for this complexity, of course, is the hope that you will be so confused that your resistance will be worn down and you will end up putting money into whatever fund is ready at hand — the one with the most effective (often misleading) advertising or sales pitch.

Another reason that mutual fund promoters encourage this craziness is that it helps deflect attention from other investment options. They want you to become obsessed with their products, because once you discover that direct involvement in markets can be easier and less expensive than access via mutual funds, you will see no justification for the high fees they charge. They don't want you to find out, for example, how easy and inexpensive it is to put together a personal portfolio of U.S. Treasury securities rather than pay high sales loads and heavy management fees for government bond funds.

Again, resist the temptation of joining the slicing-and-dicing crowd of mutual fund fanatics, because once you buy into their craziness, you've gone crazy too. On the other hand, blindly strolling along and assuming that all mutual funds are the same and can be used with equal success could be your undoing.

Follow the Rules

Just as there is a set of Mutual Fund Survival Rules for dealing — simply — with the people and sales pitches of mutual fund promoters, there are broad survival rules for choosing (or avoiding) different types of funds in different categories — money market, bond, and stock.

These rules are based primarily on the advice that was handed out in hindsight during the 1890s in Great Britain following the investment trust mania and the crisis of 1888–1890, during the 1930s following the investment trust mania and the bust of the late 1920s, and during the 1970s in reaction to the mutual fund mania of the go-go years. These are the rules observers identified during those retrospective periods that *should* have been minded instead of the ones followed by so many lambs on their way to the slaughter. In other cases the rules accommodate the observations and studies of the mutual fund investment experts — without the accompanying detailed description and statistics of how those rules were determined.

As you'll see, these rules may seem restrictive — almost laughably stodgy — in light of the investment "flexibilities" that mutual fund promoters are claiming to need to meet the investment challenges of the future. But remember that most, if not all, of these flexibilities and the "innovations" that they are breeding are not really new. They are simply revived or revised versions of old ideas that professional managers of the past proved unable to handle when tested on a grand scale.

The risks you face in the future will be the same risks that people before you faced in the past. The nature of risk hasn't changed. The type of risk involved with different types of financial markets, investment vehicles, or investment techniques hasn't changed either — no matter how the vehicles or techniques may be renamed or slightly repackaged to get you to ignore their real character and the actual risk involved. We already know how people of the past — people who had been as hopefully expectant about achieving financial security as you are today — got burned when they took with full faith the promises of "leaders." And there is no reason to believe that it is any different this time.

Because of the rapidly changing mutual fund landscape, it is not possible to list here specific funds that currently fulfill survival rules. However, as of the beginning of 1995, there were plenty of funds still able to function under these rules. They might not be at the top of the performance charts, but that's because they aren't juiced up on tricks. And if

MUTUAL FUND SURVIVAL RULES:
THE MASTER LIST

1. **Don't put your money in a fund that appears at the top of ANY chart measuring recent performance.** The list of top performers on last quarter's performance charts is best used to identify the funds you *don't* want to be in. You can be fairly certain without further investigation that the ones at the top are either juiced up to the hilt with the riskiest types of tricks available or are representing some small volatile part of the market. Funds with top long-term performance records — for example, five or ten years — need not be summarily dismissed.

2. **Avoid all funds appearing on the bottom 10 percent of recent or long-term performance charts.** The one consistency revealed on performance charts is that funds on the bottom of the performance charts are likely to stay there.

3. **Avoid any fund calling itself "high-yield" or "high-income."** These terms are the mutual fund industry's euphemisms for high-risk.

4. **Don't ever buy any shares of a mutual fund on margin.** You shouldn't further compound your risk exposure by borrowing money to send to somebody else to gamble with.

5. **Never invest in a fund using margin, puts, or calls.** Just because mutual fund promoters are reviving the excitement about the power of leverage — margin buying, puts, and calls — doesn't mean that they'll be able to prevent it all from going into reverse during a sharp market turn. If you learn only one lesson from the experience of the investment trusts of the 1920s, learn this one.

6. **Never buy shares of a new fund.** While past performance is no realistic guide to the future, a fund with no past has a greater likelihood of performance disappointment than well-established funds. In addition, when an old fund changes its investment policies (by removing investment limitations), it's really a new fund. You have to start over again.

7. **Don't buy shares of closed-end funds.** Closed-end funds — those sold as stocks via the stock exchange — require analysis not only of the fund's investment policies and holdings, but also of the stock market itself to determine market pressures on the fund's stock price. Too complicated. Additionally, these funds tend to be the most willing to embrace risky techniques, such as leverage tricks.

by the time you pick up this book you can't find a fund that still offers a prudent approach to the markets, then you'll know that it's time to get out of the whole business and lie low in wait for the bomb.

The rules, however, do not attempt to name every arcane bit of high-risk chicanery that mutual fund promoters may be foisting on you. Instead, they emphasize the most common pitfalls. Usually, however, mutual fund promoters will attempt to try their hands at time-worn high-risk tricks — such as margin buying or short selling — before moving on to the esoteric forms of derivatives or other tricks not yet invented as of this writing.

It's not going to be easy. Mutual fund promoters, as we've seen, have become very clever at covering up the actual nature of risk — even for investors who know where to look to discover what risks lie in wait and what questions to ask the promoter. For example, unlike bottles of wine that feature the words "Contains Sulfites" on labels to warn off people who are allergic to the chemical additive, mutual fund prospectuses do not carry a simple "Contains Derivatives" on the cover as a quick warning to mutual fund survivalists. Actually, mutual fund promoters' games for hiding involvement with derivatives had already been perfected by 1993. Some fund managers who used the securities simply unloaded them just before the date when they were required by law to disclose holdings of the funds' portfolios. Then, as soon as the reporting date had passed, the managers went right back into the derivative fracas.

To assure your survival you will still have to read prospectuses and understand jargon, but when approached with some degree of methodi-cal sorting, it isn't that taxing — despite what the mutual fund promoters would like you to believe — to find out which ones are really *investing* and which ones are simply playing hocus-pocus tricks with your money. (Appendix A: How to Read a Prospectus should simplify the process for you.)

Okay, maybe this isn't fair. Maybe this time our current generation of professional managers will be able to handle it all successfully. But here's the message behind the rules: Let them prove to the world that despite all their efforts to confuse you and keep secret from you the actual nature and risk of the things they are doing with your money that they really are doing what is best for you — as well as the American economy. Let them prove that the people of past generations who had attempted these same techniques and failed were simply incompetent. Let them prove that all the wisdom of money management has been refined and absorbed into the capabilities of the current generation, not only to achieve success where previous generations have failed but precisely to select from the many new "innovations" only those that will work. Let them prove that what they are doing is *not* an experiment on a grand, untested scale but is instead finally the real road to world financial stability that will create unprecedented personal wealth for the millions of people who have come to believe and depend on their promises and abilities. Indeed, let them prove it and take the full and glorious credit. But, man, don't let them prove it with *your* money.

CHAPTER 6

■ ■ ■

The Risks You Face:
Money Market Funds

The money market fund has proven to be one of the greatest financial ideas ever invented — simple and flexible. You put your money in. It earns interest that varies from week to week. You take your money out when you want to. It is a fully liquid instrument, usually providing nearly all the ease and features of a checking account. And, indeed, money market funds are most widely viewed as a type of fancy checking account.

But the money market fund is not a way of life. Too many people keep too much money in them for too long. It is only a place to park money temporarily while looking for a better alternative for it. Other options — including the boring CD — can usually give you better returns on money for a longer-term horizon — for parking purposes or otherwise. (Sometimes, however, money market funds can outperform just about anything, namely, when long-term interest rates are rising steeply and quickly, as during the late 1970s and early 1980s — and possibly the 1990s.)

As far as risk goes, once upon a time the money market fund was about as risk-free as anything you could find — inside a bank or out, insured or not. A money market fund's investments into short-term government and commercial debt should make fund manager goof-ups nearly impossible. In fact, it was the invention of this good financial idea back in 1972 — and its accompanying feature of virtual foolproof management — that helped save the mutual fund industry from total annihilation in the 1970s.

But the assumptions about the no-risk quality of money market funds changed in 1989 when a highly questionable financial services firm called Integrated Resources defaulted on about $1 billion of commercial paper.

Two money funds — one run by Value Line and one run by Mutual of New York — got stuck with more than $30 million of the worthless paper. Then in 1990 the Mortgage and Realty Trust, a real estate investment trust, defaulted on its debt, with $75 million in ten money market funds, including the T. Rowe Price Prime Reserves fund.

In both cases, the fund promoters took money out of their own pockets (although they didn't have to by law) to make sure the share price didn't go below the set one dollar net asset value that everyone automatically assumes will stay steady forever. They really did it, of course, to keep the good faith — and money — of the shareholders who otherwise would have made a run for the door not only out of the money market fund, but very likely out of the rest of the funds managed by the investment companies as well.

In reaction to these mishaps, the government added a few stronger investment restrictions on money market funds that became effective in 1991. The most important government action, however, was to require money market fund prospectuses to carry a boldly printed warning that the shares were not insured or guaranteed by the government and that there was no assurance that the fund would be able to maintain the one dollar net asset value.

Once again, the fund managers and the government were off the hook. It was now perfectly clear that everything would be *your* problem.

Despite this new, bold warning, money continued to be shifted from one money market fund to another in a seemingly endless search for the best possible yield — even if it was a tiny fraction of a percent. It was (and is) a variation on the old follow-the-S&L-CD-yields of the 1980s. And the funds accommodated this by finding new ways to circumvent regulations — and constantly upping the risk ante.

The result of this new round of recklessness came to a head in 1994 when several large money market funds almost collapsed — saved only by the fund companies' multimillion-dollar bailouts. Then in August 1994 a money fund did collapse, paying 92 cents on the dollar. The government reacted by putting on more restrictions. And the fund companies reacted by printing the "no guarantee" warning more boldly. Industry leaders started talking as if it was unreasonable for investors to expect a consistent one-dollar-a-share price in the future. In other words, the industry made it clear that bailouts should not be routinely expected.

Yet most fund promoters kept looking for ways to juice yields. They know that just a smidgen of extra yield, which gets their money market fund on the top of a performance list, can bring millions of dollars into the company. That means lots of profit — since money market funds are cheap to run — as well as getting the names of people who could then be cajoled into the promoter's other fund products.

Also, the money market fund guys know exactly what all the other money market guys are doing to crank up their yields. Thus, as long as everybody is doing about the same thing, if anything goes wrong it probably will go wrong with just about everybody. And, in typical Wall Street fashion, the blame then can't be put on one fund promoter but instead attributed to "uncontrollable market conditions" or inadequate (or unrealistic) government regulations or some other blah-blah-blah that may seem appropriate at the time.

As a mutual fund survivalist, you can't fall for this. A money market fund is not an "investment" vehicle of which you can tolerate any risk, any potential fluctuation of principal, as you would with other mutual fund products. If a loss is ever experienced with a money market fund, it will never recover. A money market fund does not represent a market with rises and declines.

You have to keep your money in the safest type of money market fund possible. In addition, as we get closer to the mutual fund crisis, you may want to have already identified a fully secure place for your money that can be used in case of a hasty retreat from other mutual fund options. This means that your money market fund will *not* be giving you the highest yield advertised. But with a little bit of careful shopping, neither will you be accepting a yield that puts you below the "average" money market fund. (As is often the case in the mutual fund world, you can be both high-risk and low-return.)

Generally, as noted in the rules at the end of this chapter, the absolutely safest money market fund is one that invests solely in Treasury bills. The interest paid on these funds also happens to be exempt from state and local taxes. However, be wary of promoters calling their funds "100 percent Treasury" or some other variation on the word "Treasury" without actually having all the money in Treasury bills. All kinds of shenanigans with derivatives can be used to camouflage the actual makeup of a fund's portfolio. A current trick of choice is the use of "floating rate notes" — notes paying variable rates tied to Treasury bill rates but with much longer maturity dates. Because of the maturity date they are not absolutely risk-free. Look for this term in the prospectus or call the fund company to see if it is used. And, if so, then the fund is not for survivalists.

Second to all-Treasury funds, funds identified as "U.S. Government and Agency" are the safest. These funds invest in Treasury bills as well as securities of government agencies like the Federal Farm Bureau and the Government National Mortgage Association. These funds may also go into "floating rate notes." If so, avoid them.

Further on the risk spectrum are taxable money market funds (those investing in commercial paper). For taxable money market funds, you want only those investing solely in the highest-grade commercial paper (no junk bond–style paper) while avoiding risky overseas forays like "Eurodollar" or "Yankee Dollar" certificates of deposit.

But when it comes to national tax-exempt money market funds (those that can invest in the securities issued by all states and cities, with interest that is free of federal taxes but not of local state or city taxes), the risk level is getting beyond a survivalist's comfort zone. That's even more true of single-state tax-exempt money market accounts. The incredible popularity of these types of funds has pushed managers to scramble for any crumb of an investment to put money in. This has forced yields down (and risks up) on many of these funds to a point that the tax savings don't make much sense any more. Also, the lack of investment outlet (decent or otherwise) has sent some managers of single-state funds outside the state — defeating the whole purpose, since you would have to pay taxes on the returns from those investments. If you've been using such a fund for a long time, don't assume that what you're getting now is the great deal you got a few years ago. In the current environment, money market funds in the other categories might be a better bet, even if taxed.

Like all areas of the mutual fund world, money market funds are in constant flux. Many performance chart listings printed in magazines or newspapers of money market funds will give information on expense ratios and average maturities. A gleaning from these lists can be a starting point. A more comprehensive and fairly up-to-date list of likely candidates for survivalists can be found in the annual money-fund handbook, *IBC/Donoghue's Money Fund Directory.* (This directory often is in public libraries, but also is available from the Donoghue Organization, P.O. Box 9104, Ashland, MA 01721-9104 at 800-343-5413.) Even this detailed annual directory can be out of date by the time you see it, so you'll have to double-check the current status of a fund either using the prospectus or, more easily, by calling the promoter's customer service line.

MONEY MARKET FUND SURVIVAL RULES

1. **For the safest money market funds use 100 percent U.S. Treasury funds or U.S. Government & Agency funds that do not hold "floating rate notes."** Make sure that the funds are fully invested in Treasuries or other government securities without any "floating rate notes."

2. **Do not go into a money market fund with an average maturity of more than sixty days.** Although the law allows money market funds a ninety-day maximum average maturity for their portfolio securities, a sixty-day cutoff is the survival maximum. Lower is better.

3. **Consider taxable money market funds only if the fund limits investments to highest-quality commercial paper.** While the law may allow a percentage of lower-than-highest-quality investments in a money market fund, a mutual fund survivalist cannot tolerate it. The question to ask is "Does the fund limit itself to A-1/P-1 paper?" (These are the terms used for the highest ratings issued, respectively, by Standard & Poor's and Moody's.) Any answer other than a simple yes is unacceptable.

4. **Do not go into any fund investing into Eurodollar or Yankee Dollar CDs.** These exotic instruments are CDs in overseas banks. They help inflate yields — and expose you to greater risk. Avoid them.

5. **Never put money in a money market fund with an expense ratio higher than 0.7.** It's better to find one with an expense ratio of 0.5 or lower.

6. **Beware of temporary waiving of management fees.** One way promoters pop up the yield to get on a top-performing list — and attract more money — is to temporarily waive some or all management expenses. Then, later, they slap the fees back on. Going into such a fund with waived fees is great if the fund fulfills the other rules —but get ready to jump out as soon as the fees go into effect.

7. **Stay away from "single-state" tax-free money market funds —and possibly national tax-exempt ones as well.** These are the highest-risk money market funds of all. The popularity of these funds has pushed managers to low-rated (and in some cases unrated) issues. Worse, some funds have had to invest in out-of-state debt, thereby making that part of the returns taxable. All in all, the tax saving, even in high-tax states, is minimal compared to the risk. Ditto for national tax-exempt funds.

Also, all money market funds with a Standard & Poor's Money Fund AAA rating fulfill the criteria of the survivalist rules. Funds with this AAA rating will often advertise the fact. However, not *all* funds fulfilling the rules are on the Standard & Poor's list. That's because a fund has to pay Standard & Poor's a high fee to get rated. A full copy of the current AAA list is available for a fee (currently, $120) from Standard & Poor's (212-208-1527).

Identifying a fund company that has an acceptable money market fund is a good starting place for finding a fund "family" likely to have bond or equity funds that fulfill survivalist rules.

CHAPTER 7

■ ■ ■

The Risks You Face: Bond Funds

For millions of shareholders of bond mutual funds, the mutual fund crisis actually started in 1994.

Up until that year the greatest growth of mutual funds during the late 1980s and early 1990s had not been in the highly visible stock funds but rather in bond funds — going from a tiny fraction of the total amount of money in mutual funds in 1980 to over one-third in 1993. Bond funds in their various versions — from government to municipal to junk — grew at an astonishing rate as people went searching for high-income alternatives to decreasing bank interest rates. Bond funds came to be viewed as steady and safe places to put money.

The reality of the bond fund game — a reality that the fund promoters didn't tell anyone about — was that the ten-year performance of bond funds that looked so good in elaborate charts in the early 1990s compared to CDs would have been virtually impossible to replicate ten years into the future. The reason for this was that bond funds had done comparatively well *because* interest rates had fallen from historically high levels to near historic lows. And when interest rates went up, the values went down. Tragically, over 50 percent of the shareholders who saw their bond fund shares plunge in value during 1994 had entered the bond market at its peak during the previous two years. These trusting folks who believed the "attractive alternatives to CDs" pitch didn't understand how bond funds worked. As a survivalist you have to keep some basics in mind (or learn) to find the opportunities in the future.

Bonds vs. Bond Funds

The most important thing to remember about bond funds is that when you put money in a fund you are not buying a bond, but rather you are investing in the bond *market*.

When you buy a single bond directly — whether some type of government bond like a Treasury bill or some type of corporate bond — you know the amount of interest that will be paid on the bond and the date when it matures. Assuming that the bond doesn't default or get "called" by the issuer, you collect the fixed-rate interest on the bond while you hold it. Then at maturity date you get back the full amount that you paid for the bond in the first place.

However, while you are holding the bond, the value of the bond itself will fluctuate based on rising or falling prevailing interest rates. If interest rates fall while you are holding the bond, the value of the bond will go up. That's because if you were to sell the bond to somebody else before it matures, the other person would be willing to pay more for the bond than you did to get the higher interest rate originally promised on that bond.

On the other hand, if interest rates go up, the value of your bond will go down. This is because no one would pay the amount you did since they could get a higher interest rate on the same amount of money somewhere else. But, although your bond would go down in value while you held it during a time of rising interest rates, it would still pay back the full amount when cashed in on maturity date. You would, therefore, get the full amount of interest and your full principal back at maturity date — as with a bank CD — even though during the holding period the value of the bond would have fluctuated.

In contrast, a bond *fund* is a collection of different bonds that mature at different dates. The money the bond fund pays on a share held in the fund is based on the amount received from all those different bonds in the fund's portfolio. The yield, therefore, on a share of a bond fund fluctuates. Actually, the fund manager is constantly buying and selling bonds — much as stocks are bought and sold — to attempt to keep the yield and possibly even the value of shares in line with what the fund promoter's marketing team has decided is the easiest or most lucrative product to sell.

More important to remember, however, is that the bond fund itself *never* matures in the same way as a bond you hold directly or a CD does.

Instead, the value of the bond fund share fluctuates constantly in reaction to changing interest rates. When interest rates go down — which happened in a general downward path throughout the 1980s and into the early 1990s, when interest rates fell from all-time highs to near all-time lows — the value of the bond fund shares goes up. (That's why so many people had a good time with them.)

But if interest rates go up, the value of the bond fund share will go down. And the bond fund share that goes down in value will *never* recover back up to its original value until interest rates come down again. This is a very important consideration when interest rates are at a low level, because from a very low level it is more likely that interest rates will go up than down.

Interest Rate Changes and Bond Maturity Dates

Long-term bonds will be affected by interest rate rises more than short-term bonds. For example, a thirty-year Treasury bond yielding 7 percent would drop in value about 11 percent if interest rates went up 1 percent. But on short-term bonds (a three-year Treasury note, for example) a 1 percent rise in interest rates would mean a decline in the value of the bond by about 2 percent.

Like individual bonds themselves, bond funds carry maturity dates of different durations based on the makeup of the bonds held in the portfolio. Generally, bond funds — any type of bond funds — can be separated into three categories based on their average maturity date of the collection of bonds in the portfolio: (1) short term, with a maturity of one to three years; (2) intermediate, with a maturity of about four to ten years; (3) long term, with a maturity that can run over ten years but usually runs anywhere from fifteen to twenty-five years.

Interest rate fluctuations vis-à-vis the maturity date of a bond fund is an extremely important consideration. The longer the maturity of the bond fund, the more wildly violent the NAV of the bond fund shares will fluctuate in reaction to changing interest rates.

A recent example of how interest rates can affect the value of a bond fund share was in 1987 when the price per share of long-term bond funds went down between 10 and 20 percent between March and October when the interest on long-term Treasury bonds rose from 9 to 10 1/2 percent.

That meant a decline of $1,000 to $2,000 on a $10,000 investment. (Luckily for the shareholders who got caught in this and held on, interest rates went down again and they recaptured their previous paper losses. Don't count on such luck from already low interest rate levels.)

Notice also that as the principal shrinks, so does the amount you get as actual yield income. For example, in the late 1970s/early 1980s, when interest rates were going up and the value of bond fund shares was going down, bond fund shareholders who weren't paying attention got a rude surprise: in 1979 a dividend yield that paid 10 percent on $10,000 provided $1,000; but by 1982, when the shares had shriveled in value to $6,200, the dividend yield of 10 percent provided only $620.

It is rare to find interest rates jumping suddenly and unexpectedly by a full percentage point. But it did happen in the 1970s and early 1980s — and it could happen again. When interest rates have more room to move up than to move down, you have to monitor the changing directions of interest rates if you want to survive intact without loss of principal in bond funds.

If you have shares in a long-term bond fund — that is, one with an average maturity of over ten years, but usually more like fifteen to twenty-five years — you should be doing this continually — daily. At the first whisper of a real rise in interest rates, you *must* get your money out of long-term bond funds. Remember it this way: every dollar you put into a long-term bond fund from now on is your bet — your speculation — that interest rates will remain the same or go down. (This is not a mutual fund survivalist perspective.)

If you stick with intermediate-term bond funds (those with average maturity dates of from six to ten years) or, for even less risk to principal fluctuation, short-term bond funds (those with maturity dates of four years or less), you won't have to monitor the changing direction of interest rates so diligently.

Of course, the longer-term bond fund is also the higher-yielding one. But the shortest-term bond fund — one with an average maturity of three years or less — can assure you that you will not likely lose principal if you don't wish to monitor interest rate changes at all. A bond fund with an average maturity of less than two years — if you could find one — would be as close as you could get to complete insulation from interest rate fluctuation. But yield would probably be only slightly higher than that of a money market fund. By paying attention to changing economic conditions just a little bit more, taking on the added risk of an intermediate-term bond fund — with a limit of eight years average maturity — should give you a more attractive yield and a fairly safe total return performance.

Whatever you do, don't get hooked into chasing yield with bond funds. Unfortunately, it is yield that the mutual fund promoters emphasize in their ads. It's yield that those performance charts in newspapers and magazines highlight. And, it seems, it's yield that bond fund investors are focused on. A focus on simple yield might have been successful as interest rates were going down. That's how so many people who were new to the bond fund game since the early 1980s apparently got lulled into thinking that the funds were as safe and secure as a bank account. But a focus on bond fund yield in circumstances other than stable or falling interest rates will not be successful.

Many mutual fund promoters (as well as some financial journalists) add to this confusion by insisting on referring to bond funds with the misleading label "fixed-income funds." Of course, these funds do not in any way provide any type of "fixed income" despite a fund manager's professed goal of "high yield with preservation of capital." And do all 12 million people with bond funds actually realize that the term "fixed income" relates to the interest paid by the bond issuers into the fund — and not to the ever-fluctuating yield paid by the fund to its shareholders? In reality, there is *nothing* "fixed" about bond funds.

Certainly, many of those millions of ignorantly happy bond fund holders will keep focusing on the yield aspect of bond funds — which, of course, is the aspect that the fund promoters are emphasizing — without even realizing that as the yield goes up along with rising interest rates, the value of the fund shares will go down — and with it the total return of the investment will go down dramatically as well.

A worse aspect of the bond funds is how the promoters are trying to juice up yields to flash all over ads and attract the money of the unwitting through the use of derivatives. Some of the most offensive are mortgage-backed securities called "interest-only strips" (or "IOs") and "inverse floaters." Interest-only strips pay only mortgage interest. Inverse floaters pay more when interest rates fall than when they rise. Don't worry about figuring out what all these tricks mean. (Some of the people using them aren't even sure.) Just avoid them. The reason that they're popular current tricks with fund promoters is that, legally speaking, mortgage-backed securities are "government backed" and therefore the promoters can truthfully claim that they are government securities and get people to think that they are safe. (Don't forget the mutual fund promoters' credo: "It's legal!") In reality, these securities are highly volatile and high-risk — and they completely distort the concept of "fixed income."

Can't you just 'see how the congressional hearings during our next period of mutual fund reform will go? The little old lady who had one day finally realized that the value of her lifetime savings put in a long-term bond fund had shriveled in the wake of rising interest rates and derivative shenanigans sitting there at the table weeping and telling the congressmen: "But the young man told me it was a fixed-income fund."

Don't be one of those people (and don't let your mother be one either). Remember that the average maturity of a bond fund — no matter how conservative the profile of the fund may otherwise be — is the single best indication of the inherent riskiness of the fund.

Volatility

The next best indication of the inherent riskiness of a bond fund — again, no matter how conservative-appearing it may otherwise be — is the fund's past record of share price volatility. You can find this information in the prospectus on the page headlined "Financial History" or "Table of Selected Per Share Data and Ratios." This is the chart near the front of the prospectus that shows all the figures about the performance and charges of the fund year by year going back ten years or for the life of the fund. The line of information of greatest interest is the one reporting the value of shares at the end of each reporting period. A comparison of these share prices — or "net asset value" (NAV) — will show you how volatile the fund has been in the past. Funds that show a widely fluctuating NAV from year to year are volatile. Funds with a steady NAV are less volatile. A simple way to determine the volatility is to find the highest NAV figure of the past and the lowest NAV figure. Subtract the lowest figure from the highest. Divide that number by the highest NAV figure and you'll get the percentage difference between high and low of the past. For example, if the NAV of a fund experienced its high in 1979 at $9.50 and its low in 1988 at $7.50, there was a difference in NAV of $2 — or 21 percent. A 21 percent variation in a bond fund NAV is an indication that the fund is very volatile. (When the value of a share of anything goes down 20 percent, it requires an advance of 25 percent to get back to the breakeven point. And it's not easy to get a 25 percent advance in any market.) Some bond funds — typically junk bond funds and mortgage-backed bond funds such as GNMA (Government National Mortgage Association) — experienced even wider swings in the 1980s, some as much as 40 percent. (When the value of a share drops 40 percent, you need a 66.7 percent advance to break even.) For a mutual fund survivalist, no bond fund with a past history of volatility greater than 15 percent (between highest and lowest NAV) is acceptable. A lower spread is better.

Risks by Fund Category

While the factors of average maturity and NAV volatility will tell you the most about the riskiness of a bond fund, there are some special shadings of risk with different broad categories of bond funds. In approximate order from least risky to riskiest, they are:

GOVERNMENT BOND FUNDS. A real government bond fund made up of 100 percent Treasury securities or other government securities — without being souped up with gimmicks such as junk bonds — can be the safest type of bond fund from a creditworthiness point of view.   The U.S. government is not likely, after all, to stop paying interest on these bonds (not likely, that is, as long as it has the power to tax you and to print money).

These real government bond funds — particularly short-term bond funds — can be a valuable place to park money temporarily in much the same way as a money market fund. But if you are attracted to government bond funds as a long-term option because you are income-oriented but conservative-minded, and you don't want to risk loss of any part of principal, then government bond funds are not doing the job for you. And you are wasting money.

For all the safety that a truly 100 percent government bond fund would give you, no such fund is safer than owning Treasuries directly. That's because when you own Treasuries directly you are always guaranteed that you will get your full principal back when they mature. That might not be the case when you want to sell your bond fund shares.

Also, owning Treasuries directly is very easy — just as easy as going into a bond fund or even a bank CD. It can all be done directly with the government — without using a broker — via the mail in a program called Treasury Direct. Over 2 million people already do it. For the information packet, write to Treasury Direct, Department of the Treasury, Bureau of the Public Debt, Dept. F, Washington, DC 20239-0001.

With Treasury Direct you can devise your own personal intermediate 100 percent Treasury fund by dividing your money, for example, in a tierlike fashion by buying Treasury notes with varying maturity dates and, thus, varying yields — two years, five years, ten years. The minimum for a two- or three-year Treasury note is $5,000. For a five- or ten-year note, $1,000. All done by mail. There's nothing safer. There's no commission. No sales charges. No need to get a certified or cashier's check to send money in to open an account. No management expenses. No complicated prospectus to decipher. The government deposits your interest payments directly into your bank account twice a year. And you get your full principal back at maturity with automatic reinvestment options taken care of by the government. Guaranteed. It's as easy as a CD and the interest is exempt from state and local taxes.

Realistically, you would need about $10,000 minimum to invest directly in Treasuries, even though the process is easy and can be done with less.

All in all, government bond funds are not worth much for anyone. They may have made sense during the period of ever-lowering interest rates when shares of the bond funds increased in value. And they could be worth something for speculators who want to bet on even lower interest rates. But they're certainly not worth much to the people who are being manipulated, successfully it seems, by the power of mutual fund promoters' sales efforts into thinking that these funds are as good and as safe as an insured bank account.

Rather than letting millions of dollars from small savers go into the sales loads and management fees of government bond funds as easy high profits for a relatively small number of people who happen to be running mutual funds, perhaps the government should promote how easy it is to buy government securities directly — a Liberty Bond–style campaign to help Win the Deficit War, for example.

If, however, despite this harangue, you still insist on keeping your money in a government bond fund, at least make sure that the fund is truly a 100 percent government bond fund — without derivatives. This is the area in which fund promoters like to use mortgage-backed derivatives — like inverse floaters and interest-only strips — since these things can be officially called government-backed securities.

Also, of course, make sure that the average maturity is less than eight years. As a money-parking alternative to a money market fund, choose a short-term fund of three years average maturity or less.

CORPORATE BOND FUNDS. A corporate bond fund with intermediate maturity focused heavily on high-grade corporate debt can be a worthwhile choice for a long-term holding with continual reinvestment of dividends and capital gains in a tax-protected account.

Finding a corporate bond fund of highest-quality corporate bonds is becoming increasingly difficult. By law a bond fund can call itself "investment-grade" with only 65 percent of the portfolio actually made up of investment-grade bonds — namely, the four highest grades of bonds, as in Standard & Poor's ratings of AAA, AA, A, and BBB. The rest of the fund can be loaded up with, well, junk. (In the late 1980s few "investment-grade" bond funds actually exercised their right to carry such a high percentage of non-investment-grade bonds. But those were the good old days when mutual fund promoters still practiced a modicum of prudence. Today you can be pretty certain that most such funds are scraping right up against the legal limits.)

Although there aren't many, a mutual fund survivalist should search out those corporate bond funds that go above "investment-grade" by limiting themselves to 80 percent of their portfolios of A-rated or better corporate debt. These funds usually identify themselves as "high-quality" or "highest-grade." The other 20 percent could be spread out through all manner of junk bonds and other types of "repos" or inverse floaters and the like. Although not ideal for a survivalist, it is risk that can be acceptable when viewed as a long-term commitment. (Such a fund will not deliver the type of potential severe drop that you would get in almost any type of stock fund during a "crash"-like event.) But, again, this type of bond fund is best used as part of a tax-protected account with dividends and capital gains reinvested. Once in such a fund, you have no need to further "diversify" to other high-risk bond funds such as pure junk bond products. You'll have *plenty* of risk in the 80 percent high-quality fund.

One tricky stunt that fund promoters attempt with these 80 percent high-quality funds is to include "government-backed securities" in that 80 percent. In other words, the promoter could be trying to sneak in those interest-only strips, inverse floaters, and other risky "government-backed securities" that have done so much to compromise so-called all-government funds. As a result, you could be right back with the legal (yet unacceptable) limit of 65 percent. Look carefully at the "investment limitations" section of the fund's prospectus or "additional statement of information" booklet to find the real story. And if you can't tell if the fund is *really* limited to highest-quality corporate debt, then contact the fund.

MUNICIPAL BOND FUNDS. The rush into tax-free municipal bond funds during the late 1980s and into the 1990s has made many of them — particularly single-state funds — nearly as risky as junk bond funds. The fund managers have thrashed around and looked under every rock to find places to put all the money that poured in. Perhaps not surprisingly, the single-state funds serving states with the highest taxes — like New York — can be filled with the lowest-quality bonds, including unrated bonds. They often don't even provide much added tax benefit anyway compared to a general, national municipal fund.

If you are in a high enough tax bracket to need the tax-exempt status of such funds, it would be better to build your own portfolio of the highest-quality of these bonds with the expectation of holding them to maturity. You would need a minimum of about $60,000 to do it.

Otherwise, for a survivalist, a general municipal fund — free of federal taxes, of course, but not exempt of state and local taxes on that part of the fund outside your state — is a safer bet. But in this case, the average maturity should be short-term — *very* short-term (under three years).

INTERNATIONAL BOND FUNDS. Here's a category of bond funds that puts your money full faith into the hands of the talents of an individual fund manager. Putting together an international bond fund is a complex — and high-risk — matter. The fund manager has to juggle all the considerations of credit risk and interest rate risk not only of one country but of many. Also, most foreign markets aren't as well organized as the U.S. marketplace. Your money can find itself exposed to markets of unstable countries or precarious economies. There are few "rules" that can assure success with an international bond fund. Actually, an investment into one is mostly a speculation about currency fluctuations. When the value of the dollar declines, the value of an international bond fund generally goes up — no matter what fund you are in. But when the dollar strengthens, the international bond fund will generally plunge. These funds are unpredictable and risky places to put money. Investors have already had a grim experience with these funds when in 1992 several international bond funds got caught on the wrong side of a European currency crisis and came up with heavy hits on their NAVs. Fund shareholders then evacuated the poor-performing funds, apparently in search of another elixir — but now with reduced funds. In short, international bond funds — or "global" money market funds — are not for true mutual fund survivalists. But for those with large portfolios, we'll revisit this product in Chapter 11.

ZERO-COUPON BOND FUNDS. Unlike other bond funds that never "mature," the zero bond fund contains securities ("strips") that all mature on the same date. If you buy shares of these funds, sometimes called "target" funds, with a strict commitment to holding them to maturity, you can expect absolute safety. The total return on the fund will be known at the time you buy the shares — without credit risk or market risk if held to maturity. However, during the holding period these are the most volatile of all bond funds. Like holding zeros directly, you have to pay taxes on the interest every year as if you received it. And, although the fund is effectively set and therefore not in need of "management," the fee you pay every year goes for nothing. It's an expensive convenience for not owning the zeros directly: zeros, that is, that are U.S. Treasury versions — not higher-risk corporate or municipal versions.

MORTGAGE-BACKED BOND FUNDS. Mortgage-backed bond funds — the well-known Ginnie Mae versions and the less well known adjustable-rate mortgage funds — have turned out to be, despite their backing by the government and basic appeal of higher-than-Treasuries yield, a volatile product. As interest rates fell and home owners refinanced their mortgages, the Ginnie Mae funds, unlike other bond funds, went down in overall value. The adjustable-rate versions have been somewhat more stable, but the yields are not particularly attractive compared to other products. These mortgage funds may have some consistency and value when interest rates begin to rise.

CONVERTIBLE DEBENTURES. These hybrid securities — sometimes called "convertible securities" — seem to come out of mothballs at every market peak. They were certainly the rage near the end of the 1920s and near the end of the 1960s. Sold as a "bond," a convertible debenture pays a certain amount of income every year while also permitting holders to convert the debenture to shares of the company's stock up to a specific

BOND FUND SURVIVAL RULES

1. **Never let yield attract you to a bond fund.** The least important thing about a bond fund is its current — certainly past — yield. It is total return that is of interest. Of greater interest to a survivalist, however, are the investment techniques used to reach that total return.

2. **Stay out of long-term bond funds. Limit bond fund investments to funds with an average maturity of no more than eight years.** Unless you are a willing speculator on interest rates — which, then, removes you from the ranks of mutual fund survivalists — stick with intermediate-term bond funds (four to eight years average maturity). Short-term is better if you are unwilling or unable to monitor the progress of changing interest rates. Maximum two years average maturity is safest, but three years is acceptable.

3. **Do not put money in a corporate bond fund with more than 20 percent of holdings in bonds rated below "highest-quality."** By law bond funds can call themselves "highest-quality" with only 65 percent of holdings in actual bonds rated AAA, AA, and A. A minimum requirement for a mutual fund survivalist is 80 percent in highest-grade bonds.

4. **Never go into a bond fund with an expense ratio higher than 0.8.** The lower the expense ratio the better. The single most important factor of return on a bond fund — a safe one at least — is the amount you *don't* pay to the fund's promoter.

5. **Avoid U.S. government bond funds of any type except as a short-term place to "park" your money.** Owning U.S. Treasury securities directly is safer, cheaper, and almost as easy as owning shares of a government bond fund. You can buy U.S. Treasury securities — T-bills, T-notes, and T-bonds — directly from the government by mail. You'll be certain of getting your full principal back at maturity date, and there are no commissions, sales charges, or management fees to pay.

6. **Avoid bond funds with a history of volatility greater than 15 percent.** An examination of the history of a fund's annual share net asset value will show the percentage spread between the highest price and the lowest. Any percentage differential greater than 15 percent indicates unacceptable volatility.

7. **Money in convertible debenture, junk bond, and unit investment trust funds is only for speculators — not for survivalists.**

date at a fixed price. The sales pitch here is that, if the company's stock price goes up, you (or, rather, the fund manager, if you are going after these things via a mutual fund) can buy the stock at a "bargain" price. And if the stock goes down, you will still have the debenture paying interest with a "floor" valuation. Generally, convertible securities are issued by small companies and carry a risk level about equal to that of junk bonds. During the late stages of a bull market, these things are popular and, for a time, successful, because at that point in the maturity of a bull market anything connected with small, emerging companies enjoys its greatest moment in the sun (after everything else is already overbought). That's what happened in the late 1920s and 1960s. Investors of those periods found that on the way down the value of the convertibles moved in tandem with the stock prices — all the way to zero. When a company (or small company market) collapses and its stock price collapses too, there isn't any "floor" for a convertible debenture. And the same goes for the convertible debenture fund. Few of the convertible debenture funds started in the 1960s survived the 1970s. They resurfaced — tellingly — in the late 1980s and early 1990s.

JUNK BOND FUNDS — A.K.A., HIGH YIELD CORPORATE BONDS. They still call them "junk" for a reason. Despite their periodic resurfacing as an apparent moneymaker, they should be avoided by all mutual fund survivalists. Don't forget that some junk bond funds declined by 50 percent in six months in 1989/1990.

UNIT INVESTMENT TRUSTS (UITs). These are fixed, closed-end portfolios that are held until maturity. In theory this idea should approximate the idea of holding your own portfolio of bonds until maturity — only the portfolio is more diversified than you could put together yourself. In reality these funds are almost always sold with a high load and are also packed with so much low-rated junk to make the yields look enticing that they are far too risky for any consideration by a survivalist.

CHAPTER 8

■ ■ ■

The Risks You Face: Stock Funds

Because stock investing — either through mutual funds or on your own — can be the most complex of any type of investment you make, it perhaps should be approached with the greatest amount of simplicity. Actually, an understanding of the inherent caprices of the stock market and the many influences that potentially push it from one side of the spectrum to the other seems more widespread than an understanding of the complexities and potential volatility of the bond market — particularly through bond fund involvement — which at first blush seems so simple. But there are many complex nuances that can be applied to bond investment (even of U.S. government securities). And there are simple concepts that can help take the mystique out of stock market investing.

You've seen examples of how simple it all can be. For instance, those amusing newspaper and magazine articles that report on contests between professional stock pickers and a monkey that throws darts at a list of stocks. The monkey, as you probably know, almost always wins. Yet, despite this ever-popular sneer at professionals and the whole process of stock market analysis, the same newspapers and magazines continue to print volumes and volumes of information and dissections of hundreds of new and old companies, both famous and obscure. They also print volumes of profiles of different investment ideas — equally famous or obscure. Ultimately, it all seems so contradictory that it can confuse even a rocket scientist.

Within Your Grasp

But the reality of stock market investing lies somewhere in between a monkey's dart and the presumed genius of rocket scientists. In fact, it lies exactly at a point within your grasp.

Over the last twenty years, however, the mutual fund industry has done a very good job of convincing people who are new to the investment world — namely, coming-of-investment-age baby boomers — that the complexities are beyond the understanding of mere mortals. As we've seen, this basic sales pitch, which has been circling the globe for over a hundred years, has been more successful this time around than at any of its previous peaks of popularity, and as a result, ownership of the shares of U.S. companies by individuals had dropped from nearly 85 percent in the late 1960s to under 50 percent in the 1990s.

Of course, the mutual fund floggers would say that their successful achievement of such a high level of popularity is a confirmation of the desirability of their products. In reality, however, it had more to do with the expensive smoke-and-mirrors marketing effort itself, along with steady — nearly unparalleled — rises in speculative markets, bringing people into the fold who would never have been involved under less lighthearted circumstances. The conversion to dependence on "professionals" was also achieved through the government's favoring of the mutual fund concept over nearly all other investment options via increasingly popular defined-contribution retirement programs, such as 401(k) plans.

But despite the "evidence" that the stock market belongs to the professionals, there is plenty of room for individual investors. In addition, there are benefits to investing directly, and, in fact, as institutional investors, including mutual funds, continue to paint themselves into a corner with their growing concentration of control of the shares of public companies, your direct involvement in the stock market can be less risky than access through mutual funds. Just as direct ownership of bonds is the best way to have complete control over your money in the bond world, the only way to be fully sure of surviving a mutual fund crisis as it may apply to stock market investments is to have your own stock portfolio. Then you can be absolutely certain that you won't be exposed to esoteric investment tricks that put you at greater risk than you would ever want or even begin to understand.

Obviously, the direct route isn't possible for everyone. If you're limited to the options of a 401(k) plan, for example, you are pretty much at the mercy of what is available through that plan. (This is a situation that will probably change during the next period of investment company reform following the mutual fund crisis. But in the meantime, be careful and don't be lulled into a sense of false security just because your employer has presented these mutual fund products to you as the only options for your retirement money.)

Also, you may not have enough money to build your own portfolio. Realistically, you would need at least $25,000 — or, more comfortably, an amount exceeding $50,000 — to begin a sufficiently diversified personal stock portfolio. But beyond those considerations, building and maintaining a personal stock portfolio — if, indeed, you have the risk tolerance for any type of involvement with the stock market — can be just as easy, if not easier, than involvement with a mutual fund. And it can be less expensive and more stable.

The fear that keeps many people from taking a direct plunge into stock market investing is, of course, one of making a mistake. And, indeed, amateur stock market investors who fail usually do so because they don't follow a set strategy, but instead go about it in a haphazard manner — ending up with a mess. Diversification is one thing. But a mess is another. (There are many professional portfolios that are haphazard messes too. But those portfolios represent other people's money, and the results of the mess aren't taken as personally as that held by one individual. Strangely, sometimes people who are shareholders of a professional's mess of a portfolio and end up losing money seem more willing to forgive the actions of the professionals than they would be to forgive themselves for mistakes they may make in their own portfolios.)

There are many different types of stock market investing strategies. And any bookstore or library offers shelves of strategic ideas to choose from. They range from very conservative "buy and hold" concepts that depend on selection of individual stocks based on "value" assessments to highly aggressive in-and-out trading strategies that attempt to play off the "momentum" of the market. Many of these strategies are very good. None work all the time to allow you to "beat the market" at its every turn. But that is part of the animal — whether ridden by yourself alone or along with a group via any mutual fund.

The important thing is to find the strategy you are comfortable with and stick with it. Stock market investing has nothing to do with following tips heard in a bar or at the gym. It also doesn't mean that you must be on an endless search for the $2 stock that will turn into a million bucks to be successful. Nor does it mean that if you don't come up with a constant flow of "ten-baggers" you're a loser. Equally, it doesn't mean that you have to change strategies every time you pick up a newspaper or magazine touting a different perspective. These publications have to constantly keep coming up with something "new" to print. Your life need not be so nomadic. In fact, if you expect long-term success in this or any other arena, it shouldn't be.

Here are three very simple — albeit boring — strategies for putting together a reliable "core" portfolio that would let you sleep with relative ease:

1. **Portfolio of Dividend-Yielding Stocks.** Stocks that have an unbroken history of paying dividends can provide a solid backbone for any "amateur" stock portfolio. There are some companies that have not missed a dividend payment in over fifty years. You can find a comprehensive list of stocks that have consistently paid and, indeed, increased dividend payments yearly over a long period of time in the annual directory *Handbook of Dividend Achievers,* published by Moody's. Any selection of fifteen, ten, or even fewer stocks from this list (hire a monkey with a dart, if you'd like) could serve you well for many years. And if one disappoints one year by omitting or lowering a dividend, replace it. Many of these companies also have automatic dividend reinvestment plans that keep building a portfolio without transaction fees.

2. **Portfolio of Widely Held Stocks.** Another simple yet comfortably conservative stock portfolio could be made up of stocks selected from a list of those that have already attracted the greatest number of shareholders. Currently the top fifteen companies with this distinction are AT&T, Ameritech, Bell Atlantic, BellSouth, Exxon, General Electric, GM, GTE, IBM, Nynex, PGE, Pacific Telesis, Sears, Southwestern Bell, and US West. The list of these companies is often found on the business pages of daily newspapers.

3. **Portfolio of Institutional Investor Favorites.** If you don't think you can beat the professionals at their game, then join them without paying them the fees for it. Just put together your own portfolio from those stocks most favored by institutional investors. You'll find that

the favorites aren't all that imaginative — which, of course, begs the question about why all this genius of institutional investors is so expensive. The list of the top companies with the greatest amount of institutional investment can be found quarterly in *Barron's* in the issues published in the final week of the months of February, May, August, and November. The current crop of institutional investor favorites are, in order of largest percentage of ownership by institution: General Electric, Exxon, AT&T, Texaco, Philip Morris, Royal Dutch, Mobil, American Express, Motorola, Eastman Kodak, Intel, General Motors, Bristol-Meyer-Squib, Amoco, Ford.

These three strategies aren't "perfect." They are not right for everybody. But a portfolio made up of about equal amounts of money invested into ten or so (or even fewer — as few as five or six) from any of these sources will give you a sufficiently diversified portfolio with steady performance that will, over time, match or likely exceed stock market benchmarks such as the S&P 500. During the last heady months of a bull market, however, these conservative portfolios are *not* likely to outperform the market. This is because during those last days the focus will be on raising the prices of "new, emerging" companies. During bear times, however, these conservative portfolios will probably beat the market. This is because when the hotshot darlings of the latter stages of a bull market start turning south, there is a rush back to the known — particularly to stocks that provide income. This is the period in the maturing process of bull markets when "old-fashioned" measurements of value go back into style. Once you have such a conservative "core" portfolio in place, then you can branch out into more precarious arenas — maybe even with a lucky bump into a big hit or two. Remember, however, during bear times "beating the market" means only that the value of a stock portfolio goes down *less* than the market. But it still goes down.

Holding a personal portfolio does not mean that you are totally immune to the actions of others — including institutional investors as they move herdlike through the market. If institutional investors start selling off in the type of professional panic displayed, for example, in the market declines of 1929, 1969, and 1987, the shares of your stocks, no matter how well chosen or conservative they may be, will go down in price as a result of their actions. But as an individual investor you don't have the same type of pressures as an institutional investor. You need not act herdlike during a panic that often features institutional sell-offs of good, and otherwise stable, stocks.

Tax Factors

Building a personal stock portfolio is a particularly compelling option over mutual funds for anyone who wants access to the stock market outside a tax-protected vehicle such as an IRA or 401(k) plan. The tax considerations become very important for mutual fund shareholders, who must pay annual taxes on fund returns. For fund shareholders in the highest tax bracket, returns on a fund can be reduced by 25 percent or 30 percent — and by even more when state and local taxes are considered.

With a stock fund you have to pay capital gains tax, of course, whenever a fund manager sells shares showing a "profit." In addition, you have to pay taxes on dividend and interest income.

The money you pay in taxes on the fund manager's actions has to come from some other source or you have to sell shares of the fund to pay the taxes. This might not be a bad thing as long as the market is rising and the overall net asset value of the shares of the fund is rising as well. But if the market drifts downward — or plunges — it won't be so attractive. The fund manager can continue turning the portfolio over to capture capital gains from the sale of stocks at a "profit" that can be shown on performance charts as part of the overall return. But at the same time, while you would be responsible for paying taxes on those "capital gains," the actual net asset value (NAV) of the fund's shares could be lower than what you had paid for them or, in fact, lower than it had been a year before — or even a few months before.

This was one of the contributing factors for the heavy redemptions of fund shares in the early 1970s. At the time, mutual funds were not held in tax-protected accounts. That became possible only after the creation of Individual Retirement Accounts (IRAs) in 1975. Fund shareholders in the early 1970s had, as the market entered a bearish period, the unhappy experience of having to fulfill tax obligations on supposed capital gains — as fund managers, particularly of the go-go funds, kept selling off the winners in the portfolios to claim as "performance" — while the NAV itself kept going down. The longer people held the funds, the deeper the hole got. People were almost forced to redeem the fund shares. The same thing could happen to you if your stock fund investment is not tax protected.

A study conducted by economists at Stanford University reveals how much of a toll taxes can take on a stock mutual fund. The study, which was based on the median return of a sample of sixty-two mutual funds, showed that $1 invested in 1962 would have grown to $21.89 by 1992 on a pretax basis. But on an aftertax basis the $1 would have grown to only $9.87.[1] And in the meantime the mutual fund investor would have had to come up with $12.02 to pay the taxes. In other words, to get the full $21.89 return over those thirty years, it cost the hypothetical shareholder the original $1 and an additional $12.02 in taxes paid out over all those years for all the reinvested capital gains, dividends, and interest on the original $1 for a total cost of $13.02 of real money shelled out to get the $21.89. The reality of this investment, therefore, is that the unsuspecting shareholder didn't even get a return in those thirty years that was double the amount of real money put into the whole experience. In contrast, $1 put into a tax-deferred — and exempt from state and local taxes — U.S. Savings Bond in 1962 became in thirty years $10.93.

When you have your own stock portfolio, you need not worry about the annual tax burden created by mutual fund portfolio turnover. Instead, you decide yourself when to sell something for a "profit." Until that time, you pay taxes only on the dividends. And in a down market you won't be backed up against the wall to make the decision to sell shares to pay the taxes on capital gains — when, in fact, the total value of your holdings is going down — or find the money to pay taxes from some other source. Instead, your view can be more long-term: to wait out the market declines while you continue collecting the dividend income. If, however, your only reasonable access to the stock market is via a fully taxed mutual fund because you don't have a large enough amount of money or simply have no interest in holding stocks directly, there are a couple of guidelines for fund selection.

First, a high portfolio turnover can jump up those capital gains obligations. For this and other reasons, the Mutual Fund Survival Rule for stock fund portfolio turnover limit is 100 percent a year. That means that the entire portfolio is effectively changed once a year. A lower turnover is better. Any portfolio turnover that is higher than 100 percent — and you can find some that are 500 percent or more — not only usually means bad news for taxed funds, but it also means unnecessary expenses. It is an indication of a manager's frantic approach to the market and accompanying heavy trading commissions that get charged to everyone in the fund, whether taxed or untaxed.

Second, a further complication in assessing stock funds in terms of tax issues is the amount a fund has on its books as "unrealized capital gains" — or, in other words, stocks the fund is carrying that have appreciated in value but have not yet been sold. Some funds carry 40 percent or more of their total asset value as unrealized capital gains. The risk here is that a fund manager, if pressured, could sell those shares to capture the capital gains that had been accumulating while you were not in the fund, but requiring that you pay the capital gains taxes nonetheless. Thus, when assessing different funds for a taxable holding, the best is the one with the lowest proportion of unrealized gains as reported in the fund's most recent shareholder report.

Yet Another Alternative

While having your own stock portfolio, as part of either a tax-protected or a taxable account, may still seem daunting, an alternative way of getting involved directly and avoiding the added layer of complication with mutual fund entanglement is via the investment club idea. While best for the gregarious person and somewhat time-consuming (because you have to go to meetings and argue with other people about the best course to take with the money), the investment club idea works somewhat like a mutual fund. Money is pooled and risks are spread out over a wider selection of investment options — either stock investments or other options — than may be possible with the money of only one person. The differences are that you know all the other people involved and you don't have to pay all those high fees. And, with an investment club, if one member tries to pull some dashing high-risk trick with your money, you can take him out back and punch him in the nose. That's an opportunity that you will not likely get to enjoy with an anonymous fund manager.

For information about investment clubs, contact the National Association of Investment Clubs, 1515 East Eleven Mile Road, Royal Oak, MI 48067. Those who do not care for the thought of making any type of committee decision may wish to contact the American Association of Individual Investors, 625 North Michigan Avenue, Chicago, IL 60611.

The Fund Way

But if these direct-involvement alternatives are not possible, then your choice, as a survivalist, of a stock mutual fund — or continuation with the one(s) you may already be in — depends on separating the romance presented by the fund promoter from the reality you can tolerate as a survivalist.

The romance, which often starts with the very name of the fund, usually is most readily evident in a fund's broadly stated "investment objective." This is the place where a fund promoter's staff of lawyers and slick marketing people can have fun concocting glamorous-sounding — or conservative-sounding, if that happens to be the investment flavor of the month — investment philosophies to ring your bell and get you salivating faster than Pavlov's dog.

There seems to be an "objective" to serve every possible view or perception of the market. There is, for example, the "value investment" concept that promises to search for companies with stocks selling for less than their real worth. There are funds that focus on "small companies," "emerging industries," "growing companies," "ethical companies," or companies in a certain region of the country, and on and on. Included in these objectives are such basic goals as "long-term growth of capital and income," "reasonable current income," and so on. Additionally, the objective can give a broad idea of the investment approach of the fund — for example, "prudent investment risk" or "aggressive investment techniques." These carefully worded objectives, however, which are always qualified with the line "there can be no assurance that the Fund will achieve its investment objectives," often have little to do with what is really going on with the fund.

For example, here's the stated objective of a fund that claims to be focused on the blue-chip segment of the market: "To increase the value of the fund's shares over the long term by investing in large, successful growth companies at the top of their industries." Sounds cozy, huh? Here's a chance, it would seem, to snuggle in with a long-term relationship with blue-chip growth companies. As the economy grows, you may think, so will your potential for return as these companies "at the top of their industries" grow along with the economy. A closer inspection of this fund, however, reveals that during the previous year it had a portfolio turnover of over 300 percent. Where's the long-term view, you may ask, when a portfolio is spun more than three times in a year? Apparently, the answer is that the fund promoter wants *you* to maintain a long-term view of the fund while the fund manager trades with little regard for any long-term performance of the stocks and, by extension, the blue-chip companies themselves. Moreover, as far as "blue-chip" goes, there simply are not three new crops of blue-chip companies born in a year that would justify this type of trading activity. Equally, there is not an annual 300 percent turnover of industries dominating the economy — no matter how volatile and changing the economy may be. This fund simply is not the conservative one that its stated objective tries to suggest. Instead, the fund is run as a trading adventure juicing up "performance" by capturing minuscule capital gains with fast in-and-out short-term trades. (Remember, for a mutual fund survivalist, the annual portfolio turnover maximum is 100 percent.) In fact, in this particular case, the fund also was involved with other high-risk tricks like foreign currency futures contracts and puts and calls. The fund's "stated objective" is just a cleverly worded lie.

As with this "blue-chip" fund, no fund can be effectively judged for its inherent riskiness on the basis of a lofty-sounding and seductive objective. Instead, you have to look beyond this to the actual investment makeup of the fund. But this isn't as difficult as it sounds. The first thing you need to do when you encounter a fund that strikes your fancy — a no-load fund, of course, encountered accidentally through advertising or publicity you may see, or through a methodical search through lists of no-load funds, or presented to you as a choice in your pension plan — is to think of it not in terms of its grand objective but in the more simplified terms of how it fits into five broad categories of funds. You can determine more about your likely future experience with a stock fund from its classification in these five categories than from a fund's specific narrow objective. The five broad fund categories, which you probably recognize, are balanced, equity income, growth and income, growth, and aggressive growth.

Funds within each of these broad categories have over the years taken on specific traditional risk profiles and historically have performed in a fairly consistent manner more related to the category than the specific funds within the category. In other words, the inherent risks of stock funds are more widely different from one category to another — as the different categories have been traditionally defined — than from one fund to another within each category. Although the profiles of these different broad categories, which we will look at in a moment, are well established via tradition and are often used by magazines, newspapers, and mutual fund tracking services to group and compare different funds, the actual categorization of a fund is determined by the fund promoter itself.

Unfortunately, the integrity of these classifications has been seriously compromised in the last few years, along with the general deterioration of integrity within the mutual fund industry, until the labeling of funds by promoters in different broad categories has little value. The promoters know, for example, that if they can get a high-risk fund using spurious investment tricks included in a conservative fund category, they are more likely to be able to place nearer the top of the performance charts for that category — at least temporarily during a period of rising markets. (Remember, aggressive tricks work well during rising markets. They are far less effective during falling markets.)

Thus, while the fund promoters get to choose which category they want their fund placed in, the burden of having to decide whether the categorization of the fund is correct enough to justify putting money into the fund is squarely on you — the person with the least amount of readily available information to decide if the categorization is appropriate or even true.

There are, however, a few quick checks that you can make to see if the fund is really what it claims to be. Here, then, are the broad categories and general risk profiles of stock funds in approximate order of ascending risk and volatility.

BALANCED. A balanced fund is commonly made up of about half bonds or other interest-bearing securities, such as preferred stocks, and half common stocks. Sometimes the fund manager has some leeway to skew the percentage of holdings of bonds or stocks one way or the other when, in the opinion of the manager, market conditions favor either stocks or bonds.

The balanced fund is the closest thing to the original British version of the investment trust — original, that is, in the conservative version that was created by the British in the wake of the Baring Crisis of 1890. When the basic idea of the investment trust was brought over to America in the 1920s, only a few of the investment trusts followed the British formula. Most of the trusts were pure common stock funds — with the added juice of tricks like leverage and short selling. One American trust founded in 1928 that did follow the old British idea was the Industrial and Power Securities Company. The trust's conservative investment policy allowed the trust to survive the 1930s and later to become known as the Wellington Fund, the name under which it continues to survive today.

The seeming conservative balanced fund might appear to be the "one-stop shopping" answer to the whole problem of where to put your money. Indeed, many people over the decades have used such funds for exactly that purpose. And those who used them during the 1980s and early 1990s had a decent time of it since falling interest rates made the value of the bond portion of the funds go up at the same time that the stock portion was going up as well.

Today, however, the mutual fund survivalist's search for a balanced fund to meet personal objectives is likely to be so complicated as to be impossible. To begin with, you may not want to have 50 percent of your money in stocks. Also, you may not want the bond portion of your money in the types of bonds that a balanced fund may be holding. For example, when choosing a balanced fund you would have to determine the average maturity of the bond portion of the fund's portfolio *and* the approach taken by the stock portion. Too complicated. It would be easier to select a bond fund (or, in fact, own your own bonds directly) and then select an appropriate stock fund. The balanced fund, in other words, does not provide the type of flexibility you are going to need. During the 1973–74 market decline of 45 percent, balanced funds as a group lost 29.3 percent of their value.

In the early 1990s the "new" — and incredibly popular — mutual fund product called an "asset-allocation fund" was really a jazzed-up version of the old balanced fund idea. The newer version, however, tended to allow greater investment "freedoms" (or, in other words, tricks) and in most cases unlimited leeway for portfolio adjustment among bond, stock, and cash alternatives. The implied promise of the new asset-allocation funds is that the managers will successfully "time" the market to have the proper balance of holdings to get maximum return under all changing conditions. These funds, which, reflecting their popularity, tend to be expensive, generally performed well in the early 1990s (but, then, so did far less expensive balanced funds). The asset-allocation funds, as of this writing, have not been tested under adverse conditions. In the past, funds that attempted different types of "timing" strategies did not succeed. The managers of the "timing" funds of the past invariably were wrong when the market took its *real* turn. For mutual fund survivalists, the asset-allocation fund is too difficult to decipher to determine its suitability.

Also, it is generally too expensive. (Another fund promoter term often used to describe a timing approach to the market is "all-weather fund." These funds also are of no interest to survivalists.)

A further extension of the old "balanced" idea that took the "asset allocation" concept to another level of elaboration was the early 1990s mutual fund product called "wrap accounts." Promoted primarily by full-service brokerages, the wrap account promised investors with $100,000 minimum investments "personalized" asset management from topflight money managers. In return for this service the investor would be levied a flat 3 percent annual fee for the money under management. An expensive service to be sure, but the sales pitch here was that these top managers — people, it would seem, who were not only professional, but were *really* professional — would not normally have anything to do with investors with such paltry amounts of money as $100,000. These were managers who were accustomed to advising millionaires, you see, and if you wanted to get close to them — although not close enough that they would actually talk with you directly — you should be willing to pay a high fee. In addition, by paying such a high fee you could avoid the potential of having your money managed by low-level brokers or "financial planners" who would be tempted to "churn" your portfolio just to generate fee income for themselves. In other words, pay the high fee from the start and the company will save you from the greedy shenanigans of other employees within the same company! In reality, this is just another marketing gimmick that plays on investors' confusion over the multitudinous choices within the mutual fund world — created, of course, by the mutual fund industry itself. Simply put, the "wrap account" idea has not been tested as of this writing under the dark clouds of falling markets, and the evidence of performance does not indicate that the price is worth it.

EQUITY INCOME. This category of fund focuses on stocks that pay dividends. Dividends on stocks have little income risk. Stock fund portfolios that emphasize stock dividends are more stable in terms of income than bond fund portfolios. Interest rates as reflected in bonds change quickly — often daily. But the decisions affecting changes in dividends at corporations are rarely made more than once a year. When bad times hit the economy, there is usually a long delay before dividend cuts reflect the bad time. Bond fund yields, however, reflect the bad times immediately and unmercifully. The net asset values of funds emphasizing dividend-yielding stocks, however, are more prone to violent swings than are the values of intermediate or short-term bond funds. Because of the potential volatility of stock prices, you are more likely to lose overall value of your money with a stock fund — even one almost completely invested in div-idend-yielding stocks — than you would in a 100 percent government or high-grade corporate bond fund.

Generally, however, stock funds emphasizing dividend yield drop less than other types of stock funds during extended down markets. These funds also tend to do better than the market itself during bad times — but do not reach the spectacular heights of more daredevil funds during peaks of a bull market. During the 1973–74 decline, the equity income category lost 30 percent. Over long periods of time, however — twenty to thirty years — the equity income fund outperforms all other categories when capital gains and income are continually reinvested. During the market's rise from 1974 to 1992, 53 percent of the advance of the S&P 500 stocks came from dividends.

To fulfill a mutual fund survivalist's minimum requirements, an equity income fund's portfolio must be made up of at least 70 percent of stocks (more would be better) that actually pay dividends. You can check this quickly by looking at the most recent annual or semiannual report of the fund. Often the annual report will identify exactly the percentage of div-idend-paying stocks in the portfolio as of the end of the reporting period. Also, each listing of stocks in these reports must identify those stocks that do not pay a dividend. This is usually identified with an asterisk or some other mark. Go through the portfolio report and cross out the ones that do not pay dividends. Count up or simply eyeball the list to see if the fund is actually pursuing dividend income. The other 30 percent of the fund could be in non-income-producing stocks or corporate and treasury bonds.

GROWTH AND INCOME. As the name of the category implies, this type of fund attempts to deliver capital gains appreciation by finding "growth stocks" that can be expected to rise in price while at the same time providing some dividend income. The dividend income would gen-erally be lower than with a more strict equity income fund. A higher percent of stocks in this type of fund would not pay any dividend at all. For a mutual fund survivalist, however, at least 50 percent of the portfolio should be dividend-paying stocks. The 1973–74 decline battered this cat-egory with a drop of 39.3 percent.

GROWTH. This category, which includes the largest number of funds, is focused on capital appreciation of stocks — rising prices of the stocks themselves instead of income from dividends. Typically, you would find that 30 percent or less of the stocks in the fund's portfolio pay dividends. During the 1973–74 bear market this category was hit with a 48 percent drop.

There is a wide range of different funds in this category. Traditionally, however, this category focuses on investment into established, "quality" companies and a "long-term" investment perspective. In addition, the funds would be expected to follow "prudent" investment policies, avoiding the tricks, for example, of leverage, short selling, ownership of restricted securities, and the like.

This category is the one abused the most by fund promoters as they have abandoned the "gentleman's agreement" about the profile of the funds they claim as simple "growth." The promoter of the "blue-chip" fund looked at earlier in this chapter put the fund into this fund category. Basically, a growth fund is a real growth fund when it is *not* an "aggressive growth fund."

AGGRESSIVE GROWTH. This category — sometimes also called *maximum capital appreciation* — was created after the 1960s go-go years to separate "standard" growth funds from the ones loaded up with go-go tricks. Today, therefore, the so-called aggressive growth funds are the formalized versions of the old go-go funds. The idea of calling a group of funds "aggressive growth" was to try to give people a better idea of what they were getting into after all the fuss in the early 1970s about how go-go promoters had misled investors. In the reform days of the 1970s, therefore, when people heard the term "aggressive growth," they knew that it was a euphemism for go-go. Since then, however, memories have faded of the time when the go-gos roamed the earth and the resulting disaster that made paupers out of the many unfortunate shareholders who had put so much faith into the "promise" of these funds. (Today, fund promoters hate being equated with the old go-go funds or having their managers redubbed "gunslingers" — even when the evidence of their resurrection of old-fashioned tricks is clear and undeniable. Actually, it's fun to hear them sputter about how things have changed, people are different, etc., etc.)

Today, fund promoters have been willing to identify fewer than 200 of the 1,900 stock funds as aggressive funds. Many, many more funds should be put into this category but are instead hiding out in the "growth" and the "growth and income" categories. Thus, we're back to the dark ages of the go-go years when it comes to trying to determine the true identity of funds.

Without a doubt, however, these are the funds that reach the highest heights during strong bull markets. But they are also hit the hardest during bears — usually wiping out all the "gains" made during the previous period up. During the 1973–74 market drop, the "average" aggressive growth fund lost 46 percent of its value.

Funds in this category have few if any stocks that pay dividends. Often they are focused on "small companies" (but you can also find funds that fit a more conservative "growth" category that is focused on "small companies"). The real tip-off that separates the aggressive fund from other categories is the tricks or, more euphemistically, the fund's investment policies. Leverage, unregistered securities, futures contracts, commodities, puts and calls — these are all typical of an aggressive fund, no matter how it may officially be categorized.

Investment Policies

When you get beyond the general historically established risk patterns of different types of funds in broad categories, the next consideration — perhaps the most important one for mutual fund survivalists — that determines the nature of risk you are exposed to is the specific investment policies of the fund. These are the written "laws" printed in the fund's prospectus and "additional statement of information" — a document that must be specially requested from the fund promoter. To find a complete list of what a fund can and cannot do with your money you need to look at the prospectus *and* the "additional statement of information" under the headings "investment restrictions" or "management policies."

Like the historically established risk patterns of different types of broadly defined funds, there are historically established investment techniques that can define the risk profile of *any* fund — or, to be more blunt, there are the tricks. As each trick is added, your risk is compounded. If, for example, a fund practices margin buying, that's one level of risk. Add to it short selling, and that's another level. Sprinkle in a high percentage ownership of "illiquid securities" or some "unseasoned companies," and you've sent someone off to the races and to gamble with your money.

Of course, you have the option of embracing those funds that use the widest range of tricks. These funds may indeed provide quite a thrilling spectacle while everything is looking good — specifically, when the stock market is on a generally positive path. But using history as your guide, you had better evacuate any such fund at the first hint of a problem with any of the tricks — either at your fund or at any other similar fund — because once the tricks start to crumble, no fund playing them is immune to the snowball effect of their collapse. You would have to monitor this continually — daily, perhaps hourly, as we get closer to the crisis — and then be ready to move fast. This is not for survivalists. You have better things to do with your life.

As we've seen, the government allows a very wide range of investment possibilities for mutual fund managers. The law requires only that the nature of the investments be disclosed. This is the place that separates the high-risk from the acceptable investment activities for mutual fund survivalists — particularly since the fund industry has been so anxious to do away with these "old-fashioned" limitations.

To avoid being caught in the downdraft of tricks, the first thing that a survivalist needs to know is revealed in the opening sentence of a mutual fund's prospectus — that is, whether or not the fund is actually "diversified." Some funds do not fulfill the legal definition of "diversified" but are instead "nondiversified."

The official definition of a "diversified" fund demands that 75 percent of the fund be diversified among stocks so that no more than 5 percent of the assets of the fund are in the securities of one company. A "nondiversified" fund need diversify only 50 percent of its assets and can put up to 25 percent of its assets in the securities of a single company.

Putting money into a nondiversified fund is unacceptable for mutual fund survivalists. Diversification, remember, was one of the good ideas that got you interested in mutual funds in the first place. (So-called sector funds or industry funds are not diversified. By definition, therefore, they are too risky for survivalists.)

After assuring yourself of the basic protection of diversification, make sure that the fund does not engage in any of the investment tricks that have in the past proved to be so consistently dangerous. The following is a list of the most prominent of these tricks. While this list is not comprehensive — such a list would fill another book — these are the most offensive tricks. They are the ones usually adopted first by reckless fund promoters before they fly off to the never-never land of more esoteric (and untested) investment practices.

To make sure, however, that a fund is not involved in these areas, you must actually *see* the words that say, for example, "The Fund may not purchase securities on margin." The limitations must be flatly stated without any qualifications. If you don't see the actual words, you can contact the fund promoter for clarification, but usually you can assume that the fund does not have a limitation against these practices and therefore is probably already engaged in them.

Margin buying. The concept of leverage and its probable dire consequences must be avoided. As we get closer to the moment of the mutual fund crisis, financial world leaders will try to convince you that leverage is a reasonable and low-risk activity. It is not. It never has been, and it never will be.

Short selling. Just as risky as margin buying, short selling techniques have invariably caught fund managers who have tried them in the past on the wrong side of the market when the market actually goes bad.

More than 5 percent of value of fund assets in one company. Even under the government's official "diversified" definition, a fund, without this limitation, can use 25 percent of its assets to buy a large stake in a company. Any such skewing of a portfolio is high-risk.

Ownership of more than 10 percent of shares of a company. High fund concentration of ownership of one company makes the shares more difficult to sell — more illiquid — and therefore adds risk to the fund.

Ownership of "unseasoned companies" greater than 5 percent of fund assets. Companies with less than three years of continuous operation are considered "unseasoned" and are among the riskiest of any type of company.

Ownership of "restricted" or illiquid securities greater than 10 percent of fund assets. The more illiquid a fund is the riskier it is. When there is no market for holdings, the "value" of the fund's shares can be difficult to ascertain accurately.

More than 10 percent of value of fund assets in one industry. Like concentrating assets of the fund in one company, a concentration in a single industry also compromises the concept of diversification, making the portfolio inherently riskier than other, more diversified funds. Typically, fund managers who concentrate their portfolios do so with small companies with thinly traded stocks — all contributing to a self-fulfilling upward movement of the fund's performance as long as the market is generally rising. In a falling market such a concentrated portfolio of thinly traded stocks becomes nearly illiquid, causing the values to drop dramatically because there are no buyers. That's why a personal portfolio of a few stocks of large companies with actively traded issues can be less risky than being in a large fund concentrated in thinly traded issues.

Ownership of shares of open-end mutual funds. You don't want a fund that simply buys shares of other funds, layering charges one on top of another. This is a characteristic of so-called multifund funds or funds of funds. Any attempt to provide multiple levels of diversification often ends up with the investment perspective practiced in one such fund canceling out the investment perspective in another.

Buying or selling of real estate. Real estate speculation adds further illiquidity to a fund's portfolio and complicates the valuation of the fund's shares.

Commodities investing. Commodities are among the riskiest types of investments.

Direct investment in oil, gas, or mineral exploration projects. Exploration projects like these are among the most speculative of all.

STOCK FUND SURVIVALIST RULES

1. **Be skeptical about the stated objective of a fund.** A fund promoter's "opinion" of the nature of the fund's investment approach can vary widely from reality. Think of the fund's "objective" only as a starting point for a general narrowing of your choices.

2. **Be sure that you are comfortable with the fund's risk profile as defined by its broad category.** All stock funds can be categorized within five broadly defined groups — balanced, equity income, growth and income, growth, and aggressive growth. Each category has a historically consistent risk performance. Accurate identification of a fund by the established profiles of these categories will tell you more about your probable future experience than looking at the "unique" profiles of the funds themselves.

3. **Never invest in a stock fund with a portfolio turnover greater than 100 percent.** If a fund manager has to buy and sell a completely new portfolio more than once a year, then the manager either doesn't know how to evaluate stocks for long-term prospects or is just interested in fast in-and-out trading to churn the portfolio.

4. **Don't invest in a nondiversified fund.** Diversification is one of the principal reasons you would be interested in mutual fund involvement in the first place.

5. **Never accept an expense ratio higher than 1.25 percent.** A lower expense ratio is better, of course.

6. **For a fund not in tax-protected accounts, make sure that you choose the most "tax-advantaged" funds.** Paying taxes on dividends, interest, and capital gains can have a big impact on the total *real* return you get from a fund that is not in a tax-protected account. Avoid funds with high turnover — perhaps even lower than the 100 percent turnover acceptable to other mutual fund survivalists. Among final selection candidates, select the one with the lowest percentage of "unrealized capital gains."

7. **Avoid all funds engaged in historically identified high-risk tricks.** Margin buying, short selling, high concentration of fund assets in a few companies, high ownership of restricted or illiquid securities, investment into unseasoned companies, and other high-risk investment policies should be avoided.

CHAPTER 9

■ ■ ■

The Risks You Face: Institutions

The worst experience you could have with a mutual fund company — or any financial institution for that matter — is out-and-out fraud. Simple theft of your money. Happily, this particular risk is the one thing that government regulations and government enforcement teams work at the hardest to protect you from suffering. Although there is always the possibility of fraud (and no financial crisis of the past has ever happened without a revelation of fraud or another type of scandal), there is nothing you personally can do beyond what is being done on your behalf by government regulators to identify whether one mutual fund company would be more likely to engage in fraud than another.

As long as you stick to established, mainstream fund companies that are listed in daily newspapers and avoid sending your money off to something that you've never heard of or because a salesman makes a telephone pitch for something, you are on equal footing with everyone else in avoiding fraud. That doesn't mean, however, that limiting your investments to the largest or best-known fund companies is an automatic safeguard against fraud. As anyone who witnessed the scandals of the 1980s and early 1990s can attest, most of the biggest and most costly scandals involved some of the biggest and previously most well respected institutions — from E. F. Hutton to Drexel Burnham Lambert to Salomon Brothers to Prudential Securities. This is a fact of life that can be traced throughout every moment of financial history. But it doesn't mean that you must avoid large mutual fund companies just because you are expecting a bomb to hit. It's just that you can never tell when you are about to be shanghaied, and, therefore, it isn't worth getting obsessively worried about it.

Another potential institutional risk that you need not worry about is the possibility of a mutual fund company going bankrupt and your money going with it. This cannot happen. Your money is not tied up with the mutual fund company itself. Instead, each fund is organized as a separate corporation. The investments of the fund are not dependent on the financial health of the company running the fund. The law protects your investments from intermingling with the business activities of the fund itself.

If a fund company goes out of business, the worst that can happen is that the investments of the fund get liquidated (or folded into another fund) and the actual liquidation value is lower than you thought it was. For example, back in the late 1960s when the once-mighty Mates Fund halted share redemption because of an inaccurate valuation of illiquid securities, the fund remained closed for redemptions for seven months. At the time that the redemptions were halted, each share of the fund was valued at $15.51. When the Mates Fund mess was finally cleaned up, the value per share was set at $3.56. But the Mates Fund nightmare was not caused by fraud or the bankruptcy of the fund company: it was simply incompetent handling of high-risk, illiquid securities. And remember that mutual fund management incompetence is not illegal. Neither is high-risk investment activity. In short, your ability to weather a mutual fund crisis will depend more on what the fund managers are doing *legally* with your money than on the financial health of the fund company itself or the likelihood of your being a victim of fraud.

Cash Redemptions

Yet, as the 1960s shareholders of the Mates Fund and other funds of the time discovered, during any period of crisis liquidity becomes very important. The high-risk nature of illiquid securities in a fund, for example, becomes even more risky during a crisis. In addition, your ability to liquidate your fund shares can become more important. Your mutual fund shares are not necessarily fully liquid for immediate redemption. During the 1987 crash, when there were heavy fund redemptions, some mutual fund companies exercised their legal rights to hold back payouts on redemptions for seven business days. Since then, many fund promoters have adopted a further redemption policy that gives them the freedom to pay fund shareholders "in kind" rather than cash. This means that a fund *could* choose to pay off redemption requests with, for example, shares of stock of a company that at the time of the redemption were worth an amount equivalent to the cash value of the shares you were redeeming — not a nice prospect for a mutual fund survivalist!

The prospectus or "additional statement of information" will tell you under the "Redemption" heading whether or not the fund has reserved this payment-in-kind proviso. Many funds with the payment-in-kind stipulation designate the redemption policy only for those shareholders who own $250,000 or more of the fund or 1 percent of the fund's assets. If this is the case, the fund promoter will have filed a document called Form 18F-1 with the SEC. Thus, if you find the payment-in-kind proviso in the prospectus, call or write the fund promoter and ask if the fund has filed a Form 18F-1. If it has, then limit your investment into the fund to under $250,000. (Not a current problem, you say?) Or, if it lists the payment-in-kind provision and has not filed Form 18F-1, then either get out of that fund or don't go into it.

The "Goldfish Bowl"

An institutional risk you face that is more critical than raw fraud or outright theft or immediate access to cash redemption of the value of your mutual fund shares is the possibility of having your money exposed to something you have no intention of being involved with. This is, of course, the central issue for a mutual fund survivalist, and it is the basis for most of the survivalist rules you've already read in this book.

Unfortunately, as previously demonstrated, many mutual fund promoters are not very cooperative when it comes to making it easy to figure out the investment reality of the funds they run. Some are worse than others. And a few little tricks surfaced in the early 1990s that made the game even more difficult to play. (The big question here is: Why does it have to be a game at all? The lack of a reasonable answer to this question is, of course, the central factor that will lead to the mutual fund crisis.)

Mutual fund enthusiasts have always claimed that mutual funds operate in a crystal-clear "goldfish bowl" unmatched by any other financial institution. And well they should. They are the least regulated of financial institutions, depending almost solely on "disclosure" as the principal protective agent. Although the "goldfish bowl" seems great in theory, a few communication policies recently adopted by some mutual fund promoters seriously compromise that concept.

One way that mutual fund promoters discovered in the early 1990s to circumvent the intentions of disclosure and cloud up the goldfish bowl was to play word games with the directives of the Investment Company Act of 1940 when it came to communicating with shareholders concerning changes made in a fund's investment policy. Back in the 1930s, when the act was drafted, the people who drafted it had seen how small investors had been burned because they had been in funds that literally changed investment direction overnight. One day the fund managers were following an investment approach that emphasized preferred shares of large companies; the next day they were putting the shareholders' money into railway lines in Argentina. The people who put together the Investment Company Act considered this ability to switch investment direction one of the most serious shareholder abuses by the managers of the old investment trusts. And one very important aspect of rebuilding faith in the idea of professional management was the promise of maintaining the consistency of the investment approach (to guard against managers flying off in all directions) and full disclosure of the progress and nature of the investment.

To make certain that changes couldn't be made with a fund's investment policies without shareholders knowing about it, the Investment Company Act dictated that any change in a "fundamental investment limitation" must be voted on by the shareholders. The list of "fundamental investment limitations" printed in the prospectus, therefore, was the *law* of the fund's investment profile. With the shareholder voting requirement, when a fund management asks for permission to change a "fundamental" investment policy, at least the shareholders would be alerted to the fact that a change was being made. This voting privilege was one of the most strongly emphasized parts of the mutual fund sales pitch of the 1940s and 1950s to those who remembered the horrors of the investment trusts of the 1920s and 1930s: "You always know that the fund you invested into yesterday is the same one today." The voting procedure provided a method for advance warning to shareholders that the nature of the fund was changing and therefore gave a shareholder time to leave the fund if the changes redefined the fund in a way that no longer matched the shareholder's risk tolerance.

In the early 1990s, however, when apparently it became important for some mutual fund promoters to keep secret from shareholders the exact nature of changing investment policies into high-risk arenas, they practiced a two-step sleight of hand so that few shareholders would notice how dramatically the fund was changing. Here's how they did it: they asked shareholders simply to vote to change the status of an investment limitation from "fundamental" to "non-fundamental." That meant, of course, in the eyes of regulators there would be no need to get further shareholder approval to change an investment policy if it was already "non-fundamental." The law required shareholder approval only for changes in "fundamental" limitations. Indeed, that is what happened. The wording of the investment limitation didn't change as it went from "fundamental" to "non-fundamental." But the fund promoter could change a "non-fundamental" limitation in any way, at any time, and in secret — without, of course, shareholder approval.

This is completely unacceptable for mutual fund survivalists. When you look at the investment policies of the funds you may be considering, therefore, look for the phrases "non-fundamental" and "can be changed without shareholder approval." If any limitation carries that qualifier, you have to assume that the limitation *will* be changed. It is better, however, simply to avoid the funds that try this little act of deception, because with it they remove the all-important "goldfish bowl" effect that shareholder voting on investment policy changes provides. Even if you wouldn't be able to understand the implications of investment policy changes, the lack of shareholder voting privileges means that things are done in such secrecy that others — such as a sharp-eyed financial journalist — couldn't be able to identify and report on the changing nature of the fund either.

At the minimum, the fund promoter must have a policy of telling you in advance that investment limitations are going to be changed so that you can have a chance to get out of the fund before it exercises the new investment "freedoms" being foisted on shareholders without their approval. (Some mutual fund promoters simply send out new prospectuses with the changes incorporated in them without highlighting for shareholders the exact nature of the changes. The only way you could detect the differences is to match a new prospectus word for word with an old one. This "disclosure" procedure isn't good enough for survivalists.) If you let your money sit in a fund that can make investment policy changes "without shareholder approval" and without prior shareholder notification of changes (for example, thirty days) you should recognize that you now have your money in what is essentially a "blind pool" that is not much different from the worst type of investment trust of the 1920s.

Actually, your first indication that something is afoot will be when you get a proxy statement asking you to vote for changes. Usually these changes — which most often include requests for changes in fees and expenses (almost always upward) or investment policy changes — are requested when the fund is experiencing good performance. Few shareholders look too closely at the changes being requested when they are happy. But the changes last forever.

If you are faced with a proxy statement that asks for your approval to make investment policy changes that redefine the fund into something more risky than you are willing to be involved with, just vote "no" and then start looking for a new, more acceptable fund. Your "no" won't mean anything. Rarely have fund management requests for changes in policies or fees been voted down by shareholders. The only way you can vote is with your feet. Theoretically, you could start a proxy fight and try to organize other shareholders against the changes, but it's not worth the effort. There are many other fish in the sea acceptable to a mutual fund survivalist's palate — although admittedly, as of this writing, their numbers are dwindling.

"Independent" Directors

All the fund's policies and operations are overseen by a board of directors that government regulations dictate must be composed of at least 40 percent of people who do not have financial ties with the mutual fund company itself. The theory is that "independent" directors can be more effective in protecting fund shareholders from self-serving activities by a fund company's management. In practice, however, a fund's "independent" directors are usually long-time friends or business associates of the fund's top managers or people with strong political ties, and they rarely challenge the actions of the fund's management. Directors, who usually attend four to twelve meetings a year, can earn annual fees topping $100,000 with pensions equal to 100 percent of their final salary. (Directors of public corporations earn on average about $34,000 a year.)[1]

While the independence of a fund's directors can rarely be assumed, you can at least hope for a fighting chance by limiting your fund involvement to those funds with a board made up of 50 percent or more of independent directors. The names of the fund's directors and their independent status are listed in either the fund's prospectus or its "additional statement of information." In those few cases when a fund's board took action against the wishes of the fund's management, it has always been when the majority of the board was independent.

Among the matters that the directors supposedly oversee is potentially self-serving investment activity on the part of employees of the funds at the expense of the fund shareholders. One recurring abuse of the past was "front running" — a fund manager's purchase of shares of a company for a personal portfolio just prior to a major purchase by the fund itself that raises the price of the company's shares, giving the fund manager a quick profit. While this particular activity is illegal, there is a wide range of policies among different mutual fund companies about the limitations put on the personal trading activities of fund employees. Some fund companies do not let their managers keep personal portfolios — particularly of any security that the fund may also own. Other fund companies actually encourage their managers to maintain personal portfolios even if they do contain securities that are also in the funds. Other fund companies claim that without the freedom to maintain a personal portfolio, unusually talented money managers wouldn't be willing to take on the job of fund management. One question that this attitude raises is whether the manager would be such a hotshot in personal investing if he didn't have so much "free" research information ready at hand that had already been paid for by the fund shareholders. Another question that seems to go unasked of fund shareholders is whether they would prefer the couple of extra percentage points a year that could possibly be delivered by such a hotshot manager or be willing to sacrifice the extra performance for the assurance that everything is kept perfectly "clean." After past crises involving the mutual fund/investment trust idea, the dominant shareholder preference became "clean" over "hotshot." Despite this past experience, some mutual fund promoters in the 1990s moved not to limit the personal trading activity of their employees and directors (and the temptations that can go along with it) but instead *expanded* it in a way that had not been permitted since the 1930s. Specifically, some fund promoters removed the long-held traditional limitation that had prohibited a fund's employees, officers, or directors from holding 5 percent or more of the shares of a company in which the fund also holds a stake. The tradition of prohibiting ownership of 5 percent or more of a company

MUTUAL FUND SURVIVAL RULES: INSTITUTIONS

1. **Make sure that the fund has a "cash only" redemption policy.** Avoid any fund that maintains a "payment-in-kind" proviso as an alternative to cash as a redemption option.

2. **Pay close attention to proxy statements.** Whenever you get a proxy statement, it usually means that major changes are being made. The changes requested are almost always to your disadvantage — the fees and expenses are going up, or the investment policies are getting more risky. Simply send the voting card back with a "no" vote on everything. Then, because your vote will mean nothing, start looking for a new fund.

3. **Avoid funds that can make investment policy changes "without shareholder approval."** When a fund company removes shareholder voting privileges, it has taken away one of the most important ingredients of disclosure. At the minimum, the fund company should have a procedure for notifying shareholders of policy changes prior to putting the changes into effect.

4. **Do not invest in a fund with a board of directors made up of less than 50 percent of "independent" directors.** While directors of funds are rarely truly independent, you won't even have a fighting chance if the fund company is run by a board with a majority of people already working for the company.

5. **Avoid funds that allow officers and directors to hold 5 percent or more of the shares of a company that is also owned by the fund.**

6. **Complain loudly whenever you feel that you have been wronged by the fund company.** Watch for errors in computing your account, and demand clear explanations of what the fund is doing with your money. Serious complaints should be directed to: Office of Consumer Affairs, U.S. Securities and Exchange Commission, 450 Fifth Street NW, Washington, DC 20549. Phone: 202-272-7440.

7. **Get answers to questions in writing.** While a fund's prospectus isn't as intimidating as it may first appear (see Appendix A: How to Read a Prospectus), any questions that you may have — particularly when trying to determine whether or not the fund fits within critical survival rules — should be submitted in writing and written answers obtained.

that the fund invested in was actually an accommodation of long-held blue-sky securities laws of certain states, but the mutual fund industry successfully lobbied to get these laws relaxed in the early 1990s. But as a mutual fund survivalist, take a tip from past generations and avoid the funds that allow such potentially damaging temptations for shareholder abuse.

The limitations about the personal investment activities of employees of the fund company may or may not be revealed in the prospectus or "additional statement of information." If anything is unclear to you about anything in a prospectus, you can usually find out answers to questions about a fund's investment policies by calling the fund company's information line. However, it's better to make written inquiries about important questions and get your answers in writing.

CHAPTER 10

■ ■ ■

The Final Scenario

The mutual fund crisis will probably come to a head some time in 1996 or 1997. If we are lucky — if for some reason the push to ease mutual fund investment limitations slows or if America's unquestioned love affair with the mutual fund idea cools — we might make it to the turn of the century.

As alarmist as this may sound, it is a simple fact that never in history was a good financial idea created that allowed the world to live happily ever after. Never. Good financial ideas come and go. They work for a while, and then they are tossed aside. When one financial idea fails, another one is found to replace it. Sometimes those replacement ideas are new. Most times, however, they are old ones that are revived — sometimes in a renamed and revised form, sometimes in their original pure forms — after memories have dimmed about the reasons for their having been thrown on the rubbish pile by an earlier generation. Even the financial idea we call "bank" has gone through many redefinitions and restructurings over the centuries.

When we think about the historic ebb and flow of good financial ideas, the most significant consideration for our time is this: historically, whenever everybody pins financial hopes to a *single* idea, the ending is always some degree of collapse. The life span of a single financial idea that becomes unusually popular has in the past varied in the number of years that the idea remained effective (and popular). But those unusually popular financial ideas have historically gone through five steps of maturity:

- **Skepticism about the idea.**
- **Acceptance of the idea.**

- **Embracement of the idea.**

- **Mania focused on the idea.**

- **Collapse of the idea.**

By the early 1990s, the popularity of the mutual fund concept in our era was well into the third stage of its maturity — embracement — if not already on its way to flirting with the next level. As we've seen, this is the fourth time in a little over one hundred years that the basic concept of large professionally managed public investment pools has achieved such a level of unquestioned popularity.

The mutual fund concept, however, is not the single financial idea that will rule most of the 1990s. Instead, the single idea is securitization. Mutual funds, pension funds, and other investment pools are simply the instruments that are allowing large groups of people — many of whom, if not most, have little understanding of what they are getting into — to participate on an unprecedented scale in this single idea of securitization, and, of course, the privatization of risk that is going along with it.

Securitization, like the basic mutual fund concept, is not new either. Over the decades it also has gone in and out of fashion as a financial idea. In the past, when the appeal of securitization heated up as a speculative moneymaking idea following a drop in interest rates on "safe" income-producing instruments (usually to below a 4 percent yield), the idea lasted on average four to six years before it burned itself out. And thus, since interest rates starting dropping below that magic 4 percent level in early 1992 and Americans almost immediately started getting slap-happy for securities as offered by the mutual fund concept, that takes us to about 1996 or 1997.

Before then, however, we can expect a continued boom in financial markets — with a few probable choppy periods. As in the past times of boom and following bust that characterize the history of capitalism, the boom will mask the underlying problems that will ultimately lead to the crisis (or bust). Actually, during periods of boom most people don't recognize how good they are having it. The good times aren't considered good enough. The expectation is for even more and better ahead. To achieve it, greater risk is assumed. Then, as each level of new risk seems to prove to be successful, yet another new level is attempted until the fatal one is finally found. Then the cycle starts over again.

This does not mean to suggest in any way that some other economic system is better. At least with capitalism you get luxuriant periods of boom. In contrast, as the recent grim undoing of Eastern European countries showed, other systems rarely deliver more than perpetual bust. And there's no reward possible in that.

In the recurring boom-and-bust cycles of capitalism (and the ebb and flow of financial ideas that go along with them), winners emerge from both extremes of a cycle. But before you can seize the opportunities of a cycle, you must first step outside the pattern of the cycle and recognize these alternating periods for what they are. Otherwise you'll just be going along with the herd and you'll likely get trampled to death.

Cyclic Patterns

Studying the apparent cyclical nature of different aspects of life on earth has fascinated people since at least the time that humans were able to write down their thoughts — and certainly long before then. When, for example, Joseph in the Bible's Old Testament helped the Pharaoh identify the cyclical pattern of the Nile River's rise and fall as the central cause of "seven fat years followed by seven lean years," he created an impression that has loomed heavily over the Judeo-Christian world ever since.

The study of different types of financial cycles — whether called economic cycles or business cycles or market cycles or some other kind of cycle — has produced a rich body of literature over the centuries. You can find a full shelf of books at the library devoted to the analysis and description of financial cycles. Such famous cycle theories as the Elliot Wave Theory, the Schumpeterian System, and the Kondratieff Wave, as well as many, many not-so-famous cycle theories, attempt to identify when and how cycles move and the forces that push them. The Kondratieff Wave, for example, claims that capitalism goes through fifty-five-year evolutionary cycles that build up to an intense period of speculative excess (a boom) and then a purge of excesses (a bust). This theory claims to have accurately predicted the 1930s depression and predicts that the cyclic fifty-five-year return of a great depression is scheduled for the 1990s.

While different theorists have different ideas about why cycles happen, they usually acknowledge that the root explanation boils down to a consistent pattern of human behavior and crowd psychology — actions taken by people as a group because of expectations or hopes about the future and memories of the past. As financial wizard Bernard Baruch observed in the early 1930s: "All economic movements, by their very nature, are motivated by crowd psychology. . . . Without due recognition of crowd-thinking (which often seems crowd-madness) our theories of economics leave much to be desired."[1] For economist John Kenneth Galbraith, the idea of crowd behavior provides a cyclic pattern that shows that "the financial memory should be assumed to last, at the maximum, no more than 20 years. This is normally the time it takes for the recollection of one disaster to be erased and for some variant on previous dementia to come forward to capture the financial mind. It is also the time generally required for a new generation to enter the scene, impressed as had been its predecessors, with its own innovative genius."[2] (Each time such a variant on previous dementia is revived it tends to last somewhat longer and to be experienced in a somewhat bigger way than the last manifestation, all adding to the temporary illusion that the new generation had indeed been able to accomplish what previous ones had failed at.)

While Galbraith sees a cycle of twenty years and Kondratieff a fifty-five-year timetable for his cycle, others see cycles of two, five, or ten years. In fact, there are about as many timetables for cycles as there are cycle theorists. Therefore, attempting to pinpoint a timetable of rising speculation toward a moment of crisis (and following bust) is really a parlor game of no particular value. Also, while a whole unorganized army of economists is constantly massaging tons of financial statistics to measure current economic conditions, the statistics rarely have been helpful in predicting impending crisis.

But while time frames and financial statistics may vary, past financial crises have followed a highly consistent pattern of events that served as the original spark to the crisis and carried through to the actual crisis. Also, the groups of people involved in the events leading up to the crisis display a consistent pattern of behavior that provides identifiable outward symptoms leading up to crisis. One of the earliest studies of these consistent patterns of events and symptoms of group behavior was Charles Mackay's 1841 classic book, *Extraordinary Popular Delusions and the Madness of Crowds*. This book is still *must* reading — at least the first three chapters — for anyone who wants to understand the power of crowd thinking. Many scholars since Mackay have built on his observations. (The single best and most readable summary of financial crises throughout history and analyses of how they grew and died is *Manias, Panics, and Crashes: A History of Financial Crises* by Charles P. Kindleberger.)[3]

The work of Mackay, Kindleberger, and other crisis analysts has shown that the historical similarities of one financial crisis to another are so consistent, in fact, that they can serve as milestones to mark the progress of an unusually popular financial idea as it moves through its phases of embracement and mania before the crisis of its collapse. These milestones can occur over long periods of time — months or years — or can happen quickly — compressed into weeks, days, or even hours. Sometimes the milestones happen concurrently with each other. In other cases some milestone events or symptoms are skipped altogether. But generally they take a consistently steady course of one step after another that is so submissively adhered to by the ultimate victims of the impending crisis that it is almost heart-wrenching to track.

It is perhaps important to mention here that some scholars who study financial crises say that no attempt should be made to identify the gathering symptoms of an impending crisis. The crisis should not be avoided. It should be allowed to run its course as part of the ever-expanding spiraling progress of economic history. We are to learn from each specific crisis, take our lumps, and then go on to something else. The scholars who make such assertions, however, tend to be those with university positions carrying full job tenure and a government-guaranteed pension plan. For others who do not have these certainties — individuals who not only are part of the big global historical picture, but also must consider the immediacy of personal interests — finding out what crisis scholars have learned from their research (much of which was paid for by the taxpayers via government grants) may be of greater value than having that knowledge languish in dusty volumes of scholarly journals or whispered in the meeting rooms of ill-attended academic symposia.

Here, then, are the milestones as applied to our current experience with the mutual fund concept. As of this writing, at the beginning of 1995, some of the milestones have been passed. Hopefully, you will pick up this book before we reach the last one.

Nine Milestones on the Way to Crisis

1. Financial Displacement
Sometimes something happens that changes the way people view the world and their future in it. For example, the outbreak of war can force people to change the way they must live their lives. Crisis scholars call

this type of development a "displacement." It is "some outside event that changes horizons, expectations, profit opportunities, behavior."[4] These types of events can trigger other events that lead to speculative mania and then on to crisis. For example, the opening of a new market or the creation of a new innovative product can cause a "displacement" as attention is moved to something new and may in turn cause a speculative mania focused on that new development. In the nineteenth century, for example, the invention of the railroad touched off a railroad investment mania and, later, a collapse of that market. (Earlier in the century, before the invention of the railroad, there was a mania — and later collapse — focused on canal construction.)

When such an event forces people to move their money from one place to another, it is called "financial displacement." A financial displacement is often caused by some government action. One classic example was the March 1888 British conversion of government debt consols that lowered interest yield from 3 percent to 2.5 percent. Another classic example was the 1924 redemption of Liberty Bonds by the U.S. government. In both cases, as we now know, many people who got "displaced" turned to the investment trust idea for financial answers — and each time sparked a mania and later a collapse.

In the 1960s the U.S. government action was somewhat less classic, but had a similar effect on American "savers." In September 1966, when interest rates were on the rise, the government put a limit on the amount of interest that savings and loan companies could pay depositors. This limit was 4.25 percent. The government's goal was to keep people from taking money out of commercial banks — which were already limited by law to paying 4 percent interest on deposits — and putting it in S&Ls. That interest payment ceiling, however, was lower than prevailing market interest rates. In fact, Treasury bills yielded more, so there was first a partial shift directly to Treasury bills. But with the minimum denomination of a Treasury bill at $1,000, it was out of the range of many small savers.[5] (Remember that money market funds were not invented until 1972.) In addition, U.S. Savings Bonds at the time were paying even less than bank and S&L savings accounts. All this played into the hands of the mutual fund promoters, who were waving sensible-looking — not to mention very attractive — performance charts of the previous twenty years. Here was *proof* of success. And the low minimum initial investment required by the mutual funds — which at the time was as low as $10 — made them available to anybody. Thus, many "savers" became "investors," and the mutual fund idea got pushed to its mania status during 1967–68. (Later that crummy 4.25 percent S&L rate looked pretty good after the new "investors" saw 50 percent of the value of their money evaporate in the bear market of the 1970s.)

The financial displacement that launched our current era can be traced back to January 1, 1989. Remember that date. Financial historians of the future will have a field day with it. That was the deadline day when profit-sharing retirement plans that had become illegal based on laws and court decisions going back to the passage of the Tax Code of 1986 had to be halted. The legal status of these plans changed to do away with profit sharing that favored high-paid executives over lower-level employees. Many of the pre-1989 plans earmarked a higher percentage of profits for the executives' company-sponsored retirement packages than for others. The old plans were dissolved and new ones were devised. This was the period when the idea of 401(k) plans exploded, since these plans treat employees more equally. But as the old plans were closed, many companies simply started over again by paying out the money in the old plans throughout 1989 and 1990 as cash "roll-over" distributions to employees.

Suddenly, many of the most affluent people of our society had to find somewhere to put billions of dollars from these dissolved retirement plans. With equal suddenness, these people were expected to have become financial experts in selecting the best places for their money. Billions of retirement dollars had moved from corporate responsibility to personal responsibility (just as the 1924 Liberty Bond redemption moved money from government responsibility to personal responsibility). With the declining interest yields on "safe" instruments, it is no wonder so many of these newly displaced people found the promises of the mutual fund idea so alluring.

Closely following this financial displacement was another of almost equal size. This one came in the form of additional billions paid out as "early retirement" cash packages to the innumerable people who lost their jobs as part of the massive "downsizing" of corporate America in the early and middle 1990s. This second great roll-over within five years of the first added even more fuel to the mutual fund furnace.

The sad part about the second lump of roll-over money is that many of the people who got the cash remain unemployed today while others are at best underemployed — and perhaps will remain so for the rest of their working lives. Yet much of that money was aggressively invested with the hope that it would provide high returns to transform a cash nest egg into substantial wealth by retirement time. The question is, however, Where is this mystical land of stable, fast-growing businesses that will deliver handsome investment returns to permit a comfortable retirement, but in the meantime cannot accommodate the full employment of bright, capable, and experienced people? Those who can justifiably ask that question may discover that the answer is the same one that previous generations of the financially displaced discovered: It doesn't exist. It's not true. At least it's not true in a large enough manifestation to satisfy the hopes and expectations of so many people.

2. Evidence of recovery from economic slump or financial jolt

Most speculative manias in history began after some rattling economic disappointment or shock turned out *not* to be the mark of the beginning of the catastrophe that it originally was thought to be. Instead of expected disaster, there is a relatively quick recovery from the shock. This shock could be, for example, a recession that didn't turn out to be a depression; or it could be a stock market crash that didn't turn out to be the beginning of an extended bear market; or it could be some similar type of economic disappointment — such as the failure of financial institutions (e.g., banks) — without an accompanying loss of depositors' money.

These seemingly painless recoveries give the impression that somehow the world has learned how to deal successfully with economic dynamics so that future shocks or disappointments will be equally painless and short-lived. When a few of these economic shocks happen in rapid succession and recoveries happen equally fast, the future becomes viewed confidently as perpetually going through a process of two fast giant steps forward and one short baby step back.

It is this buildup of confidence over time that characterizes the beginnings of major speculative periods. Manias grow in a tierlike fashion. They rarely spring full blown spontaneously. Moreover, most of the people involved in the mania rarely recognize it as such. It isn't as if everyone is running around wide-eyed and lolly-jawed trying to grab onto something that is viewed as simply temporary. Rather, manias are characterized by a sense of confident certainty about the long-term successful future of whatever is the focus of the mania. This was the pattern seen during both the 1920s and 1960s.

In the 1920s short recessions and equally short market setbacks *increased* confidence with each recovery. For example, the 1926 collapse of the Florida land speculation bubble that had been going on since 1924 made people nervous that such a panic would spread to other markets. When that did not happen, people became even more confident about those markets, although at the time those markets *were* overheated and long overdue for a sharp correction.

In the 1960s, the recovery from the 1962 market drop of 27 percent — with an advance of 86 percent by 1966 — and the quick rebound of the 1966 market drop of 25 percent provided "proof" that recoveries were easy. This, on top of the 1966 financial displacement, added another impetus toward the mutual fund mania of 1967–68.

Just as the fast recoveries of those periods set the stage for the speculative manias that followed, the recovery in the 1980s and the early 1990s from an unprecedented string of financial jolts — from the S&L collapse to insider trading scandals to the 1987 and 1989 stock market crashes to recession and so on — provided similar "proof" to a new generation. These jolts, however, were not solved by human genius to assure smoothness in the future. Instead, the solutions provided only temporary Band-Aid treatment and were very, very expensive: billions of dollars borrowed from our grandchildren to bail out S&Ls; more billions in the form of lost jobs and liquidation of American businesses to pay off greedy corporate raiders and their sleight-of-hand comrades. And as far as the initial financing of recoveries of speculative bond and stock markets went, see Milestone 1.

There are some economists — particularly the cycle theorists — who believe that whenever a sharp economic decline is artificially averted it simply delays matters and makes the next decline bigger and more serious. Excesses of a past period of expansion, they say, *must* be completely worked off before a new period of true prosperity can begin. Some economic historians, for example, claim that the world was ready for a deep economic decline just before World War I broke out and that the war itself artificially delayed the inevitable. And then, in the United States at least, continual lowering of interest rates during the 1920s to keep a sense of prosperity afloat artificially delayed it further. As a result, the 1929 experience was far more devastating than it would have been if the "cycle" had been permitted to follow its natural course fifteen years earlier.

When we consider how many truly dire catastrophes have been artificially (and expensively) avoided in the last decade, it makes the prospects of meeting up with another one more troubling. Let's face it, there's not much left in the till to soften the blow of another financial jolt — either in this country or anywhere else in the world. And, certainly, there's nothing promised from the U.S. government's dwindling till that will help you personally soften the blow of any jolt from your "investments" in mutual funds.

3. A positive event sparks confidence in the future

Crowd perceptions of financial markets do not exist in isolation from perceptions of the rest of the world. Confidence in a financial idea that has previously been considered risky is often provided by some positive incident outside the financial world.

For example, some historians point to Charles Lindbergh's solo transatlantic flight of May 20–21, 1927, as the kickoff event of the final stage of the 1920s financial mania. Lindbergh's high-risk conquering of the Atlantic provided irrefutable proof of America's can-do future and the high reward that comes with high risk.

A generation later, America began the decade of the 1960s with seeming lost stature in the world after the Soviets' building of the Berlin Wall, the embarrassing loss of face following the ill-fated Cuban Bay of Pigs invasion, and the United States' lag in progress in space exploration. A shot in the arm came, however, in 1962 with success against the Soviets in the Cuban missile crisis and the first American manned space orbit during the same year. This new self-assurance (coinciding with lowering interest rates) launched the 1962–66 bull market. Then, by the middle 1960s, politicians' promises of a "Great Society" and assurances to business that recessions would never be permitted again, along with the belief that the United States was "winning" in Vietnam, combined to give confidence in the unerring future of financial markets. Then it was on to the mania of 1967–68.

In the early 1990s, the 1991 success of the United States' military action in the Middle East — Operation Desert Storm — sparked the beginning of a raging bull stock market. This was closely followed by the fall of Communist control of the Soviet Union. Capitalism, it seemed, had "won."

4. New groups of inexperienced and uninformed people join the idea

Legend has it that Joseph P. Kennedy Sr. pulled out of the stock market in early 1929 (and thereby saved the family fortune) because a guy who shined his shoes one morning touted a stock that Kennedy himself owned. For crowd watchers like Kennedy, the shoe-shine guy provided the evidence that the crowd was getting too big. Too many people had jumped on the bandwagon.

The bandwagon phenomenon is created by a force, as some crisis scholars believe, called "informational cascade."[6] New groups of people seize on an idea simply because they see that other groups of people have been successful with it before. The information about the idea "cascades" from one group to another. And with each cascade, the information becomes more simplified. Each new group asks fewer questions, since there is so much "proof" of easy success. Latecomers to an idea just follow "pathfinders" without assessing the appropriateness of the idea for themselves. (The term "informational cascade" is really a polite rephrasing of "the blind leading the blind.")

To trace the progress of our current cascade, you don't need to have your shoes shined every day. Instead, as in the past, the promoters of the financial idea themselves will give the best clues on how widespread the idea is getting. This is because the promoters will become increasingly desperate to expand the circle of new recruits to keep the money coming in. This becomes particularly pressing after the surge of new money from a financial displacement has been absorbed into the financial idea. Afterward, the leaders of the financial idea try to keep up the inflow pace to match that first new-money surge. (Ultimately it is never possible.)

One way of expanding the circle of new recruits is by constantly lowering the "admission fee" to make it available to as many people as possible. During the 1920s and 1960s, investment trust sponsors and, later, mutual fund promoters kept lowering the initial investment requirements from a few thousand dollars to a few hundred and ever downward until near the end of each period they were pleading with potential investors to send in "just $10 a month." (It is an interesting question to consider whether speculative bond or stock markets are the best places for the money of people who have but $10 a month to put aside.)

As the sources of loose cash dry up, the next step is to try to convince people to make sacrifices in their lives to send even more money into the financial idea. Similar to the appeal from a TV evangelist with vague promises of a place in heaven, the promoters of the financial idea castigate the believers for not committing more of their resources to the idea. The appeal for the money is urgent, and people are made to feel actually irresponsible for not sending in more money immediately. (The urgency, of course, is the promoter's need to fulfill this month's sales goals.)

After this approach is tried, the leaders of the financial idea try to convince people to *borrow* money to send in to them. During the 1920s this was the *real* motivation behind Wall Street's heavy promotion to small investors of the joys of leverage and margin buying.

By 1993, many large mutual fund companies were already advertising initial investments of only $100, with additional investments of $50. Also by 1993 discount broker Charles Schwab and the brokerage arm of Fidelity Investments were letting customers buy shares of mutual funds on 50 percent margin, although promotion of the idea was not yet aggressive. Remember that it is the actions of leaders of financial ideas as they pursue their own insatiable greed that ultimately lead to crisis — not the actions of the "little guy" who looks to leaders for truthful guidance.

While lowering the admission fee, promoters will also try to target special demographic groups that traditionally have not been involved. This will include trying to get retired people out of their fixed-income instruments and into more lucratively priced aggressive growth funds. (The appeal will go: "You're living longer than ever. You *have* to take the long-term view of common stock investment.") Other demographic groups — geographic, racial, age, religious — will all come under special focus as the idea matures.

When we are told stories about the late days of the speculative frenzy of the 1920s, we often hear that near the end not only was the shoe-shine guy involved but so was the mail room kid. Today we laugh about the absurdity (yet poignancy) of this image. But by the middle of the 1990s, that mail room kid was back again actively speculating in the stock market, and in a manner that is a perfect example of how history can repeat itself exactly — but in a completely different way. In the late 1920s the mail room kid played the market directly — often with an easy-to-obtain margin account — in imitation of business leaders who appeared to be getting rich from these types of investments. Today that kid, instead of imitating the leaders, is being told by them that speculating in the market — via defined-contribution plans such as a company's 401(k) — is a good thing to do. In reality, however, business leaders are simply anxious to get that mail room kid involved as an inexpensive way of unloading the pension responsibility that business leaders had previously assumed off their shoulders and onto the shoulders of the uninformed and innocently unsuspecting — namely the mail room kid. And very likely, sixty years from now, when people of another generation look back on this episode, they will laugh with the same type of astonishment that we laugh at the deluded kid of 1929. That kid thought that the leaders knew what they were doing. And the kid today thinks the same thing.

The mutual fund promoters handling the money of the defined-contribution plans don't care what happens to the mail room kid. They just want his money. And they want to get it by providing only the sketchiest amount of information or guidance legally possible — both about their own products and about other possible options for that kid's money.

It should be noted that historically one of the final groups of people to be targeted as a special separate group are women. That doesn't mean that women haven't been involved from the beginning. (In fact about half of all mutual fund shareholders are women.) Rather, the promoters of the financial idea try to get *all* women to join in. The sales pitch here is to admonish women that by not taking an active role in their own financial destiny they are forsaking their independent right to personal wealth achievement.

In the late 1920s this calculated appeal manifested itself with souped-up articles on investment trusts that appeared in such magazines as *Ladies' Home Journal.* (Brokerage firms had, by the late 1920s, set up special "ladies parlors" for women who wanted to watch the progress of the advancing ticker.)

This was the case again during the peak of the 1960s mania when *Better Homes and Gardens* and other traditional "women's-interest" magazines started featuring bullish articles on the ease of mutual fund investment. A particularly telling — and cynical — how-to book published in 1967 for the throngs of mutual fund salespeople then actively canvassing friends and neighbors was titled *How to Sell More Mutual Funds — Especially to Women.*[7] If, then, you should notice that *Woman's Day, Family Circle,* or some other general-circulation "women's-interest" magazine is running an article extolling the simplicity of mutual fund investment, you'll know that there's not much life left in this financial idea.

5. Long-established standards of value and risk assessment are rejected

As each new generation gets its chance to swing the speculative bat, the "rules" of the previous generation become viewed simply as old-fashioned silliness. Prices rise to levels out of proportion to historical precedents. Investment techniques that had once been universally considered high-risk — such as margin buying, short selling, decrease in liquidity of portfolio, and high portfolio turnover — now become commonplace and seemingly risk-free.

In an attempt to get people to continue along a path of speculative action, promoters of the frenzy try to characterize these ever-rising prices and ever-riskier investment techniques as just part of the definition of a "new era." By the mid-1990s we were already seeing proclamations of an emerging "new economy" and claims of "new-age financing" that have gone along with the sloughing of "old-fashioned" investment policies and procedures at many mutual funds.

As the pronouncement of the "new era" becomes louder and more widely assumed to be true, the closer you'll be to discovering that it is not true. Often the final clue of the impending close of a "new era" comes when a leader outside the financial world heralds the speculative financial idea that is reflecting the "new era" as nearly risk-free. More often than not this comes from a political leader or government official. In January 1929, for example, President Calvin Coolidge confidently declared that stocks were "cheap at current prices." In 1967 it was Vice President Hubert Humphrey who told Americans that mutual fund investment was a great idea. Unlike Coolidge, who did not own any shares of common stock at the time of his firm declaration (or, indeed, at any other time of his life), Humphrey punctuated his endorsement of mutual funds with the revelation that he himself was a mutual fund shareholder. In each case the testimony of the leader was widely promoted by Wall Street to attract the money of the remaining holdouts.

6. Proliferation of new, "innovative" financial products

After the standards of the past are effectively destroyed, then comes an obsession with *anything* new. It is the very newness or the claim that something is "innovative" that becomes the primary appeal. It's thought of as "good" simply because it is new. The secondary appeal is that the new product offers a quick and wide road to riches. This was the dynamic, for example, behind the clamor for shares of new companies during the hottest days of the manias of the late 1960s, 1920s, and, in Great Britain, the late 1880s.

As pandemonium for the "new" increases, there also is an increase in the obsession for leverage instruments — margin accounts, futures, and options — all promising the accumulation of wealth and the control of large amounts of assets with the use of small amounts of actual money. (Whenever real estate has had its recurring periods of speculative mania, the obsession with leverage is proclaimed by promoters of the mania with the promise of success with "no money down." Watch for similar claims by mutual fund promoters.)

After the obsession with leverage gets digested into the consciousness, then you'll see the rising popularity of financial products that promise to hedge against possible losses. Hedge funds were popular in the late 1920s and late 1960s. They didn't work in either period. In the mid 1980s, as the stock market was heating up, "portfolio insurance" became a popular idea. That idea didn't work either when tested by the 1987 crash.

Behind this obsession with hedging techniques is, of course, the gnawing feeling — an accurate one as it usually turns out — that the pricing of the original products has gone beyond a level of reality. Much of the distorted pricing has been created by tricks — such as leverage — and therefore needs more tricks — such as puts and shorting — to save people from the effects of earlier tricks. That's how manias end up as a pileup of tricks upon tricks upon tricks.

Code words used by mutual fund promoters that will appear near the end of it all will be claims that funds are "using investment techniques designed to help protect you from sudden shifts in the market." The historical fact is that there really isn't any such investment technique that has ever worked on a large scale when actually put to the test. And it's not likely that anything "new" will deliver the goods this time either.

As mentioned previously (and repeatedly), with so many "derivatives" already being tossed about as supposed hedging products, it's impossible to identify exactly which one now promising to be the magic bullet to save everyone from disaster will actually be the fatal disappointment. But one of them will. And, again, the only way not to be trapped by it is to avoid *all* of them.

7. Involvement with the financial idea becomes fun and success easy

When speculative manias are in their early stages, strong concerns are voiced about the gathering tidal wave of enthusiasm for the idea. However, by the last leg of the mania, the accumulating "proof" of success after the destruction of past measurements of value and the introduction of "new" investment products quiets the nay-sayers. In fact, as the last leg turns the final bend, many of the former nay-sayers become converts to the idea. Initial concerns appear to have been unwarranted in the face of obvious success.

Often, the "pathfinders" who have been the first to adopt the idea leave it during the first stages of the gathering mania when everything seems to be reaching a high point. But then after it goes higher, the pathfinders *return* to it when it appears to be delivering even greater (and easier) success. (Those returning pathfinders often end up losing not only the gains they had made from their original involvement with the idea, but also the original stake they started out with.) At this point few people ask any questions, and an everybody-ought-to-be-rich giddiness takes over. The financial elixir that has eluded every generation since Adam and Eve has been found!

People who just a couple of years before didn't know their assets from a liability get caught up in the fun of it all by swapping success stories (and sometimes stories of isolated bad experiences) at parties, work, on the street, and at church socials. This fun attitude is often expressed by leaders of the financial idea itself just before the despair starts setting in. They, by this time, have become pretty cocky about their own powers and abilities to make money easily. Even leaders who previously may have issued words of caution now talk as if all is certain.

Incredibly, leaders of financial ideas often will acknowledge that the idea has gone beyond a breaking point but, curiously, find that it is all just part of the fun. For example, in the mid-1980s Ivan Boesky signed his name as author to a book, titled *Merger Mania,* that chronicled, with a sense of fun and adventure, his experiences as a power broker during the takeover/merger excitement of the 1980s. The book was later revealed to be riddled with lies after Boesky was arrested and his real activities were exposed. But the important thing is that at the time the book was published it provided the view that one of the principal players in the madness of the 1980s had readily embraced the concept of mania as a fun idea — as did, apparently, his publisher as well as the readers of the book — without any consideration of the consequences that has marked *every* financial mania in history. Boesky, however, was already in jail by the time it became clear how costly the mania he so joyously celebrated would be in terms of lost American jobs and defaulted debt.

By the early 1990s some mutual fund leaders were ready to say that the mutual fund idea had been pushed into mania. Some of them expressed concern. Others, however, found the situation exciting and challenging. In February 1993, the manager of Fidelity's Magellan Fund, Jeff Vinik, agreed with a reporter from the *Atlanta Journal-Constitution* that a mutual fund mania was in progress. He qualified this, however, by saying that "this seems to be just the beginning" and offering an assurance that manias need not be bad.[8] If Vinik's assessment was accurate, then, considering the fact that full-blown manias historically have a life span of no more than two to three years, that gives us 1995 to 1996 as dates to mark on our parlor game calendar.

8. *The financial idea becomes an object of ridicule*

It can be a short jump from the giddiness of fun to the absurdities of funny. Often, near the end of the maturing process of a mania the financial idea becomes the butt of jokes. Lots and lots of jokes. And these jokes are readily understood and laughed at by large, diverse groups of people.

This has been a feature of manias at least as far back as the South Sea Bubble of eighteenth-century England. When the South Sea companies were all the rage, popular comic songs and ribald poems about the companies expressed the jokey feeling of the time. This sense of ridicule culminated just before the bubble burst with the publishing of a pack of playing cards, called "Bubble Cards," that satirized in picture and verse the absurdities of the various companies. (Incidentally, South Sea Bubble cards are collectible items today. The South Sea companies may be gone, but the cards that made fun of them continue to have value.)

The reason that it becomes possible for comedians to joke about a financial idea as it reaches its maniacal peak is not that the idea becomes funny in itself or is somehow funnier than it was before. (Ridiculous, maybe. Funny, never.) Instead, the reason that audiences can laugh is that so many people are involved in the idea that there are enough people in a large audience to understand what is being made fun of. Comedians can make fun of something only when they are sure that the audience knows what they're talking about. And when the complex terms of a previously esoteric financial idea become so well understood that large audiences easily grasp jokes about it, then it is a symptom of that "wider and wider group of people seeking to become rich"[9] that defines mania. Not only has a large group come to understand the terms of the idea, they also have become so confident about it (see Milestone 7) that they are willing to laugh about it.

Historically, one of the places to find early signs of a good idea beginning to come under ridicule is the New York theater — which draws its audiences from a high concentration of people working within the financial world who are ready to laugh (confidently for a while) at their own foibles. In 1925, for example, the Marx brothers appeared in the musical *The Coconuts,* a stinging satire on the Florida land boom that opened just a few months before the boom's collapse. (As an aggressive Florida land salesman in the musical, Groucho announces: "Now is the time to buy. The new boom is on. Remember that old saying, 'A new boom sweeps clean.'") By 1929 virtually every musical, comedy, and vaudeville act (including Will Rogers) had some crack to make about Wall Street, stocks, bonds, and investment trusts. A generation later, at the peak of the 1960s stock market/mutual fund mania, a Broadway musical called *How Now, Dow Jones* kept audiences in 1968 laughing and singing along as it told the story of a bunch of fun folks trying to manipulate the stock market. The giddy go-go years would start to unravel later that year. In the late 1980s, New York audiences chortled over the capers of a ruthless corporate raider in the play (and later movie) *Other People's Money* that opened just months before the collapse of the junk bond market effectively ended the era of the corporate raider.

Sometimes the beginnings of financial panics that can accompany crises are likened to the image of someone yelling fire in a crowded theater. Perhaps a more accurate correlation between panic and the theater is that panics are often foretold by the theater itself when it yells fire through the satiric message on its stage. (At the beginning of 1994 a new Broadway musical spoof of Wall Street was announced for a spring 1994 opening. A sequel to the previous hit *The Best Little Whorehouse in Texas,* the new musical promised to satirize the idea of raising capital in *The Best Little Whorehouse Goes Public.*)

There's no need, however, to monitor the New York theater scene to sensitize yourself to signals of emerging ridicule. When you start hearing jokes about mutual funds on late-night TV talk shows or in situation comedies or see them in newspaper cartoons — those media intended to reach a large *general* audience and not a small financially oriented audience such as that of public television's *Wall Street Week* — it is a concrete sign that the idea is overpopulated. And if Alfred E. Newman should ever appear on the cover of *Mad* magazine fashioned after the image of a mutual fund manager or shareholder, you'll know that everything is nearly over, because if this financial idea ever gets viewed as that funny it will be no laughing matter.

9. Revelations of fraud

As anyone who lived through the 1980s knows, when a lot of money is being flung with little question at a financial idea, it is only a matter of time before the crooks move in. Unfortunately, crooks can get away with a lot before the actual nature of the dishonesty becomes known. Crisis scholar Charles Kindleberger calls this stage of impending crisis "the emergence of swindles." Other crisis scholars call it the period of "shady transactions." The more polite observers try to candycoat it a little with the simple label of an all-inclusive "abuse of trust."

Virtually every financial crisis in history has involved revelations of swindles. They have ranged from skimming off the profits of investors by leaders of the ideas — such as during the railroad frenzy prior to the Panic of 1873 — to simple embezzlement of the investors' money — a perennial favorite dating back to at least the South Sea companies and revisiting us during the 1980s savings and loan jamboree. Historically, these revelations usually start at the fringe of the idea, then invariably move to the center to focus ultimately on one or more of the foremost leaders of the idea. As we saw in the 1980s, such revelations brought down some of the biggest names on Wall Street. That experience, of course, was not unique to the 1980s. In the 1930s, for example, the unfolding scandals even featured jail time by the president of the New York Stock Exchange, Richard Whitney.

The up-and-down history of the investment trust/mutual fund idea has slavishly followed this pattern. The end of the British investment trust mania of the late 1880s was prompted by the collapse of the Baring investment trusts — first because of investment management error and later because of questionable placement of shares of "new issues" in the trusts that had been underwritten by the company's own brokerage arm.

At the end of the 1920s mania, the collapse in September 1929 of a giant British investment trust promoter called Hatry following revelations that the company had been issuing phony securities sent shock waves throughout the industry on both sides of the Atlantic. (Some historians claim that the Hatry scandal was actually the event that sparked the October 1929 crash.) Later, Americans had plenty of scandal-rife stories from among their own investment trusts to ponder.

In the late 1960s, first came questions about the valuation of "letter stock" and other illiquid investments of mutual funds. Then the collapse in the early 1970s of a previously successful mutual fund promoter called Investors Overseas Services (IOS) sent a new charge of shock waves through the industry. This mutual fund company, although forbidden by the Securities and Exchange Commission to sell shares of its many funds in the United States, had amassed millions by selling to Americans abroad — military personnel and expatriates. (Later the SEC banned all Americans from buying shares from IOS.) The whole thing was created by a colorful former social worker named Bernie Cornfield. The empire he put together included not only mutual funds but also banks, insurance companies, and other financial services companies. His company was also the one to create the 1960s version of a "fund of funds" that others copied to the later chagrin of shareholders after their collapse and eventual disappearance during the 1970s. Most of all, however, Cornfield is remembered for putting together an aggressive sales force that worked on a compensation program requiring the recruiting of more and more salespeople for a larger and larger cut of the money being brought in. It was a classic pyramid scheme — with little of the investors' money left over for actual investment. All this was accomplished under Cornfield's famous rallying cry "Do you sincerely want to be rich?" (This theme was revived and only slightly revised for a 1993 mail promotion campaign for Fidelity's *Worth* magazine with the tantalizing dare "Find out if you really want to be filthy rich.") When Cornfield was squeezed out of this setup in the early 1970s, another colorful character named Robert Vesco (a good friend of and campaign contributor to Richard Nixon) took over, making a big play about his intentions of putting the company back on its feet to save the money of so many investors. He used his time at the helm, however, to take what remained in the coffers before disappearing with it — apparently to a comfortable outpost in Costa Rica and later Cuba.

Later, another successful mutual fund promoter called Equity Funding collapsed after it was revealed to be a sham. Mutual fund shareholders — already shell-shocked by the collapse of these large companies and fearful of another shoe dropping — then started viewing smaller transgressions as major examples of abuse of trust. In 1971, for example, Fidelity lost a shareholders' lawsuit that revealed that the mutual fund promoter had been taking cash kickbacks from brokers on the commissions paid for the funds' securities transactions but charged to the fund shareholders for the full commission amount. Fidelity fought the lawsuit, claiming that the practice — euphemistically called "give ups" at the time — was legal and widespread throughout the industry. As accurate as that may have been, many small investors interpreted the action as unfair.

Of course, these and other events of the period prompted the reform. And as the mutual funds' unquestioned popularity waned and their assets shrank, the crooks found other venues — namely, the insurance game and the S&Ls.

By the late 1980s the mutual fund industry, compared to the chaos of other crumbling and scandal-ridden financial institutions of the 1980s, looked squeaky clean. The mutual fund industry had survived the decade virtually unscathed. By the early 1990s, however, cracks in the armor were already beginning to show. By early 1993 there had been several indictments, convictions, and government enforcement actions against a variety of mutual fund misadventures, ranging from illegal insider trading by fund managers to raw fraud via sales practices. And there had already been at least one discovery in 1993 of a "boiler-room" operation that had bilked over $1.5 million from people in forty-seven states by selling shares in nine fictitious mutual funds.

As of this writing, none of the actions was significant. In the larger scheme of things, all were petty crimes. But as Willie Sutton, the famous bank robber, once said of his interest in banks: "That's where the money is." In the 1990s, mutual funds is where the money is.

And Then the Crisis

Just as manias for financial ideas grow in a tierlike fashion, they decompose step-by-step in a way that is nearly as consistently followed. The disillusionment behind the breakdown almost never arrives in a single blow. Instead, the realization that the high hopes pinned to the idea were completely out of proportion to reality dawns slowly. But then the depth of the disillusionment reaches a point that almost always precisely mirrors the height of the previous illusion.

Crisis scholars sometimes refer to the height of financial illusion as an "error of optimism." This occurs sometime during Milestone 7. Conversely, they call the depth of the disillusionment an "error of pessimism." Both extremes are unjustified. But they never seem so at the time.

The beginning stage of the actual crisis — or disillusionment with the financial idea — is often prompted by a tightening of the money supply. Invariably, the mania focused on the financial idea was first launched by an easing of money — e.g., lower interest rates. (In crisis literature this is called "monetary expansion.") During the expansion period the leaders of financial ideas mobilize interest in the speculative pursuit of making money from money with the cry of "cash is trash." When, however, the money supply tightens — and interest rates rise in reaction to the overheated condition prompted by the money expansion — then "cash is king." The conversion to cash out of illiquid or noncash securities is sometimes a crash or a panic. But crisis need not feature a crash or panic. Sometimes it can just be a drift away from one idea to another — maybe over a long period of time.

This crash or panic or beginning of a drift often corresponds to some jolt, such as a revelation of fraud. Then the psychology of the crowd changes and a general weariness about the financial idea sets in. Those focused with enthusiasm or giddiness on an idea simply get tired of it. Giddy expectation succumbs to exhaustion — and, more important, disappointment. The "promises" turn out to be wrong.

Next, all the characteristics of the rise of mania are played in reverse. For example, just as positive events external to the financial idea affect perceptions of the future of financial markets, negative external events can affect markets when fatigue replaces euphoria. In the early 1930s every announcement of layoffs by big employers was interpreted as a negative sign of shrinking consumer buying power while such announcements of big layoffs in the late 1920s were interpreted, following the Wall Street perspective, as positive signs pointing toward productivity gains. On top of this, world stability, which was presumed to have been achieved after World War I, started unraveling in the early 1930s with the growing political chaos in Germany and Spain. Even Charles Lindbergh, who had served as such an important symbol of personal invincibility during the self-confident days of the late 1920s, became in the distraught year of 1932 a national symbol of personal vulnerability when his young son was tragically kidnapped and murdered.

The next generation experienced the same thing in the early 1970s. The "Great Society," the appearance of imminent victory in Vietnam, and the joyfulness of Woodstock gave way to riots and death on college campuses, retreat from Vietnam, Watergate, and a world held hostage by skyrocketing OPEC oil prices.

Confident Assumptions Overturned

One consistent characteristic of crisis is the realization — often startling for the people who must face it — that the single most certain, perhaps the most popular and unquestioned, aspect of the entire maniacal episode turns out to be the most fragile and unworthy of such confidence. In the 1920s, leverage and the powers of margin buying that had been used with such unquestioning aggressiveness — by amateurs and even more so by professionals — turned out to be the executioner.

As for investors' use of public investment pools overseen by "professional managers," a consistent reaction in the past to the excesses of managed portfolios was a switch to dependence on unmanaged investment decisions. In the early 1930s this bred the pursuit of "fixed-investment trusts." Typically, these trusts were set portfolios containing twenty stocks of the largest companies at the time — each making up exactly 5 percent of the portfolio. If the price of one of the stocks went up, that portion of the holdings for that stock would be sold and reinvested or paid out to the trust shareholders so that the portfolio would be always in perfect balance without any human intervention. As these fixed-investment trusts became more popular, they had a self-fulfilling impact on the prices of the twenty stocks. All the fixed-investment trusts were buying the same stocks. And, ultimately, this had the effect of raising the prices of those twenty stocks completely out of proportion to their actual value. Then this idea, too, failed. By the late 1930s few of the fixed trusts, so popular during the early part of the decade, were still in existence. (Today's unit investment trust is the direct descendant of this early-1930s idea — an idea that was revived in the late 1980s and generally was as disappointing as it had been sixty years before.)

Any financial idea that takes on a life of its own to the point where it distorts the valuation of the actual underlying investments can never continue forever without a reassessment event — either one of a short duration or one that extends over a long period of time. The prices that get inflated artificially because of the overuse of a financial idea *always* go back into relationship with reality sooner or later. Usually when a pricing distortion is caused by the popularity of such a simplistic idea as the fixed trusts of the early 1930s, the idea itself disappears when the moment of revaluation of artificially inflated prices back to a level of reality occurs.

In the early 1970s, a similar reaction to the mistakes of picking stocks during the "new issues" craze of the late 1960s, which brought down so many of the hotshot go-go fund managers, created another version of the fixed trust idea. The 1970s version, too, focused on large companies with proven records. This idea was nicknamed "Nifty Fifty," and it was aggressively followed by institutional investors. The Nifty Fifty game was based on a list of fifty favored stocks — including Avon, Johnson & Johnson, Tropicana, Polaroid, and Disney — that represented solid business growth histories, as opposed to the unseasoned companies that had been the rage in the late 1960s. The Nifty Fifty stocks were considered by institutional investors as "one-decision stocks." (They were really *no*-decision stocks.) You could buy them, the institutional investors thought, with no regard to their current prices or to overall market conditions. The projected future growth for the companies would even everything out over time. For a while, this approach worked as more institutional investors jumped on the Nifty Fifty bandwagon. The stocks of the Nifty Fifty outpaced the market in 1972 by 4 to 1. Ultimately the stock prices got elevated to at least 60 times earnings. (Disney got up to 80 times earnings; Polaroid up to 115 times earnings.) Then, of course, the idea collapsed. And today we laugh at the fools who were deluded by the idea. (Note, however, that even delusion can bring profits if you jump out in time. But most people don't. When you think you're getting rich, you only want more. Read: greed.)

Right after that idea collapsed, another antiprofessional management idea started taking form. This one was called Index Investing. If managers couldn't "beat the market" on a consistent basis against such benchmark measurements as the Standard & Poor's 500 list of leading American companies, then perhaps it is better simply to invest in the entire list of stocks making up the index.

Like the Nifty Fifty idea, index investing has become particularly attractive to institutional investors. The amount of money going into the stocks that make up various indexes is astronomical. For example, the top fifteen private and public pension plans alone nearly doubled the amount they put into indexes in the two years from September 1988 to September 1990 — from $76 billion to $144 billion. Like the institutional investor appeal of Nifty Fifty, the appeal today of index investing provides a ready excuse to shift the blame onto the markets themselves if anything should go wrong.[10] Without a management decision process, who can blame the manager for a mistake?

The early 1990s saw a scramble among fund promoters and financial information service companies to create new indexes. There was the S&P 400 Mid-Cap Index of companies not big enough to get on the S&P 500. The S&P 400 Mid-Cap was introduced in 1990. The stocks of that index were quickly bought up, and then other indexes were invented. By 1993, two indexes being touted were the Russell 2000 and the Wilshire 5000 — lists of 2,000 and 5,000 of the most actively traded stocks across all stock exchanges. With so much money trying to fit into the stocks of limited indexes, the solution was to put money in an index that represented the stocks of virtually every public company. This offered the ultimate in diversification — as well as a widened playing field that could take a while longer to fill up. Also, it saved those looking to avoid blame for decisions from picking the wrong index from among the many being invented.

By the early 1990s the popularity of index investing had clearly started to distort the original good idea into a classic example of financial self-obsession — an obsession completely unrelated to the actual reality represented by the businesses behind the stocks. Actually, index investing is really Nifty Fifty all over again except on a bigger scale. In the case of S&P 500 indexes, the scale is exactly ten times bigger than Nifty Fifty. (And with a Wilshire 5000 index, it's a hundred times bigger.) Maybe as an idea, S&P 500 index investing will last ten times longer than Nifty Fifty, which lasted for about two years. The first S&P 500 index fund got formed in 1976. Perhaps, then, you should underline 1996 on your parlor game calendar.

Advent of the Unknown

Just as the assumptions of the present — the "answers" that seem so right — turn out to be wrong, something offbeat, unnoticed, or dismissed will emerge as the "answer" during the crisis period to set us up for the next era. In the 1920s, the closed-end trust was the rage, then the problem. The unnoticed open-end trust, unscathed by the blame heaped on the closed-end funds, emerged as the next answer. After the 1960s debacle, the load funds got the blame, and the no-loads, nearly completely unheard of until the early 1970s, emerged as a viable alternative.

In the early 1930s, it wasn't as if there was anything essentially different in the investment pool structure between closed-end and open-end trusts except that the open-end trust had a policy of redeeming shares at net asset value. Still, this little segment of the investment company world captured immediate attention. For example, the Massachusetts Investors Trust had fewer than 300,000 outstanding shares at the time of the 1929 crash. But in the depths of the 1932 market, Massachusetts Investors Trust had nearly 1 million outstanding shares. The rapid good publicity about the trust attracted a lot of investors — as the most popular closed-end trusts of the late 1920s virtually disappeared.

The real reason that this and other open-end trusts of the time survived to become a model for a period of reform and rebirth was the tradition of conservative investment policy followed by these trusts. It could have been the other way around. The open-end trusts could have started life in the 1920s as the high-risk, high-leverage pools that the closed-end trusts actually became noted for. If so, today we might find the closed-end getting all the attention instead of the open-end.

Equally, in the aftermath of the 1960s go-go years, the no-load fund — which accounted for only about one-twentieth of the total assets of mutual funds at the peak of the 1960s mania — emerged as a viable alternative to the load funds not only because the no-loads were less costly, but because the no-loads had generally represented the "old-fashioned" conservative perspective while the load funds had to chase after every risky trick to try to justify the costliness of their funds. The no-loads then went on to capture over 40 percent of the mutual fund world. And today we are probably overlooking some obscure or easily dismissed idea that will become the next answer.

But before then how deep will the disillusionment — the crisis — go? What will it mean in lost dollars? Who knows. Could it be the same as the "average" mutual fund loss of 48 percent following the 1960s mania? Or the "average" investment trust loss of 92 percent after the 1920s mania? Or the "average" 60 percent loss for British investors after the nineteenth-century investment trust mania?

For mutual fund promoters, however, such considerations aren't as intense as they may be for the fund shareholders. By gradually raising fees charged shareholders over the last decade, the promoters have increased their average profit margins from about 33 percent on every fee-paid dollar to nearly 50 percent. Not only has this given the mutual fund industry a nice windfall during a period of incredible growth and popularity, it has also provided a comfortable buffer against sudden loss of fees. With a current 50 percent profit margin, today's highly successful mutual fund promoter could lose about half the total value of the assets under its management and still stay in business. And if such a thing should ever occur and you stick with the idea, you'll continue paying the fee. A lesson, as one learns when visiting Las Vegas or Atlantic City, that no matter how your fortunes turn out the "house" *never* loses.

CHAPTER 11

■ ■ ■

Winning Now...
And Bailing Out
in Time

If you are currently a mutual fund shareholder, it should be pretty clear to you by now that you are a participant in a financial phenomenon. There's nothing new or wrong about financial phenomena. They have been going on in one form or another for centuries. And they will continue to go on in different forms for centuries to come.

Don't think that anyone can halt the direction of our current phenomenon. It's already too late. It's beyond the control of any one person or even a group of people. Those people who could halt it — leaders of the industry who are profiting from the phenomenon and government officials who are encouraging it as a way of providing a general sense of financial well-being (albeit a temporary one) — do not have the motivational self-interest to halt it or even to control it.

The primary self-interest of the leaders of a financial phenomenon is simple: to "win" personally within the high-stakes, highly competitive environment of the phenomenon. These leaders are focused entirely in their day-to-day work on expanding the phenomenon and capturing the biggest amount of its market share to reap the personal reward that accompanies the biggest-possible market share. They don't care that as individuals their actions may be contributing, along with the actions of their compatriots, to building a crisis. And why should they care? Why should one individual act prudently within a phenomenon when phenomena do not reward prudence? We've seen this acted out repeatedly in financial history. The leaders of the investment trusts of the 1920s didn't care. The go-go guys of the 1960s didn't care. More recently, individual junk bond dealers didn't care. S&L executives didn't care. "Corporate raiders" and the investment bankers who encouraged them didn't care. And government officials and politicians certainly didn't care until, in typical fashion, the phenomena reached crisis points.

Faced with this knowledge, you yourself can do nothing about the phenomenon as it hurtles along toward its inevitable crisis except not to care either about what the broad consequences may be — who may be hurt or the effect it may have on the economy. All you should care about is squeezing the most out of this phenomenon for yourself (as leaders of the phenomenon are already doing) — and then making sure you've exited the phenomenon before it reaches its moment of crisis.

Starting Point

The single best strategy for getting the most out of our current financial phenomenon is to go to work within the mutual fund industry, because the quickest road to riches today, as it has always been, is the leapfrog shortcut over shimmering pools of other people's money. The second best strategy is to get on the receiving end of the money that fund managers are so freely throwing around. There are, for example, the job opportunities for overseeing American interests in all those "emerging global economies" that you have been hearing so much about. Also, with increasing relaxation of standards for issuing shares of newly public and, indeed, "unseasoned companies," your chances for getting some idea off the ground is greater now than ever — and as the obsession with new companies mounts, the wackier the idea the better. Just think, the bank that wouldn't give you a loan for a new or existing business, because it was considered too risky, can now open its arms to you as part of the "unseasoned companies" investment portion of the assets the bank manages in its mutual fund products. If you fail, few people will notice, nobody will really care, and you won't be punished as you would be if you default on a bank loan. And if the shareholders of the mutual fund lose some of their money because your idea fails, that's their problem. They should have read the fine print of the prospectus that told them how risky it was to invest their savings into "unseasoned companies." (See how much fun securitization can be?)

Barring these possibilities, however, you must start with this image in mind: You're standing in the middle of the railroad tracks and there's a train careening toward you at eighty miles per hour. You're playing a game of chicken with that train that could require some nimble footwork to avoid certain death. (If you don't care to play any part in this game of chicken, you need to move to another part of town. Review the options for your money in Appendix B. And get out of mutual funds now.)

One quick indication of your tolerance for playing chicken with the coming crisis is whether you picked up this book with the question in mind: *When* is the crisis going to happen and *when* should I get out? If that was your question — particularly if you turned to this chapter first looking for the quick answer — then you have actually answered your own question. While your head may be telling you that you have high risk tolerance, your emotional self is actually focused on low risk. If that's the case, then for you the simple answer to a simple When? is Now.

If you want to play for a while longer, you must review all your current mutual fund holdings in view of the risk exposure survival rules — as well as the cost rules — outlined in earlier chapters. If you are in a mutual fund that violates *any* of those rules, you're out on the edge. You're living on borrowed time. And no matter how well these funds may have performed for you in the past, get out of them now.

And if you're involved with mutual funds via a 401(k) retirement plan or some other type of defined-contribution plan and the choices and costs do not conform to these rules — or, worse, if you have not been given enough information to even know — then you had better start complaining to your company's management to get a decent plan. It's time to make a noisy fuss. Yell, scream, and stamp your feet, now.

Freed from Tricks

Once you get out of your involvement with funds packed with high-risk investment tricks or ones charging you exorbitant fees, you will have made a huge leap toward surviving the coming mutual fund crisis. You will have rid yourself of the garbage that in the early 1990s got heaped on top of the original good idea of the mutual fund. Remember that your involvement with mutual funds is simply a way for you to get convenient, diversified access to different investment markets — or segments of those markets. Mutual funds are not an end in themselves.

As an investor using mutual funds to reach different markets, you want to make sure that the fund or funds you choose represent those markets in their *purest* form possible. That's why, for example, as a survivalist, if you decide that a portion of your money should be earmarked for investment-grade bonds, make sure that you don't put that money into a fund simply passing itself off as representing the investment-grade bond market when in reality it is loaded up with 35 percent of junk bonds. Making a decision about being in investment-grade bonds is one thing. Making a decision about putting 35 percent of the money you want to allocate to bonds into *junk* bonds is quite another thing. And *you* should make the decision and not let a mutual fund promoter, through misrepresention of a fund's profile (whether "legal" or not), make the decision for you. That's why mutual fund survivalists have to be very, very careful — at least until the crisis is over and we enter another (refreshing) period of reform.

Once you have rid yourself of funds with sleight-of-hand tricks, then you have to make sure that you are involved only in those funds representing the investment markets that you are comfortable with — the funds that expose your money only to that amount of risk you fully understand and are willing to accept. After you've done that you have made another huge leap toward crisis survival, because when it comes to making the best decision about what to do with your money, the right decision is *always* the decision *you* feel is right based on your comfort level. That decision may or may not include mutual funds.

You can go wrong with your money only when you get yourself talked into something that you don't understand or something that vaguely promises extraordinary future rewards if you would only take on "just a little more risk." Remember that reward does *not* automatically follow risk. In other words, if you have no further risk tolerance than government-insured bank CDs or U.S. Treasury bills with varying maturities, then you have made a decision for your money that is *perfect*. And don't let anyone convince you otherwise — including the people working in your bank telling you to get out of those CDs and into mutual funds that the bank is selling.

Still, you don't have to isolate yourself solely in risk-free instruments to insure your survival. Actually, as you've most certainly discovered in your life, *nothing* is risk-free. There's always the chance (although seemingly remote as of this writing) that the government will halt insurance on existing bank CDs or even renege on paying interest on Treasury bills. It's just that the more you deviate from options as completely risk-free as CDs and Treasury bills, the more time and thought you'll have to put into understanding and assessing your investment decisions.

That doesn't mean, however, that you need to have your life consumed with learning and tracking the minutia of financial markets for rational and prudent involvement in a wider range of options — with a *minimum* amount of active fuss. A very basic — very conservative — avenue, for example, could be a portfolio of equal amounts of money divided into the following four savings/investment categories:

1. **Cash**

   - 100 percent Treasury money market funds

   - Short-term Treasury bills (thirteen- or twenty-six-week maturities)

   - CDs

2. **Intermediate-term U.S. government securities**

   - 100 percent government securities funds with average maturity no longer than eight years

   - Self-directed portfolio of Treasury bills, notes, bonds, or zero coupons with varying maturity dates (for example, equal amounts of money continually reinvested in two-, five-, and ten-year Treasury notes)

   - EE Savings Bonds

3. **Highest-quality commercial or municipal bonds**

   - Intermediate-term funds — with average maturity no longer than eight years — of highest-rated commercial bonds (for tax-protected portfolios) or municipals (for taxed portfolios)

   - Self-directed portfolio of highest-rated *uncallable* commercial or municipal bonds with varying maturities — including long maturities of twenty-five years or more

4. **Dividend-yielding stocks of U.S. companies**

   - Equity income stock funds without foreign holdings

   - Self-directed portfolio limited to dividend-yielding stocks of U.S. companies

With equal amounts of money committed to each of these categories — and readjusted once a year to keep the amounts equal — you will have a portfolio with very little likelihood of loss to original capital even during a mutual fund crisis. By emphasizing investment into income-producing instruments and minimizing exposure to speculative capital appreciation options, you achieve portfolio stability with a *minimum* amount of your time and thought.

In addition, the equal split among these four categories accommodates changes in different economic conditions. One or more of the categories will be "winning" at any point to counteract the possible negatives in other categories — while at the same time generally moving forward and upward with its delivery of a steady flow of compounding interest and dividend income. If inflation and interest rates rise rapidly, so will the relative returns on the short-term "cash" instruments compared to the longer-term government securities. The effects of recession and lowering interest rates will be eased by the intermediate U.S. government securities. An economic turn to deflation is offset by government securities as well as corporate or municipal bonds. And buoyant good times will be financially expressed by the general upward movement of the stock category, while, through an emphasis on dividend-yielding U.S. stocks, minimizing exposure to the shock of a major stock market setback or foreign market instabilities.

You'll notice that this portfolio division could be achieved successfully through mutual funds or, less expensively, on your own. Do as much as you can on your own — such as building your own government securities portfolio — before turning to mutual funds. (When you cook at home instead of going to a restaurant, it's usually cheaper and you always know how fresh the ingredients are.)

Beyond this basic approach, higher-risk additions could be made — for example, real estate investment. However, if you currently are a mortgage-paying home owner, you are already a real estate investor. And if you are like most Americans, this aspect of your financial commitment is already way out of proportion to your overall assets. If you are not encumbered by a mortgage, however, real estate — such as direct ownership of income-producing properties or dividend-paying real estate–oriented stocks or real estate funds (but *not* a mortgage-backed fund) — would add a further dimension to a portfolio of different broad *income-oriented* investment categories.

Several so-called all-weather mutual funds offer some type of variation on this approach of equal division of money in different broad investment categories. Although somewhat different from either a balanced fund, which usually sticks to a rigid division of 50 percent stocks and 50 percent bonds, or an asset-allocation fund, which gives the manager wide freedoms for moving money around based on market timing strategies, the all-weather fund that follows a set division of money among different investment categories may appear, like its close balanced and asset-allocation cousins, to offer a one-stop shopping choice. But, as with the balanced and asset-allocation ideas, it is more difficult for you to attempt to assess what a fund manager is doing with the different parts of a multifaceted fund under one umbrella than it is to choose different, more specialized, funds to fit each separate segment of this (or any other) portfolio. By choosing different funds to fulfill the specific characteristics of each category, you can be more certain that each choice meets all the criteria for that category. In fact, when you find the right specific fund for such a portfolio, you have to monitor the fund periodically to make sure that it hasn't changed its course. This is particularly important for a conservative fund that could get drawn into the growing speculative frenzy (as long as it may last before the crisis) to join in on high-risk tricks.

This approach of dividing your money equally among different broad categories — while making sure that you use only those mutual funds that represent the categories *purely* and without tricks — doesn't require that you know very much about the forces affecting any specific investment market category. You won't really have to know what's going on with interest rates, foreign trade balances, freezes on Florida orange crops, or any of the other large and small factors that push markets. All it requires is that you have the discipline to maintain the equal division no matter what may happen to the money in each category. Once you go beyond an approach as conservative as this, however, your game of chicken with that oncoming crisis gets more daring.

The Roar of the Crowd

When financial markets take on the characteristics of a speculative phenomenon, there are few hard-and-fast rules that can be used to measure that moment when you should jump off the rails. A true speculator — one who wants to test the absolute last moment before succumbing to a sense of self-preservation — is a momentum player. He or she is a person who doesn't mind buying high if there's a chance to sell even higher. This type of speculator, however thrilling the prospect of being one may be, is not a mutual fund survivalist.

Instead, a survivalist listens to the crowd. The louder the crowd yells, the more it adamantly claims that all is going higher, that all is different than ever before — the more you should retreat in the secure contrarian belief that whatever *everybody* is doing is wrong.

While the mutual fund phenomenon continues along on its path to crisis, mutual fund promoters will try to convince you and others that "everybody" isn't wrong. Charts will prove it. But fundamentally, the quality of investments — bonds, stocks, money market — will deteriorate to accommodate all the people so anxious to do the same thing at the same time.

And the more investment quality deteriorates — even if it appears that others are getting rich in the process — the more you must have the discipline to demand higher and higher standards for your money, while retreating into increasingly conservative arenas as others scamper to grab "easy" wealth. Your ability to time this retreat will depend on how well you read the crowd. But this is not a "timing" strategy. A timing strategy attempts to shift assets to try to find the highest returns possible based on shifts in markets. A mutual fund survival strategy is reading shifts in risk exposure in order to abandon markets that get too treacherous. You'll have plenty of time after the crisis to practice more aggressive pursuits of making money from money — when the herd moves on to some other elixir and the quality of investment options improves.

The retreat you may want to make with your bond investments will depend on the direction of interest rates along with continual review of the creditworthiness of your bond fund holdings and average maturity dates. (Your money market commitments should be limited to mutual fund survival rules now. There is no room for "speculation" on money market commitments.)

Your continued stock market involvement — assuming that you don't plan to weather a possible storm by remaining entirely within the most conservative, dividend-yielding portfolio — can be the most difficult moment to seize. (Keep in mind, however, the old adage: It's better to be one year early than one minute late.)

At the end of major stock market bulls, the crowd can roar convincingly for quite a long time. In fact, one of the great dangers faced by otherwise prudent investors of the past is to evacuate a heated market and then jump back in at an ever higher price when others seem to be getting rich with ease. For those uncomfortable with such a seemingly vague way of making a decision about when to shift money, there are a couple of numerical measurements of market tops that have served as consistent past rules of thumb:

- **Price/earnings ratio of S&P 500 goes over 20.** When the stock market as a whole is priced so that it is selling for 20 times reported earnings from the previous four quarters, it is getting into historically untested territory. Prior to the October 1987 crash the S&P 500 p/e ratio was 21. This figure is widely reported, including weekly in *Barron's* and in the Monday edition of the *Wall Street Journal*. Take it seriously.

- **Dividend yield of S&P 500 goes below 3 percent.** The amount people are willing to pay for stocks with dividends goes up during market tops — resulting in a lower dividend yield.

Although these are two very simple numbers, don't ignore them. Price/earnings ratios may go higher. They will certainly go higher within certain segments of the market. But they have *always* come down from these levels — and the higher they go above them, the farther they fall.

During the great bull market in Japan during the 1980s, that market's p/e ratio ultimately got to 60. At that time, financial experts were declaring that Japan was operating on an entirely different set of rules of market valuations. Entire books were written about how different it was. And, indeed, it was different for a while. But the bubble started bursting in 1991 and continued bursting until, by the beginning of 1994, the p/e ratio of the Japan market was 10.

Just as there are numerical identifiers for the top, there are identifiers for bottoms. Don't worry about not having a chance in your lifetime to experience the good buying opportunity of the grim times that these guidelines represent. That time *will* come. But you will be able to take advantage of it only if you have the money to do so.

- **Price/earnings ratio of S&P 500 goes under 12.** Few people will be touting stocks — and certainly mutual funds — when the S&P 500 hits such a p/e ratio. At the lowest point of the 1970s bear market, specifically December 6, 1974, the p/e ratio was 4.8. There was no problem getting a seat at a Wall Street lunch counter in those days.

- **Dividend yield of S&P 500 goes above 5 percent.** During bear markets the aversion to stocks is reflected in the higher percentage dividend yield. The dividend yield at the December 6, 1974, bottom was a hefty-seeming 7.8 percent. (It didn't seem like such a great return at the time because interest rates on no-risk instruments were higher. But in the 1990s this was the date that mutual fund promoters always referred to, as in "If you had only put $10,000 into the market in 1974 . . .)

A bear market that could deliver these types of bargain-basement levels could take a long time to develop.

And don't believe that a market drop is necessarily a good time to jump back into the market. It will depend on the mood of the crowd. If the drop is widely viewed as a buying opportunity, then it probably isn't. If it's viewed as the mark of the end, then the crowd is probably wrong again. After the crash of 1987, the common view was that that event marked the end of the bull market. The further drop in 1989 confirmed it for the crowd. The 1991 rebound was a "surprise."

Back in the 1960s, the market drop in 1962 was widely considered the signal of the end of the 1950s bull market. The subsequent rebound was a "surprise." Then the market drop of 1966 was viewed as the end. This view was also proved wrong with the 1967–68 rebound. But now conditioned by rapid rebounds from market drops, small investors shrugged off the 1969 decline and pumped the greatest amount of money into stock mutual funds in the industry's history as they sought to take advantage of market "bargains." The 1969 decline was actually the forerunner of the decade-long bear to follow.

Typically, it takes 12 to 18 months of feeble rallies and ever-deeper drops for a bear market to show its full furry face and big teeth. And, thus, another old adage: The most successful investor is usually the one who knows when to do nothing. And yet another adage: It's not how much you make on paper that counts, it's how much you get to keep.

Ridiculous Notions

In the time left before the coming mutual fund crisis, your decision about when to increase or decrease your exposure to speculative markets — or, perhaps more important, when to do nothing — should be focused on the opportunities or dangers of those markets. Don't be dissuaded from this view by claims from mutual fund promoters (and the financial advisers who parrot the promoter's expensively prepared publicity handouts) that looking at established measurements of market risk — such as p/e ratios and dividend yields — is not worthwhile.

Mutual fund promoters have over the years come up with a couple of clever ways of getting you to ignore immediate and long-term market risk and keep sending in more money, particularly into their highest-risk products, which also happen to be their biggest profit makers, for as long as possible. These little marketing mind games sound logical until you look at them closely.

One popular gimmick of the early 1990s was to try to convince you that asset allocation of your money should be determined based on your age. No doubt you have seen the pie charts showing different versions of the asset-allocation formulas. Typically, they show that younger people should have a higher percentage of assets in high-risk investments — aggressive stock growth funds, for example — while older people reaching retirement age should lower their exposure to speculative stocks and allocate an increasing percentage to income-producing vehicles. Also typical of the asset-allocation-by-age formulas touted by mutual funds is that the vehicles you are told to use are invariably limited to mutual fund products. For example, an older investor may be told to put a percentage of assets into a government bond fund, but is never told how easy — and less expensive it is — to own government securities directly.

Seemingly, the asset-allocation-by-age formulas can be applied as a template to anyone within a specific age group. Thus, for example, people in their early forties — with twenty years or so to go before retirement — are assigned a typical template allocation of 50 percent in conservative or blue-chip stock funds, 25 percent in aggressive or "small cap, emerging" stock funds, 10 percent in a corporate bond fund, and 15 percent in foreign stocks or bonds. (Some template schemes tell people in their twenties and thirties to hold 80 or 90 percent in stocks.) Then, when these folks reach their fifties, an adjustment is made to lower their stock ownership to a total of 35 percent (emphasizing dividend-paying stocks) and boost their ownership of various income-producing funds — corporate bond, municipal bond, government bond, and money market.

These asset-allocation-by-age ideas make the assumption that each stage of the investment will be successful, that, indeed, the heavy commitment to stocks by people in their forties will without question achieve such satisfactory returns that they will simply move the money over to another style of investment when the calendar page gets flipped over and friends and relatives are gathered around singing "Happy Birthday." This is a ridiculous and dangerous assumption.

An ever-fluctuating speculative market does *not* deliver success just because it would be convenient for you based on your age. Speculative markets are unflinchingly cold and uncaring of your personal needs and expectations. Making a commitment of cash assets as large as 50 to 90 percent of your money to the stock market, as many of the asset-allocation-by-age schemes suggest, should not be based on *your* age but rather on the age of the markets. Your age is irrelevant to such a drastic decision. Just because you happen to be young (or youngish) and feeling spunky and aggressive doesn't mean that the stock market (or any other single speculative market, whether gold or real estate or pork bellies) is going to naturally accommodate that spunky feeling to the unquestioned tune of 50 to 90 percent of your money. There *may* be a point during your life when 50 to 90 percent of your money would be well situated in the stock market. That could happen, for example, when a wobbly-legged newborn bull starts to stumble out of a dark bear cave. But when and if that happens, it will have nothing to do with your age.

The mutual fund floggers make the age-allocation idea sound logical by pulling out the old, trusty charts showing that the past "worst-case" experience of stock market investing is a "breakeven" of a duration no longer than fifteen years — and usually five or ten years at most. (This isn't entirely the truth, however. The hypothetical investors who went into the stock market at the peak of the 1929 madness and broke even fifteen years later, in 1944, were those who had dividend-yielding stocks. It was the accumulated dividends paid out over the fifteen years that got those hypothetical stockholders back to the breakeven point — not the recovery of the stock prices themselves, which didn't occur until 1954. In addition, in 1929, dividend-yielding stocks were objects of scorn belittled as suitable only for the weak-kneed. The hot idea of 1929 was the pursuit of pure capital appreciation on non-income-producing stocks. And, as a result, the losers of 1929 were losers forever. The same was true of the losers of the 1960s go-go fever.) Today, however, by assuring you that all setbacks will be settled in the future with "just a little bit of time," the fund promoters hope to make the risks seem distant and remote.

But here's the raw bottom line on tying up 50 to 90 percent of your money in one place for fifteen years — or for five or ten years for that matter: "breakeven" ain't good enough. And when the time comes when it looks as if there won't be a "breakeven" for five, ten, or fifteen years, after, for example, you see the value of your holdings cut in half, you won't stick around — no matter what your intentions for toughing it out may be today — because whatever would cause the stock market to experience such a blow will spark another financial idea into life. And then all the people who are telling you today that you should commit your money to stock funds, stock funds, stock funds (the same people, you may recall, who told you CDs, CDs, CDs ten years ago, and told you gold, gold, gold a few years before that) will be pushing some other blueprint for wealth achievement. They will also try to make you look like a fool for not having started in it earlier. (You know how they will put it: "If ten years ago you had only put $10,000 into . . .")

Actually, many fund promoters who push the asset-allocation-by-age concept don't really believe it themselves, because while they present this idea out of one side of their mouths, out of the other side they are trying to sell you their asset-allocation fund, which bases its shifting allocation formula on the progress of different advancing market conditions, not on the progress of your advancing age.

A more suitable idea for young (or youngish) people putting money aside for retirement but who do not have the interest or inclination to watch the broad forces that push markets is to put that money into the most conservative, capital-preserving, income-earning options to build a solid nest egg *without* speculation. Then when you get into your fifties you can take that nest egg and be in a better position to judge the "age" of various speculative markets *at that time* to get the most out of the nest egg during the countdown years to retirement. In addition, by that time perhaps you'll have enough life experience — particularly with investment companies — to have a skeptical eyebrow permanently raised.

But in the meantime, *please* don't just blindly commit 50 percent or more of your money to *any* single fluctuating financial market — whether stock, commercial bond, municipal bond, or any other, including a fund that represents the market of long-term government securities — without knowing a lot about that market (far more than you can get from this book) and being willing to watch that baby very carefully.

Another ridiculous idea that seems reasonable on first hearing but can crumble in practice is "dollar cost averaging." This idea, like the age-allocation idea, fits neatly in with a fund promoter's self-interest of seeking a constant inflow of new money that is blindly and automatically handed over by unquestioning "investors." The dollar-cost-averaging pitch goes like this: By committing the same amount of money to a fund at regular intervals (the fund guys would like it monthly, but they'll settle for quarterly) you end up purchasing some shares when prices are high, but more shares when prices are low. After a while, then, the overall price you pay ends up being "averaged" to a price lower than the shares' actual average market price. To be successful with this idea you are supposed to ignore completely current market valuations and market fluctuations. You are to commit money continually with the secure faith that over time (five years? ten years? fifteen years?), whatever happens, the stock market will eventually recoup its position and grow on. That's the theory.

The reality of a well-intentioned dollar-cost-averaging program is that you will commit to it during fair weather, when things seem to be going generally in a good direction, but when bad times come you will continue for only a short time as the value of your holdings goes down and it starts looking like you are just throwing good money after bad. At that point you will sell in an attempt to cut your losses. And the result will be that you will have bought high and sold low.

This was precisely the experience of many small investors when the idea of dollar cost averaging was tried on a grand and formal scale in the 1960s. During the mutual fund mania of that era, one of the most popular ways of mutual fund "investing" was via monthly payments to a fund under a "contractual plan." Sold in ways similar to an insurance policy, the contractual plan featured an actual signed promissory contract that committed an investor to monthly installments over a set period of time — usually ten years — toward a set total "investment" of, for example, $1,200, or $120 a year. Since these plans were sold by salespeople, they carried a front-end load (usually 8½ percent). The special ugly feature of the concept was that the sales charge for the entire anticipated ten-year commitment had to be paid up in the first few years of the contract — with up to 50 percent of the total sales load coming out of the first year's monthly "investments." This meant, of course, that little of the money being sent in every month actually got to be invested until the third or fourth year of the installments.

Yet this idea made sense to a lot of people in the go-go 1960s when the market was booming and mutual funds were booming bigger. In 1961 about 12 percent of all mutual fund shareholders were in some type of contractual plan. And by the end of the 1960s over 40 percent of all shareholders were investing monthly under these plans. The investments ended, however, during the bear market of the 1970s. And by 1980 the contractual plan idea had virtually disappeared. (Tellingly, this idea was brought out of mothballs in the early 1990s and promoted with particular gusto to young, financially inexperienced people on military bases.) Very few investors in the 1960s and 1970s completed the contractual plans. Studies show that between 30 and 50 percent of people drop out of contractual plans in the first two years. Many states now have laws that force fund promoters to pay back most of the heavy load charges to people if they drop out in the first two years.

The failure of the contractual plan (and the idea of dollar cost averaging that it represented) is one of the reasons you probably have never heard of an actual living person who started investing in mutual funds during the height of the mutual fund craze of the 1960s and who then continued along with a dollar-cost-averaging program throughout the grim days of the 1970s to emerge during the 1980s and into the 1990s with great (and easy) wealth. Where are all these hundreds of thousands — in fact, millions — of people now in their seventies who were made into multimillionaires by mutual funds because thirty years ago while in their forties they actually did what mutual fund promoters say you should do automatically month after month? Did even one person really do it? Not likely. And you won't either.

Here's the lesson. Dollar cost averaging — or a less rigid program of simply staggering investment commitments over an extended period of several months or more — is a fine strategy as a way of easing gradually into a fund (or funds) when it makes sense to do such a thing: when things, for example, favor entry into a market or segments of a market, as when speculative markets are depressed and there appears to be a reason to expect a recovery. But blindly committing a set amount to any market without periodic appraisal of the maturing "age" of the market will disappoint you as surely as it disappointed so many people who got talked into contractual plans in the 1960s.

That doesn't mean, however, that you should avoid forced *savings* through a 401(k) or other automatic method of putting money aside. It only means that you should not commit to forced investing (or, perhaps more accurately, speculating) without a little bit of sensitivity to the issues of timing — even rough timing.

Diverting Attention

While trying to get you to hand over your money automatically and blindly without considering the risks, the mutual fund guys (and their advertising and public relations agencies) will also try to get you to focus on one set of issues — namely those that may play on your sense of fear or greed — to keep you from looking at other issues, such as the risks of the products they are trying to talk you into or the actual appropriateness of those products to your financial needs. No mutual fund survivalist can afford to let his or her guard down against their persuasive half-truths.

There is a consistent set of investment themes that you will be bombarded with — themes repeatedly hammered during past peaks of mutual fund/investment trust manias. Those themes are inflation, education expenses for children, retirement, "new" company investing, and international investing.

Inflation

The whole concept of inflation and its potential to erode your spending power — either out of your pocket today or from the money you've put aside in savings for the future — has to be kept in perspective. First, inflation, particularly as projected by mutual fund promoters in bar charts showing a mountain of ever-rising bars, is not to be feared in the sense that your life is going to be ravaged because of some sudden and unexpected leap in inflation rates. When inflation goes up dramatically, as those who lived and worked through the 1970s and early 1980s know, personal income generally goes up along with it, and so do interest rates on fixed-rate financial instruments (such as CDs and government securities).

There may, however, be a time delay between rising inflation rates and your experience of rising income — either via employment income or fixed-rate investment income. But, equally, when inflation rates go down, the general direction of your employment income as well as your fixed-rate investment income usually will lag as well. (Many people in the early 1990s still had high-yielding CDs and other fixed-rate products that kept on paying a high rate long after interest rates dropped.) During your lifetime fluctuating inflation rates will hurt you at some times and benefit you at other times. But over the long haul gains and losses will even out so that you should be able to plan and adjust your life accordingly. So just because someone shows you a chart projecting that a loaf of bread will cost $5.00 in twenty years, it doesn't mean that you will have to buy that loaf of bread with today's money — no matter what income you may be making or where you may be putting your savings today.

Before you become agitated about inflation and your savings or investment returns, remember that the primary goal in your search for return should focus on *real rate of return*. Real rate of return is defined as your aftertax return minus the inflation rate. Historically, achieving a 1 to 3 percent real rate is great. When, back in the 1980s, you were getting no-risk interest rates on bank CDs of 10 percent, the inflation rate was 7 or 8 percent. Not much of a spread. As of this writing the inflation rate stands at a little over 3 percent and the average money market rate is just under 6 percent. That's not going to make you rich. But it's a spread similar to the one you got back in the high-interest/high-inflation days.

The question of investing to beat inflation became clouded in the early 1990s when so many retired people saw interest rates drop in half in tandem with a drop in inflation. The problem for these people was not inflation, even though mutual fund promoters tried to imply that it was. The problem was that ten years ago, when individuals were making plans about a retirement life-style, the interest rates being paid on no-risk and low-risk products were assumed to be the type of returns that could be expected perpetually. If you were one of those people, the assumption you made about that interest income was not your fault. Very few people were predicting that interest rates would fall so dramatically — even though those rates were at the highest level at any time in financial history. (The mistake made — a mistake that can be made today as well — is assuming that whatever happened in the recent past is an indication of what will happen into the foreseeable future and beyond. Actually, it is more consistent to expect the complete opposite in the future of what occurred in the immediate past.)

Certainly, the bankers who sold you CDs ten years ago and told you to stay away from mutual funds were wrong. And just because those bankers can sell mutual funds today (when they couldn't ten years ago) doesn't mean that their telling you today to go into mutual funds and stay away from CDs reflects any better idea (beyond their own self-interest of making money from your money) of what the future will bring in the next ten years.

As difficult as it may be, the most important thing for you to do is not to change your risk tolerance just because you want more money. If you wouldn't do something ten years ago because you thought it was too risky for you, there is no reason to change that risk perspective. The inherent riskiness of different options that you thought were too risky for you ten years ago has not changed in those ten years. In fact, the riskiness of those options actually has increased because so many more people are trying to get so much more blood out of the same rock and the quality of the rock has deteriorated.

As we progress toward the mutual fund crisis, you shouldn't worry as much about inflation eroding your savings as you should worry about the risk you expose those savings to that could "erode" your money in an overnight vanishing act. Once you refocus attention away from what you would *like* to get on your money back to the real issue of inflation, such conservative instruments as money market funds, ninety-day Treasury bills, and even EE Savings Bonds historically beat inflation by a respectable real rate of return.

Mutual fund people don't want you to know that. They prefer that you believe that their most aggressive (and lucrative, for them) products — namely, pure capital appreciation stock funds and "high-yielding" bond funds — would do a better job of it. Certainly, you've seen the charts showing how, over the last seventy years, stocks — as represented by a hypothetical "average" rather than any real-life experience — outperformed other alternatives as an inflation hedge.

While that may be true over such a long period of time, stock market investing has a decidedly uneven history when it comes to beating inflation over shorter periods. During those time periods that may actually match a living person's realistic savings/investment life span, which is almost always far shorter than seventy years, the stock market is not always cooperative. Actually, in the war against inflation, the stock market is a fair-weather soldier, going up when things are generally "good" — that is, when inflation is "normal" or the inflation rate is falling.

But when things turn bad, when inflation heats up — either in real terms or when there is simply *anticipation* of higher inflation — then the stock market generally goes into a bearish mode. (The fair-weather-soldier personality of stocks is a thorny aspect of stock market investing that is always evident when things in the world are generally going poorly. During periods of distress — such as the onset of war or when the economy is experiencing either high inflation or deflation — the distress usually shows up in the stock market's behavior as it beats a retreat.)

For example, a portfolio of the S&P 500 stocks purchased during the closing days of the 1960s mutual fund mania at the end of 1969 (a purchase that actually could not have been made, since the first index fund of S&P 500 stocks was not started until 1976) would have delivered by the end of 1979 an advance of only 4.8 percent for the entire decade. The dividends on that portfolio would have brought the total return to 53.8 percent. That works out to a compound yearly average of only 4.4 percent. During that decade the inflation rate averaged 7.4 percent a year and ninety-day T-bills delivered an annualized 9.6 percent. (Even as late as 1989, T-bills paid 8 percent when the inflation rate was 4 percent.)

Even over longer periods of time stocks don't provide a spectacular difference considering the unknowns involved. For example, from the end of 1971 to the end of 1991 the S&P 500 stock index provided an annualized return of 11.9 percent. Over the same time frame, intermediate-term Treasury notes (ten-year) had a 9.4 percent annualized return and ninety-day Treasury bills delivered 7.7 percent. The inflation rate during the period averaged 6.3 percent.[1] Obviously, stocks during this period — a period that included one of the biggest bull markets of all time — did very well against inflation. However, the stock investment delivered its full punch against inflation only to those people who had all their money fully invested in stocks throughout the entire twenty-year period. And you can be sure that nobody in the world during this period, which included the worst bear market since the 1930s, had all of his or her money in stocks. More realistically, an investment portfolio would have been made up of, for example, a collection of one-third in stocks (with an 11.9 percent annualized return), one-third in ninety-day Treasury bills or equivalent, such as a money market account (returning 7.7 percent annualized return), and one-third in ten-year Treasury notes (returning an annualized 9.4 percent).

With such a portfolio, however, you will notice that the most conservative portion — the ninety-day Treasury bills — canceled out the most aggressive portion — the stock portfolio — to deliver a return nearly exactly the same as if 100 percent of the money had been put into the middle-road investment — ten-year Treasury notes. This isn't to say that some other time frame would have seen the stock portfolio carrying more of its weight against inflation, but don't let anyone tell you that you *have* to have a stock portfolio — particularly a high-risk portfolio — to beat inflation. Generally, an intermediate-term Treasury portfolio can do the job.

If you have a long-term perspective, you don't even need to go through the bother of putting together a Treasury portfolio — or certainly paying a fee to be in a bond fund, because the good old EE Savings Bond can do all that you need. The Savings Bond pays a variable interest rate tied to Treasury securities. During the first five years of holding the bond, you are paid interest every six months equal to 85 percent of six-month Treasury bills, and after the first five years you get 85 percent of five-year Treasury notes. In addition, the government guarantees to double your original purchase price in the seventeenth year of holding the bond if it had not already doubled by that time. At an annual rate of 5 percent a double is reached in fourteen and a half years; at 6 percent it doubles in twelve years. (If you don't think that a guaranteed seventeen-year double is good enough, remember that no one who went into any stock mutual fund beginning in any year during the bull market period from 1956 through 1968 had a double seventeen years later.) In addition, the interest is free of state and local taxes and tax-deferred from federal taxes for as long as you hold the bonds. You can hold them for thirty years and convert them to HH Savings Bonds for another ten years. If used for college education purposes, the bonds cashed in are completely tax-free depending on adjusted gross income if used that year to pay tuitions for college, university, or authorized technical school.

In the war against a period of rapidly rising inflation, however, the single biggest cannon is gold. Although few investment markets are as volatile as gold, the metal has consistently shown its true worth at exactly those times of distress — such as inflation or war or deflation — when the stock market (and often the corporate bond market) heads south. Even a small portion — as small as 5 percent — of gold as part of a large portfolio ($100,000 or more) can help hedge against steep drops in the value of other parts of a portfolio. Gold won't have this power, however, if it is bought after it becomes evident that it is needed. Like nearly all speculative decisions — and gold is a highly speculative option — the best path is to buy low (when gold is out of favor and prices are depressed) and not when the herd is rushing to buy because a general-interest money advice magazine is featuring it on its cover this month.

Education Expenses

In the early 1990s mutual fund promoters, along with the cooperation of supposedly disinterested investment advisers, started heavily promoting the idea of putting money aside for children's education via stock and bond mutual funds. This pitch, however, is another example of mutual fund promoters who have been rummaging in the "good ideas" attic. It is a carbon-copy revival of one used during the 1960s mutual fund mania.

The investing-for-college theme was popular in the 1960s, of course, because of all those baby boomers who had to be sent through college. And in the 1990s there are now the kids of the baby boomers — the mini-boomers — with minds to be molded in our colleges and universities a decade or so from now.

Here's how a book called *The Money Managers: Professional Investment Through Mutual Funds,* published in 1967 (under the auspices of the mutual fund industry's professional organization, Investment Company Institute) at the peak of that era's mania, addressed the college cost issue:

> . . . college costs are still rocketing skyward. Rexford G. Moom of the College Entrance Examination Board has predicted that by the late 1970s they will reach $12,480 for four years at a state university [up from $6,000 in the mid-1960s] and more than $20,000 at a private school [up from $9,100]. None of these figures includes such additional expense items as books, clothing, travel, allowance, and the like. A family with three children may thus face a college-education bill amounting to about $25,000 and as much as $60,000 in the late 1970s. A substantial group of mutual fund shareholders are justifiably concerned about this trend and are trying to do something about it.[2]

Sounds familiar, huh?

For the parents in the late 1960s who followed the example of this "substantial group," things didn't turn out as expected by the late 1970s. By that time four years of public university education, from 1977 through 1980, would actually cost $16,000, and private college would cost $37,000.[3] But an investment into any mutual fund during the late 1960s would not have gotten anyone anywhere by the late 1970s. In the fall of 1977 the Dow stood at almost the precise level as in the fall of 1967. (And, don't forget, few mutual funds then or today — including index funds — match, let alone beat, the market.) Moreover, as mentioned previously, in terms of inflation the stock market peaked in 1966 and declined thereafter for seventeen years before beginning in 1982 a new period when it regained its status as a positive inflation hedge.

By 1993, however, the 1960s advice of putting money into high-risk stocks as a "savings" vehicle for college expenses was being promoted with equal assurance and made to sound just as easy and risk-free. Here's a quote from a widely circulated investment advice book published in 1992: "Growth funds emphasize long-term gains. You can transfer profits from riskier funds into safer ones as your child gets closer to college age. Regular contributions are convenient, and may even be arranged as a payroll deduction."[4] Like the asset-allocation-by-age gambit, this advice begins with the assumption that there *will* be profits when needed. And, again, that's quite an assumption! It was the same assumption — incorrect as it turned out — made back in the late 1960s.

Don't let yourself be lulled by that assumption, because today, as in the 1960s or any other decade, as far as putting money aside for children's education expenses goes, a mutual fund representing any type of fluctuating market — whether bond, gold, stock, or commodities — is the *worst* place for it. The kid can't wait for markets to rebound to start school. Despite whatever interest rates may be today, traditional savings instruments for college expenses that are certain to deliver or to mature at a set date at a set amount are still the best — EE Savings Bonds, zero coupon bonds, T-bills, T-notes.

You'll be far better off — and happier in the long run no matter which way speculative markets may go in the next decade or so — buying boring Savings Bonds monthly, for example, than taking a crap shot on the stock market with your child's future. Even if you're not able to put enough aside or get enough fixed interest to pay for all the college costs, it's still better than watching it vanish as some hotshot fund manager gambles it away. The child probably shouldn't get a totally free ride anyway. Did you?

Retirement

One common pitch used by investment companies to get you to allocate more of your money to their control is their time-honored portrayal of your future decline into lonely, poverty-stricken old age. (This is the one that hooked a lot of people into high-risk gambles during the investment trust days of the 1920s, when so few Americans had any type of retirement assurance.) The more fear they can instill in you to get you thinking that you need to achieve and lock up your retirement wealth *immediately,* the more likely you are to buy into the most risky types of investment pools — which are usually the most lucrative (and fun) types of pools to run.

The particular fear that mutual fund promoters currently are trying to exploit is that the Social Security program as we know it today will not be around for a decent payoff by the time baby boomers are ready to retire. To save yourself from such a grim prospect, the mutual fund floggers say, you had better start aggressive commitments to stocks, stocks, stocks by sending your money into them, them, them.

While no responsible person could expect to live on Social Security alone, the Social Security issue, like the inflation issue, needs to be put into perspective. Like any other argument used to whip up your sense of fear (or greed), don't let this one get your goat so much that you allow yourself to be talked into taking on more risk than you feel comfortable with.

Simple numbers are on your side. If you are a baby boomer, by the time you are ready to start collecting those monthly checks you will be part of the most powerful voting block of people this country has ever known. If you think that your parents have political clout today to get inordinate retirement benefits from the government, just wait and see how good the benefits will be for the baby boomer generation. They will likely be much, much better than today's. (If Social Security benefits are declining today, it's because the biggest voting block is among tax-paying baby boomers who don't want to foot a big bill for their parents. That attitude will change when baby boomers decide it's time to get *their* entitlements. Then there will be no compunction about bleeding dry the tax-paying Americans who today are teens and toddlers.)

The only way that the Social Security system will decline in the face of the political clout of so many people is if the American economy declines so severely that no money can be found for the baby-boomer payoff. Don't forget that Social Security was started during the 1930s, when the United States was in its worst financial shape in history. It was voter demands on the government to "do something" that prompted the creation of Social Security and the first government payouts — not a Treasury bulging with excess cash looking for a home.

And if in the next twenty years the American economy declines so severely that baby boomers are left high and dry, aggressive commitments today to mutual funds investing in stocks of American companies — prices of which tend to reflect the American economy — will decline just as severely, if not more so. Therefore, if long-term fear of decline in Social Security benefits (which is really a fear of long-term decline of the American economy) motivates you in any way in investment decisions today, you should be concentrating on the most conservative long-term investment avenues, not high-risk, aggressive ones.

More important than allocating your money to the most aggressive markets possible (or the most conservative) is taking as full advantage as possible of tax-protected retirement options. That means, of course, the fullest limits of any defined-contribution plan (while making sure that the options available are of survivalist quality) as well as IRA or Keough plans.

Any cash left over should first go into tax-deferred options like EE Savings Bonds (which are limited to $17,000 a year) or fixed-rate annuities issued by AAA-rated insurance companies. Then the options chosen could expand into tax-limited options like U.S. Treasuries and municipal bonds.

New Companies

The final stage of a major bull market is characterized by an obsession with new companies. Partly this is caused by the overpricing of the stocks of established companies. It becomes clear that those established companies won't be able to continue growing rapidly enough to justify ever higher and higher prices of their stocks. But because more money keeps pumping into the speculative markets, there has to be a bigger and bigger playing field. That's when the vagueness of unlimited future possibilities of new companies becomes attractive.

The height of the obsession with new companies at the very top of big bull markets — just prior to major declines — is usually identified by a focus on new companies offering a new technology. In the nineteenth century the new technologies were at different times railroads, telegraph technology, and telephones. In the late 1920s that new technology was radio (and a new thing being hinted at called television). In the late 1960s the obsession was with the promise of computers. In all these cases, as we now know, the interpretation that these new technologies would deliver big riches was correct. But it wasn't correct quickly. It took years for the technologies to develop into viable businesses — to become technically perfected and then accepted by enough people to make them hugely profitable — and deliver a real investment payoff. The mistake consistently made during these periods of obsession with new technologies is that the payoff will be fast. And the salespeople hawking the new technologies, when first capturing investor attention, try to goad the unsuspecting along with the urgency of "you have to get in on the ground floor." That ground-floor opportunity, however, is rarely available when it's being broadcast from the cover of a slick magazine you view on your way through the grocery-store checkout line. The ground-floor opportunity actually comes after the speculative fever breaks, the market for the technology stocks crumbles, and the dust starts to settle. Then will be the time — when everybody else is disgusted with the idea — that you'll be able to find the jewels.

The roulette wheel of Wall Street turns very quickly compared to the grinding gears of corporate America. Development and acceptance of new technology rarely accommodates investors' timetables for personal wealth achievement. But, consistently, the last moment of every bull market reveals that many investors think that this time it will.

Near the very end you will see that small company sectors outperform the general market by huge percentages. They won't be able to sustain it — and their fall will signal a return to known, larger companies.

International Investment

Perhaps the most persistent investment concept that will be pounded on during the waning days of the twentieth century will be the opportunities to be found in foreign investment. Here, you will be told, is where the new economies — and the great, fast growth — will be, where the best returns on your money will be found. (These foreign climes will also be the places that people handling your money would prefer to find investment opportunities. It's a lot more fun to go to China and get fêted with exotic banquets than to go looking for investment opportunities in Kansas and have to face the same old medium-rare steak and baked potato.)

Claims about all the riches overseas need to be kept in perspective as clearly as other claims.

First, some of the mutual fund promoters who are suggesting that investments into foreign markets are a good thing for you to do are at the same time suggesting to investors in those foreign countries that it would be a good thing for them to invest in American markets. Remember, mutual fund promoters sell their products based on *your* perception of market opportunities, not on what they believe to be true. They produce and run products to sell, not to change people's minds or to educate investors about what should be done with excess personal wealth.

If you are sitting in America and not seeing how speculative markets can continue to rise appreciably because there appears to be little real business growth — your friends have lost their jobs, factories are closed down in your town, big corporations are continuing to lay off massive numbers of highly paid people, businesses up and down the street are shuttered — the facts and figures of investment markets in other countries start looking good. Mutual fund promoters have shown you the proof. You've seen the charts — growth prospects based on population and industrial and consumer demand showing near unlimited possibilities, and so on.

But while you are looking at all that proof, small investors in other countries are looking at all the mutual fund promoters' proof of the vitality of American markets. The people sitting in those other countries are also looking around at the economic situation of their part of the world. They, too, see few immediate positive prospects for the future. And mutual fund promoters with worldwide outposts are waving economic statistics and performance charts of American markets that "prove" how robust and stable American opportunities are.

From where you are sitting you can't tell what the full reality is in other countries. And the people with investment money in those other countries can't tell what the full reality is here. They, like you, depend on information from leaders of financial institutions. But those leaders selectively present data to reinforce already-established widespread preconceptions — whether valid, based on the leaders' full store of information, or not.

The result can be that money crisscrosses oceans from one group of investors looking for opportunities in markets that are foreign to them while the people in those markets want to go into equally foreign markets.

While this money crisscrosses oceans, the fund promoters, of course, get to grab a little bit of it for themselves on each journey.

In addition, don't think that investing in international markets will provide international diversification as an insurance policy against a big U.S. stock market crash. In a global economy all economies are so interconnected that the sudden realization of whatever it is that prompts a U.S. stock market crash will spread quickly around the world. The October 1987 market crash was simultaneously played out throughout most of the world's markets (with the notable exception of the Tokyo exchange, which waited until 1991 to stage its crash). The crash of 1929 also was a worldwide stunner — and those days were supposed to have been far less global than ours.[5]

Moreover, if you are looking to foreign investment as a way of tapping into global economic growth that may in the years ahead outstrip the American economy, you need only look as far as the stocks that make up the Standard & Poor's list of 500 leading American companies. Forty percent of the revenue of those companies comes from foreign sales. The spectacular rises that you may be seeing in foreign stock markets have more to do with the emerging *markets* than the emerging economies. Jumping into them is as speculative as jumping into the American market when it is overheated. Equally, unusually high interest rates or dividend rates of foreign stock and bonds carry a much higher risk than the riskiest type of home-grown equivalents.

The trick of timing an entry into foreign markets is — like the matter of finding the jewels among small, emerging companies or industries — *not* to jump when everybody is telling you to. When the covers of general-interest magazines shout the news of foreign investment possibilities, you can be fairly certain that it is the *wrong* time to consider such a move.

Take a lesson from the British investors of the nineteenth century who through their investment trust obsession pumped money into American expansion and other emerging economies. When in 1873 young Robert Fleming introduced to the people of Dundee, Scotland, the idea that would become the first real investment trust, it was after nearly three years of trying to sell people on it. Fleming had made a trip to the United States in 1870 and had seen how people were getting rich in the development of railroads in America. He monitored the U.S. railroad market, showing Dundee residents the riches they were missing. But the galloping American railroad market that he watched actually turned out to be the first American speculative financial bubble following the Civil War. The bubble peaked in March 1873 and collapsed that September in what became known as the Panic of 1873. Fleming, however, didn't start his investment trust until the summer of 1873. He had invested less than half the money he raised by the time of the September panic and had never invested any of the money at what turned out to be the peak of the bubble. Over half the money Fleming ultimately invested with his first investment trust venture was at post-panic fire-sale prices. Fleming, like many pivotal figures in history, had been plain lucky. If he had been able to convince Dundee residents just a few months earlier to support his investment pool idea, you probably wouldn't be sitting there today thinking about a concept called mutual funds. Fleming's Dundee investors would have been wiped out, and Fleming, along with his investment trust idea, very likely would have melted into obscurity. As it happened, however, Fleming's railroad securities eventually increased in value from their fire-sale prices, and that performance earned Fleming a reputation as investment genius that served him for the rest of his life.

Interestingly, in 1929 a similar stroke of luck cemented the reputation of Lehman Brothers. The investment company started an investment trust in September 1929 and was only one-half invested by the time of the October 1929 crash. The Lehman trust, because of its huge cash position, came through the period as one of the best performers. During the 1930s when so much negative attention was being heaped on investment trusts, the performance of the Lehman trust was continually brought up as an example of prudent investment management. In reality, however, Lehman had missed the fury of the 1929 bubble primarily because the company's investment trust hadn't been organized soon enough to participate.

For Fleming, who, as the development of the American west expanded, added American real estate to his railroad interests, the lesson of his near brush with investment death at the start of his career apparently was well learned. In the late 1880s when British investors aggressively embraced the idea of investment trusts to raise it to mania status, Fleming retreated to a highly conservative position while other investment trust managers pursued the securities and bonds of rapidly rising markets around the world with unbridled confidence. When it started to collapse in 1890 and British investors generally retreated from the investment trust idea, Fleming was for the second time in his career able to sift through the rubble left behind to find the jewels. These jewels, while not delivering the type of get-rich-quick returns that the bubble of the late 1880s seemed to promise, did, however, give a slow-but-steady return over the next thirty years that tracked the general growth and prosperity of late-nineteenth/early-twentieth-century America.

For today's investor looking to potential foreign involvement via mutual funds, Fleming's lesson has to be assumed personally. Modern mutual funds are chartered to invest at whatever the current market situation may be. It is your decision whether to be involved in those markets or not. And when all looks great — everybody seems to be making money easily and quickly — it is likely not the time to jump on the foreign investment bandwagon. For today's large portfolio, however, a commitment of 5 or 10 percent of the total to international investment of stocks and bonds (perhaps a "balanced" fund) could be a way of keeping an informed foot in the door. You are then in a position to look for more aggressive commitments when markets deflate and opportunities look more enticing.

Profitable Aftermath

The people who became repelled by the idea of investment trusts following the crises of the 1890s and early 1930s as well as those who became equally repelled by the idea of mutual funds during the early 1970s missed the real opportunities of their lives. While anxious to take on risk when everything looked so bright and so easy during the mania stage, they became equally anxious *not* to take on risk when the excess and overconfidence of this mania triggered a crisis. But, as Robert Fleming found at least twice in his lifetime, the time to build great fortunes is in the crisis aftermath of manias.

During a crisis, the exciting anticipation of riches that had previously made so many people so anxious to get in on the idea turns to disappointment. Disappointment can be initially sparked by a variety of different possibilities. For example, a decline in markets that lasts longer or goes deeper than the people involved can tolerate, or the revelation that a previously admired person or company had been involved in fraud, or a turnaround in the trust in something that previously had been considered an easy assumption. The crisis then breeds disillusionment. If the disillusionment comes quickly it can touch off a panic, which is nothing more than a rush to get out of an idea that is as strong as (and usually stronger than) the rush to get into it. Both cases — the mania to get in and the panic to get out — are prompted by impatience. But impatience did not make Robert Fleming, for example, rich and famous.

When the atmosphere turns to impatience to get out, the true bargains in speculative markets are found. The full atmosphere of impatience, however, can take a long time to develop. Typically, after an initial event that sparks crisis is absorbed, it is discarded as an aberration and the enthusiasm is built up again — but this time it does not rise to the previous height. Another event happens and causes another crisis of trust or confidence. This too will be shrugged aside and another attempt at rejuvenation will occur. But then, typically, a third event of crisis marks the point when the full feeling of disillusionment and impatience is felt. By that time so many people who had joined the idea at the peak of its mania have lost so much that they are willing to crawl away wounded and vow never to venture out again. Afterward, the abuses of trust by leaders of the idea become in retrospect important points for reform. True reform, however, is never possible until something catastrophic takes place or a lot of people get hurt badly.

Then the cycle of opportunity begins again — as Robert Fleming found in 1873 and in the 1890s, as investors found at the depth of the 1930s depression and as the real risk takers had the good fortune to discover in the mid-1970s. The unscrupulous get weeded out. The measurements of "value" become stringent. The "innovations" created at the peak of overconfidence and then failed get discarded. And leaders of the idea who, during the peak of their unquestioned popularity had grown contemptuous of the people that they promised to serve, work hard to regain trust. It is then, when the world seems so littered with debris, that the makings of grand beginnings can be found.

In whatever way our next crisis may manifest itself and ultimately work itself out, you are living proof that the world has survived every crisis it has ever faced. But while the world as a whole survived these crises, many individuals did not. Perhaps people in your own family did not survive, but here you are today. Whatever circumstances got you here, you are living a privileged life. You probably would like to have a better one, but it's still a life of incredible wealth compared with most of the people on this planet. You obviously have enough extra money to concern yourself with the ways of making more with it. Unless that money was given to you, you didn't accumulate it by being lazy. You probably had to put up with a lot of unpleasant experiences to get it. And, also, you're smart. You have, for example, the attention span and reading skills to get through a book (even if you don't agree with a word of it) and have the intellectual curiosity to have searched it out in the first place. That's rare. When compared to all the people living in this world today and all the people who have lived and died, you and your family are among the smallest number of the most fortunate few ever to have been on this earth. So don't blow it.

APPENDIX A

■ ■ ■

How to Read a Mutual Fund Prospectus

hether you want to assess your current fund holdings in view of survival rules or are looking for new fund candidates, the process is the same. For new funds, limit yourself solely to those that claim to be no-load funds. (A careful reading of the prospectus will tell you if they are telling the truth.) Lists of appropriate no-load funds can be gathered from magazine or newspaper performance charts of funds that identify no-loads as such. Or, more methodically, you can put together lists from *The Individual Investor's Guide to No-Load Mutual Funds* (American Association of Individual Investors, 625 North Michigan Avenue, Chicago, IL 60611), *The Handbook for No-Load Fund Investors* (P.O. Box 318, Irvington, NY 10533), "No-Load Directory" (100% No-Load Council, 1501 Broadway, New York, NY 10036), and *Mutual Fund Sourcebook* (Morningstar, Inc., 225 West Wacker Drive, Chicago, IL 60606). Most large public libraries will have one or more of these directories.

Call or write for materials from each candidate on your list. After getting materials from the funds, throw away all the promotional literature without reading it. You want to buy the steak, not the sizzle. The documents you will actually need are (1) a copy of each fund's prospectus, (2) a copy of each fund's "additional statement of information," and (3) a copy of each fund's latest annual or semiannual report.

Step One: Check on Expenses and Fees

Near the front of the prospectus there will be a chart showing "Shareholder Transaction Expenses" and a chart showing "Annual Fund Operating Expenses." The chart of "Shareholder Transaction Expenses" should look something like this:

Sales Load on Purchases	NONE
Sales Load on Reinvested Dividends	NONE
Deferred Sales Load	NONE
Redemption Fees	NONE
Exchange Fees	NONE

If there are *any* charges for transactions, the fund is no longer a candidate. Throw away all materials. This is the chart that would also tell you if there are various classes of shares — Class A, Class B, etc. If the fund has more than one class of shares, it is unacceptable. Throw it away.

If you are already in a fund where you have paid a sales load or will be charged a fee for redemption, then if the fund fulfills the other criteria, stay with it — particularly if the deferred sales load or redemption fees decrease by holding the shares longer.

Directly under this chart, you will find the chart listing "Annual Fund Operating Expenses." These expenses are made up of four possible elements:

- Management fees (money that goes to the investment adviser)

- 12b-1 fees (money that goes to "distribution expenses" but is really used for advertising/marketing)

- Service fees (money spent on maintaining telephone switching services, etc.)

- Other expenses (money spent on broker's commissions, postage, etc.)

The expenses associated with each of these elements — including the controversial 12b-1 fee — are not as important to you as the figure showing the "Total Fund Operating Expenses." This is the "Expense Ratio." As long as the total is within an acceptable survivalist amount, then the fund stays on your candidate list. Otherwise, throw it away.

Acceptable highest expense ratios are:

Money market funds	0.70%
Government bond funds	0.80%
Corporate bond funds	1.00%
Stock funds	1.25%
International funds	1.40%

Step Two: Make Sure the Fund Is Accurately Categorized

To determine if a fund actually matches the profile that you believe that it has — or have been led to believe that it has — use the fund's most recent annual or semiannual report as a guide. Although you will not be able to analyze the fund's portfolio, there are a few things to look for to fulfill survivalist standards.

For Money Market Funds

- Turn to the end of the fund's listing of holdings. For the absolutely safest fund the list should include 100 percent U.S. Treasury bills without "floating rate notes." For fully taxable funds, be sure that there is no listing for "Eurodollar" or "Yankee Dollar" CDs. In addition, look at the listing of bonds to make sure there are no commercial bonds with ratings other than A-1 or P-1.

- Check on average maturity, usually stated in the front of the report, to make sure that it is no longer than sixty days. Call the fund company to reconfirm.

For Bond Funds

- For all bond fund categories, make sure that the maturity date —usually stated in the front pages of the report — is no longer than eight years. Call the fund company to confirm.

- Check the volatility of the fund on the "financial history" chart —usually found at the back of the report. The highest figure for any one year beside the "Net asset value, end of period" entry should not be more than 15 percent different from the lowest figure for any of the other years shown.

- For an "investment-grade" or "high-quality" commercial bond fund, look for a summary chart giving percentage breakdown of holdings or cross out all entries in the listing of holdings rated below AAA, AA, A. The percentage of holdings below these ratings or crossed-out entries should not exceed 20 percent of the total.

For Stock Funds

- Look on the first page of the prospectus to make sure that the fund is officially a "diversified investment company." If it is identified as a "non-diversified investment company," stop considering the fund.

- On the "financial history" chart, check the "Portfolio turnover rate." It should not be higher than 100 percent.

- On the list of holdings, cross out all entries marked as *not* paying dividends. The remaining entries, paying dividends, should roughly match the profile for different fund categories:

Equity income	70%
Growth and income	50%
Growth	30% or less
Aggressive growth	0%

Step Three: Check for Investment Tricks

In the prospectus and "additional statement of information," find the sections labeled "investment limitations" or "management policies." The fund's limitations should prohibit all of the following. The fewer of these limitations included, the more risky the fund. If any of these limitations are defined as "subject to change without shareholder approval," stop considering the fund:

- No margin buying

- No short selling

- No dealing in puts and calls

- No more than 5 percent of value of fund assets in one company (except U.S. government securities)

- No more than 10 percent ownership of shares of one company

- No more than 5 percent total assets in "unseasoned companies"

- No more than 10 percent total assets in restricted or illiquid securities

- No ownership of shares of open-end mutual funds

- No direct buying and selling of real estate

- No commodities investing

- No direct investment into oil, gas, or mineral exploration projects

- No more than 10 percent of value of fund assets in one industry.

APPENDIX B

■ ■ ■

Ways – Other than Mutual Funds – to Make Money from Money

Y ou are probably aware of most of these different ways of making money from your money. Perhaps it's time to revisit the potential of at least some of them. Some are very good — some aren't. They are listed here in approximate order of safety and ease of use.

1. PAY OFF DEBT. The single best way to make money from your money is to pay off every dime of your debt — except, possibly, your mortgage. Then stay out of debt. You can't begin to think about tidy financial gains in your future until you've cleaned up the mess of your past.

2. SAVINGS ACCOUNT. The passbook savings account at a bank, an S&L, or a credit union is one idea that is truly old-fashioned and outdated. Even the most risk-averse "saver" doesn't need this dinosaur — except perhaps as a training tool for children.

3. NOW ACCOUNT. Fully insured, this bank product tied to a checking account usually pays the same (low) rate as a savings account. It's really useful only if you can maintain the minimum balance and get "free" checking privileges. And if you can get *really* free checking someplace else, then change banks and you won't need a NOW account.

4. MONEY MARKET DEPOSIT ACCOUNT (MMDA). This bank/ S&L/credit union product is the government-insured version of mutual fund money markets. Generally, an MMDA pays more than a passbook savings account, but about 0.5 to 2 percent less than the mutual fund version and about 0.5 percent below six-month Treasury bills. Best-yield information can be found in *Barron's, Money,* and the Sunday edition of the *New York Times.*

5. CERTIFICATE OF DEPOSIT (CD). This is the government-insured savings product — first introduced in the 1960s — that gave Americans the taste for safe, high-yield money-from-money return during the unprecedented days of high interest rates in the late 1970s and throughout most of the 1980s. They are still safe, and even when the interest yield seems low, they still tend to pay at a yield that is slightly higher than the current inflation rate. A six-month CD pays about the same as a money market mutual fund. CDs with longer terms usually pay a little more than Treasury securities held for the same amount of time. Again, best-yield information can be found in *Barron's, Money,* and the Sunday edition of the *New York Times.* Make sure when comparing yield that you are looking at "effective annual yield." CD interest can be compounded daily, weekly, or quarterly. Only "effective annual yield" tells the whole story.

6. U.S. SAVINGS BONDS. Series EE bonds pay a variable interest rate based on market rates. During the first five years of holding the bond, the interest rate is paid every six months, equaling 85 percent of six-month Treasury bills, and after five years the rate is 85 percent of five-year Treasury notes. In addition, bonds held for seventeen years have a minimum guarantee to double their original purchase price in the seventeenth year. All income is exempt from local and state taxes. Federal income tax is deferred until the bond is redeemed — or until it has been held for thirty years. (You can defer this a further ten years by reinvesting money from maturing EE bonds into Series HH Savings Bonds.) Bonds redeemed to pay tuition and fees (but not room and board) at colleges, universities, and some technical schools can be exempt from federal taxes if taxable household income is within certain limits at the time of redemption.

7. BROKER CERTIFICATE OF DEPOSIT. Government-insured just like bank CDs, broker CDs are issued by banks and S&Ls but are available *only* through brokers. These CDs normally pay more than you can get at a bank — sometimes as high as 1 percent more. The banks or S&Ls issuing the CDs pay the broker's commission, so the yield quoted is the full amount you'll get.

8. TREASURY BILLS (T-BILLS). T-bills have maturities of three, six, or twelve months. They are available in a minimum denomination of $10,000 with additional increments of $5,000. The actual cost of the T-bills is determined by auctions held every week. Bidders buy them at a discount of the actual denomination. That discount price compared to the face value that the government pays upon maturity determines the interest yield. (It changes every week.) Money earned is exempt from state and local taxes. You can buy T-bills through a broker. You can avoid the broker's commission fee by buying directly from the government through the mail or in person. For information on setting up an account for investment into government securities via the mail, write: Treasury Direct, Department of the Treasury, Bureau of the Public Debt, Dept. F, Washington, DC 20239-0001. With this program, the government deposits your interest directly into your bank account, and there's an automatic reinvestment program.

9. TREASURY NOTES (T-NOTES). T-notes are issued in $1,000 and $5,000 denominations and mature at various periods between one and ten years. They pay a fixed interest rate that is set at the time of the purchase. The interest is paid twice a year. The interest paid is usually higher than that paid on T-bills. Interest is exempt from state and local taxes. T-notes can be bought through a broker or direct — see #8.

10. TREASURY BONDS (T-BONDS). These bonds mature at periods of ten to thirty years to pay their face value of denominations ranging from $1,000 to $1 million. Interest is paid twice a year and is exempt from state and local taxes. Like T-bills and T-notes, T-bonds can be bought through a broker or direct — see #8.

11. LIFE INSURANCE. Life insurance is only for those who *need* to be concerned about leaving an estate for young children or perhaps to help pay off a mortgage. Whole life pays a set death benefit and premiums build up tax-free cash value. But the interest rates paid are minuscule. Variable life insurance is really just a mutual fund (and usually an expensive and lousy one) that is ultimately worth only as much as investments pay off. Term insurance covers you only as long as you pay the premiums — and has no investment value. Still, term is best to cover those estate issues. Then put the rest someplace else.

12. FIXED ANNUITIES. Possibly useful as a supplement to other retirement plans, a fixed annuity — bought through an insurance company — accumulates tax-deferred interest until at retirement time a single lump-sum payment is paid out or monthly payments are made until death. "Variable" annuities are simply mutual funds with no guarantees. The biggest risk factor with fixed annuities is the soundness of the insurance company sponsoring the annuity. It could go under and you would lose everything. Information on highest-paying fixed annuities can be found in *Comparative Annuity Reports Newsletter,* P.O. Box 1268, Fair Oaks, CA 95628. Buy such products only from top-rated insurance companies. That means the highest safety rating from the various agencies that rate insurance companies: Standard & Poor's, AAA; Moody's, Aaa; A.M. Best, A+. For the current Standard & Poor's rating on a specific company, call 212–208–1527. For Moody's, call 212–553–0377. For A.M. Best's, 900–420–0400, for which there is a per-minute charge.

13. MORTGAGE LOANS TO RELATIVES. Helping relatives with their mortgages (and with greater risk, helping acquaintances; and with even greater risk, helping strangers) can yield higher-than-market returns on your money while letting the borrowers pay lower-than-market rates for their mortgages.

14. ZERO COUPON BONDS. To get the full value from zero coupon bonds they *must* be held to maturity because of their high volatility during the holding period. Zero coupon bonds — particularly U.S. Treasury versions — can be a worthwhile part of a tax-protected account. Zeros not in a tax-protected account are subject to annual taxes every year as if you actually got the interest that year, even though you do not get the interest until the bond matures.

15. INVESTMENT CLUBS. The earliest versions of mutual funds in this country were made up of people who knew each other — family or friends. The increasingly popular investment club is the same idea. You and others you know make the decisions — without paying fees and trying to hazard a guess about what strangers in a distant office are doing with your money. For information on investment clubs, contact the National Association of Investment Clubs, 1515 East Eleven Mile Road, Royal Oak, MI 48067.

16. MUNICIPAL BONDS. Your own portfolio of high-grade municipal bonds (rated AA or AAA) held to maturity can be far less risky than a mutual fund of municipal bonds. At least with your own portfolio you'll be certain to know what's in it. This is one area where a full-service broker can be helpful. Once a portfolio is set up you won't need to do much trading — and therefore fees are usually paid only once. A good primer for this market is *An Investor's Guide to Tax-Exempt Securities,* available for 45 cents from Public Securities Association, 40 Broad Street, New York, NY 10004.

17. PORTFOLIO OF STOCKS. If you want to take your first incursion into direct stock market investing, building a portfolio of equal amounts of money invested into six to ten stocks with steady histories of annual dividend increases will yield a decent, stable income. The overall performance of such a portfolio will very likely mirror the market. Although not likely to "beat the market" during the late stages of a bull market, it should perform better than the overall market during an extended bear. You can find a comprehensive list of these stocks in the annual directory *Handbook of Dividend Achievers,* published by Moody's. Some of these companies also offer automatic Dividend Reinvestment Plans. Any stock-selection strategy beyond this basic approach becomes more and more risky — although not necessarily as risky as the most conservative-sounding stock mutual fund.

18. CORPORATE BONDS. A portfolio of high-grade (meaning a rating by Moody's of Aa and Aaa or by Standard & Poor's of AA or AAA) corporate bonds that are held to maturity will yield low-risk income that is greater than that achieved with government bonds, CDs, money market funds, or dividend-yielding stocks. A simple introduction to this area is *How the Bond Market Works* available free from Standard & Poor's Corporation, 25 Broadway, New York, NY 10004.

19. INCOME-PRODUCING REAL ESTATE. During periods of unusually low interest rates, using your cash and a low-interest mortgage to buy income-producing real estate can provide a powerful long-term return on your money — particularly if you buy when real estate markets are depressed.

20. GINNIE MAE CERTIFICATES. Although the highest-yielding security carrying the full government guarantee, these mortgage pass-through certificates can be volatile. A minimum Ginnie Mae certificate is $25,000. Unlike Treasury securities, the interest is not exempt from state and local taxes.

21. BUSINESS LOANS TO RELATIVES (OR OTHERS). You can be your own venture capitalist or business loan operation with low risk if you investigate the business. Lending money to your brother-in-law to start a new business, for example, may not be a bad idea after all. It sure beats the mystery of handing your money over to a mutual fund manager so that he can lend it to *his* brother-in-law. (And, if your brother-in-law's business goes sour, you will have something to hang over your sister's head for the rest of her life.)

22. BETTING ON YOURSELF. You will never get rich sending your money off to somebody else. You are not likely to get rich even if you bet directly on the efforts of others — as you do via investments into bonds or stocks. You *may* get rich, however, by putting your financial resources at risk to back your own business idea of what is needed in this world. This can be the biggest risk. Over 50 percent of new businesses fail in the first year. But they say that following your dreams can bring a new level of happiness despite the hard work involved or the financial outcome.

APPENDIX C

■ ■ ■

Ways Not to Make Money
from Money

D on't let your pursuit of making money from money lead you
into any of these dangerous arenas:

1. COLLATERALIZED MORTGAGE OBLIGATIONS (CMOs). These
complex bondlike securities are made up of mortgage-backed securities.
When invented in 1983 CMOs were thought to offer steady high-yield
income, but the actual experience has not been good. They've turned into
high-risk, uneven performers that seem to have bitten everyone who has
had the misfortune to have been hoodwinked into them. The nightmare
that people have had with these securities is a harbinger of the horror to
come from further securitization of the financial world.

2. PENNY STOCKS. The get-rich-quick appeal of penny stocks has
recurrent vogue as new generations come around to hear legendary
stories of how someone, in some distant land or time, had indeed paid a
dime or a dollar for a stock and made a million bucks. Here's the truth:
You're not that lucky. You are doomed for life to have to work for a living.

3. JUNK BONDS. You wouldn't want them in a mutual fund, and you
certainly don't want to own them directly.

4. CONVERTIBLE DEBENTURES. This hybrid security is a "bond"
that pays interest but can also be converted to shares of the company's
stock at a fixed price by a certain date. Although often touted as the "best
of both worlds" — by allowing you to buy a stock that is on the rise at a
"bargain" price while at the same time offering an interest-paying "floor"

if the stock's price goes down — it is a gimmick that gets a lot of attention at market peaks before proving to be a disaster. Convertible debs are usually issued by small companies with low credit ratings — putting the convertible debs on about the same level as junk bonds. When the company's stock price goes down, so does the value of the convertible deb. All the way to zero. Stay away, directly or via mutual funds.

5. COLLECTIBLES. Don't get hooked into "collectibles" — coins, stamps, books, plates, baseball cards, etc. — because you think you're going to be cool-headed enough actually to make money from these things. You'll be attracted to whatever the collectible is because you feel some emotional attachment to the item. You won't want to give up the one item that should be sold at the moment it could fetch the best price. Go ahead and collect stuff, but don't kid yourself that you're doing it to make money. You can, however, pass the collectibles on to your heirs and let them sell them, because you can be sure that whatever you like, they won't.

6. LIMITED PARTNERSHIPS. You as the "limited" partner in a limited partnership — or more accurately, the *silent* partner — of an investment setup about which you can get little information puts you at high risk for exposure to simple fraud. Maybe if you have a lot of money and can do enough research along with a lawyer to determine that it's not actually fraud, it might have some value. But limited partnerships are far too risky for most people.

7. COMMODITY FUTURES PARTNERSHIPS OR FUNDS. These are complex gambles at best and often disasters.

8. NEW ISSUES. When new issues come to market, the good ones are snapped up by brokerages and "insiders." The rest are sold to the general public (namely, you). The price of the new issue typically plunges shortly after coming to market, often never to recover.

9. UNIT INVESTMENT TRUSTS (UITs). These are fixed, closed-end portfolios that are held until maturity. In theory, this idea would emulate that of holding your own portfolio of bonds until maturity — except that it would be more diversified than you could put together yourself. In reality, these funds are almost always sold with a high load and are also packed with a lot of low-rated junk to make the yields look enticing.

Notes

■ ■ ■

Chapter 1

1. Charles P. Kindleberger, *Manias, Panics, and Crashes: A History of Financial Crises* (New York: Basic Books, 1989), p. 34.
2. Martin Mayer, *Stealing the Market* (New York: Basic Books, 1992), p. 40.
3. Fred Williams, "Banks gain 20% of pool," *Pensions & Investments*, February 9, 1993, p. 26.
4. Susan Antilla, "Alternatives to C.D.'s: The Ads Skip the Risks," *New York Times*, November 7, 1992, p. 33.
5. Penelope Wang, "Ways to Fight High Fund Fees," *Money*, July 1992, p. 122.
6. Leslie Eaton, "No More Mr. Nice Guy?" *Barron's*, October 14, 1991, p. 31.
7. Ibid.
8. Diana B. Henriques, "Fidelity's Secret Agent Man," *New York Times*, January 27, 1991, p. F1.
9. Allen R. Myerson, "The New Activism at Fidelity," *New York Times*, August 8, 1993, p. F15.

Chapter 2

1. Howard C. Rowe, "Starting at Age 40 On the Road to Financial Independence," *Magazine of Wall Street*, August 27, 1927, p. 778.
2. Irving Fisher, "This Era of Investment Trusts," *North American Review*, July 1929, pp. 71–77.
3. *Saturday Evening Post*, November 5, 1927, p. 34; *Independent*, October 15, 1927, p. 383; *Literary Digest*, March 3, 1924, p. 81; *Forbes*, December 1, 1927, p. 21; *Forbes*, September 15, 1927, p. 15; *Outlook*, June 9, 1926, p. 224; *Review of Reviews*, August 1929, p. 102; *Magazine of Business*, February 1929, p. 162; *Forbes*, October 15, 1929, p. 74; *Magazine of Business*, March 1929, p. 268; *Delin*, September 1928, p. 102.
4. *Good Housekeeping*, November 29, 1929, p. 96.
5. *New York Times*, October 16, 1929.
6. Leland Rex Robinson, *Investment Trust: Organization and Management* (New York: Ronald Press, 1929), p. 30.
7. John M. Waggoner, *Money Madness* (Homewood, IL: Business One Irwin, 1991), p. 116.
8. Richard S. Wallace, "Investment Trust Capital Gains a Billion," *Forbes*, May 15, 1928, p. 90.

9. Hugh Bullock, *The Story of Investment Companies* (New York: Columbia University Press, 1959), p. 47.
10. Bullock, p. 40.
11. *Barron's*, May 13, 1929, p. 2.
12. See, "British Investment Trusts — A Warning," *Atlantic Monthly*, October 1927, p. 94.
13. J. C. Gilbert, *A History of Investment Trusts in Dundee, 1873–1938* (London: P. S. King, 1939), p. 48.
14. Turrentine Jackson, *The Enterprising Scot: Investors in the American West after 1873* (Edinburgh: Edinburgh University Press, 1968), p. 315.
15. J. W. Fortescue, "The New South Sea Bubble," *Nineteenth Century*, July 1893, p. 22.
16. Gerald Krefetz and Ruth Marossi, *Money Makes Money: The Men Who Are Wall Street* (New York: World Publishing, 1970), p. 59.
17. Krefetz and Marossi, p. 66.
18. John F. Lawrence and Paul E. Steiger, *The '70s Crash and How to Survive It* (New York: World Publishing, 1970), p. 19.
19. *Fortune*, June 1960.
20. George Bush, "Ten Most Misunderstood Facts About Mutual Funds," *Better Homes and Gardens*, May 1968, p. 47.
21. "The Reader's Digest Fund," *Newsweek*, October 9, 1967, p. 64.
22. "What Ails the Mutual Fund Industry," *Business Week*, March 3, 1973, p. 48.

Chapter 3

1. John Brooks, *The Go-Go-Years* (New York: Weybright & Talley, 1973), p. 135.
2. Christopher Elias, *Fleecing the Lambs* (Chicago: Henry Regenery, 1971), p. 228.
3. Susan Antilla, "Wall Street: A Watchdog From the Other Side," *New York Times*, October 10, 1993, p. F13.
4. Sylvia Porter, *Sylvia Porter's Money Book* (New York: Doubleday, 1975), p. 896.
5. Jonathan R. Laing, "Errors of Commission," *Barron's*, September 7, 1992, p. 8.
6. Suzanne Woolley, "'You Can Securitize Virtually Everything,'" *Business Week*, July 20, 1992, p. 78.
7. "A Boom in New Issues," Associated Press Newswire, December 10, 1993, 11:52 p.m.
8. Irving Fisher, "This Era of Investment Trusts," *North American Review*, July 1929, p. 76.
9. J. Woodrow Thomas, "The Investment Company Act of 1940," *George Washington Law Review*, August 1941, p. 921.
10. "Big-block Buyers May Speak Up," *Business Week*, November 26, 1966, p. 139.
11. Judith H. Dobrzynski, "Relationship Investing," *Business Week*, March 15, 1993, p. 68.
12. Arlene Hershman, "Will the Funds Run Companies?" *Dun's Review*, July 1968, p. 75.
13. Leslie Wayne, "Money Manager's 'Reality Check,'" *New York Times*, June 22, 1993, p. D1.
14. Tim Golden, "Mexico Pulls Out of Fund That Has Roiled Trade Issue," *New York Times*, February 18, 1993, p. D1.
15. Michael Quint, "Teachers' Fund Gets a Taste of Its Own Medicine," *New York Times*, October 7, 1993, p. D7.
16. Kevin G. Salwen, "SEC Alters Proxy Policy on Job Issues," Dow Jones/News Retrieval, October 20, 1992, 9:22 a.m.

Chapter 4

1. Richard D. Crawford and William W. Sihler, *The Troubled Money Business: The Death of an Old Order and the Rise of a New Order* (New York: HarperBusiness, 1991), p. 203.
2. Stan Hinden, "Banks Pitching Mutual Funds Face Questions on Disclosure of Risks," *Washington Post*, March 24, 1993, p. F3.
3. Gary Belsky, "How Your Broker Makes a Buck," *Money*, June 1992, p. 143.
4. Carole Gould, "'Churning' Is Not Just for Stocks," *New York Times*, June 7, 1992, p. F16.
5. Susan Antilla, "Few Financial Advisers Qualify as Unbiased," *New York Times*, March 13, 1993, p. 33.
6. Linda Koco, "401(k) Plans Will Continue to Grow," *National Underwriter*, March 15, 1993, p. 17.
7. *What Every Salesman Should Know About Mutual Investment Funds* (New York: National Securities & Research Corp., 1959), p. 17.
8. Tom Petruno, "Reforming Mutual Funds: Start at the Top," *Los Angeles Times*, May 22, 1992, p. D1.
9. Jason Zweig and Mary Beth Grover, "Fee Madness," *Forbes*, February 15, 1993, p. 160.

Chapter 7

1. Randall W. Forsyth, "Baffled Investors," *Barron's*, March 18, 1991, p. 39.

Chapter 8

1. Gene Koretz, "Top-Rated Mutual Funds: All They're Cracked Up to Be?" *Business Week*, September 6, 1993, p. 16.

Chapter 9

1. Ruth Simon, "How Fund Directors Are Letting You Down," *Money*, September 1993, p. 104.

Chapter 10

1. Foreword in 1932 reprinting of Charles Mackay, *Extraordinary Popular Delusions and the Madness of Crowds*, 1852 edition.
2. John Kenneth Galbraith, *A Short History of Financial Euphoria* (New York: Viking, 1992), p. 87.
3. Charles P. Kindleberger, *Manias, Panics, and Crashes: A History of Financial Crisis* (New York: Basic Books, 1989). Other valuable books on cycles and crises are Jacob Bernstein, *Cycles of Profit* (New York: HarperBusiness, 1991); F. T. Haner, *Financial Crisis: Causes and Solutions* (New York: Praeger, 1985); Alvin H. Hansen, *Business Cycles and National Income* (New York: W. W. Norton, 1957); George Hildebrand, *Business Cycle Indicators and Measures* (Chicago: Probus, 1991); A. W. Mullineux, *Business Cycles and Financial Crises* (New York: Harvester Wheatsheaf, 1990); Allen Oakley, *Schumpeter's Theory of Capitalist Motion* (Brookfield, VT.: Gower, 1990); Dick A. Stoken, *Cycles: What They Are, What They Mean, How to Profit by Them* (New York: McGraw-Hill, 1978); Eugene White, ed., *Crashes and Panics: The Lessons from History* (Homewood, IL.: Dow-Jones–Irwin, 1990).
4. Kindleberger, p. 46.

5. Harold A. Black and Robert L. Schweitzer, "Did regulatory actions discourage consumer demand for Treasury bills?" *Journal of Banking and Finance,* February 1992, pp. 19–26.
6. Sushil Bikhchandani, David Hirshleifer, Ivo Welch, "A Theory of Fads, Fashion, Custom, and Cultural Change as Informational Cascades," *Journal of Political Economy,* Spring 1992, pp. 992–1026.
7. Loren Dunton, *How to Sell More Mutual Funds* (New York: Echo House, 1967).
8. Bill Hendrick, "Americans Dive Headlong into Mutual Funds," *Atlanta Journal-Constitution,* February 28, 1993, p. F1.
9. Kindleberger, p. 39.
10. William M. O'Barr and John M. Conley, *Fortune and Folly: The Wealth and Power of Institutional Investing* (Homewood, IL: Business One Irwin, 1992), pp. 53, 88.

Chapter 11

1. Ibbotson Associates as quoted in *The T. Rowe Price Report,* Spring 1992, p. 1.
2. Investment Company Institute, *The Money Managers: Professional Investment Through Mutual Funds* (New York: McGraw-Hill, 1967), p. 15.
3. U.S. Department of Education, National Center for Education Statistics, *Digest of Education Statistics, 1991,* Table 291.
4. Kenneth M. Morris and Alan M. Siegel, *The Wall Street Journal Guide to Understanding Personal Finance* (New York: Lightbulb Press, 1992), p. 89.
5. Charles P. Kindleberger, *Manias, Panics, and Crashes: A History of Financial Crises* (New York: Basic Books, 1989), p. 131.

Further Reading/
Acknowledgments

■ ■ ■

The most difficult part of writing a book on a topic as large and
potentially complex as mutual funds and the investment arenas
that mutual funds represent is deciding on what to leave out.
Nearly every individual sentence in this book could be expanded on to
fill a book of its own. While reading as many books as such a number
would represent wouldn't really be worth the effort, there are a few books
that provide worthwhile expansion on what has been written here.

No investor can understand the present or the potentials of the future
without knowledge and some understanding of the past. The best historical overview of the 1920s, covering the period's sociological and financial dynamics, is *Only Yesterday* by Frederick Lewis Allen (New York:
Harper & Brothers, 1931). For a detailed explanation of the financial
aspects, including the influence of investment trusts, of the decade, see
The Great Crash, 1929 by John Kenneth Galbraith (Boston: Houghton
Mifflin, 1954, rev. 1988). For scholars of the period, the single best con-
temporary chronicle of the waning days of the 1920s investment trust
movement can be found in the issues of *Keane's Investment Trust Monthly,*
which began publication in November 1929 and ceased publishing in
September 1932. The magazine vividly reflects the changing mood about
investment trusts during that period — from still-cocky enthusiasm just
after the October 1929 crash to apologia when the investment trust scandals started to be revealed and then, when the entire concept went into
its rapid descent, to a simple catalog of liquidation values of the trusts as
they went out of business. A highly influential book of the time that
detailed the abuses and deficiencies of the closed-end trusts while cham-
pioning the approach of prudent investment policy and full disclosure
practiced by most of the then little-noticed open-end trusts was *Invest-*

■ 251 ■

ment Trusts Gone Wrong! by John T. Flynn (New York: New Republic, 1931). A generation later when the mutual fund industry suffered a period of disgrace almost as intense as that experienced by the investment trusts during the 1930s, Flynn's book was reprinted (Ayer, 1974) as an example of how things never change.

Descriptions of the development and early trials of the British version of the investment trust can be found in *A History of Investment Trusts in Dundee, 1873–1938* by John C. Gilbert (London: P. S. King, 1939) and *The Evolution of the Money Market (1385–1915)* by Ellis T. Powell (London: Financial News, 1915).

The days of reform in the United States during the 1930s leading up to the passage of the Investment Company Act of 1940 are covered along with a fairly accurate and reasonably balanced history of the industry in *The Story of Investment Companies* by Hugh Bullock (New York: Columbia University Press, 1959). Bullock, whose father was a mutual fund industry leader and one of its reformers during the 1930s, offers a particularly eerie warning of the potential abuse of the mutual fund idea.

The single best book giving a retrospective overview of the 1960s is *The Go-Go Years* by John Brooks (New York: Weybright & Talley, 1973). Also, *The Money Game* by "Adam Smith," pseudonym of George L. Goodman (New York: Random House, 1967), written at the height of the madness of the 1960s and chronicling the excesses of institutional investors, remains lively and fascinating reading today. Other valuable books to give a sense of the role of mutual funds and other institutional investors in American life during the 1960s are *The '70s Crash and How to Survive It* by John F. Lawrence and Paul E. Steiger (New York: World, 1970), *Fleecing the Lambs* by Christopher Elias (Chicago: Henry Regenery, 1973), and *Do You Sincerely Want to Be Rich?* by Charles Raw, Bruce Page, and Godfrey Hodgson (New York: Viking Press, 1971).

For in-depth surveys of the growing phenomenon of institutional investment in the 1990s, see *Bear Trap: Why Wall Street Doesn't Work* by Paul Gibson (New York: Atlantic Monthly Press, 1993), *Fortune and Folly: The Wealth and Power of Institutional Investing* by William M. O'Barr and John M. Conley (Homewood, IL: Business One Irwin, 1992), *Stealing the Market* by Martin Mayer (New York: Basic Books, 1992), and *The Troubled Money Business* by Richard D. Crawford and William W. Sihler (New York: HarperBusiness, 1991).

As an introduction to the rich body of literature on the history and theories of financial crises, the essential starting place is *Manias, Panics, and Crashes: A History of Financial Crises* by Charles P. Kindleberger (New York: Basic Books, 1989). Also valuable is Galbraith's *A Short History of Financial Euphoria* (New York: Whittle/Viking, 1993). And for a highly readable overview of the considerations of crowd psychology along with many practical applications for investment decisions, see *Contrary Investing for the '90s: How to Profit by Going Against the Crowd* by Richard E. Band (New York: St. Martin's Press, 1989).

For an overview of investment options and strategies emphasizing income — from CDs to bonds to dividend-paying stocks (and mutual funds) — see *The Income Investor* by Donald R. Nichols (Chicago: Longman Financial Service, 1988). For a comprehensive description of the world of bond investment and effective strategies for getting the most out of it — either directly or via mutual funds — there is *The Bond Book* by Annette Tau (Chicago: Probus, 1992). For an understanding of the power of capital appreciation via stock market investing and a good starting place for novices (and a good refresher course for experienced investors who may have forgotten that ultimately things *do* make sense), there are few books better than *The Intelligent Investor* by Benjamin Graham (New York: Harper & Row, 1965).

While none of the currently available books focused on mutual funds provides a balanced view of mutual funds compared to other options, a careful gleaning of *How to Pick the Best No-Load Mutual Funds for Solid Growth and Safety* by Sheldon Jacobs (Homewood, IL: Business One Irwin, 1992) and *Kurt Brouwer's Guide to Mutual Funds* by Kurt Brouwer (New York: John Wiley & Sons, 1990) offers many helpful tips for fine-tuning a mutual fund investment strategy.

While these and other sources have been helpful to me in writing this book, there also have been many individuals whose time and ideas I have relied on with selfish abandon. Without the endless supply of suggestions and encouragement of Caroline Latham this book simply could not have been written. The patience and thoroughness of the staff of the Research division of the New York Public Library and the crew on the fourth floor of the Mid-Manhattan branch of the New York Public Library led me to a treasure trove of over one hundred years of published and unpublished materials on investment trusts and mutual funds. I am indebted to Jon Bloomberg, Philip Carroll, Harold Chayefsky, Joe W. Scallorns, Alan Schwartz, and my friends in the mutual fund industry, who for some reason don't wish to be acknowledged publicly, for their many helpful comments and suggestions. Also, my thanks to my agent Alice Martell for believing in the book from the beginning and my editor at Little, Brown, Jennifer Josephy, for speeding the manuscript through the publishing process so that it could be published this year. And of course, there is the immeasurable contribution from my wife, Jo, who had to endure a lot, not the least of which was repeatedly listening to it all in full, unexpurgated detail.

Index

■ ■ ■